Binxing Fang, Yan Jia (Eds.)
Online Social Network Analysis

Also of interest

Online Social Network Analysis, Volume 1
B. Fang, Y. Jia, 2018
ISBN 978-3-11-059606-9, e-ISBN (PDF) 978-3-11-059937-4,
e-ISBN (EPUB) 978-3-11-059807-0

Online Social Network Analysis, Volume 2
B. Fang, Y. Jia, 2018
ISBN 978-3-11-059777-6, e-ISBN (PDF) 978-3-11-059941-1,
e-ISBN (EPUB) 978-3-11-059792-9

Web Applications with Javascript or Java, Volume 1
G. Wagner, M. Diaconescu, 2018
ISBN 978-3-11-049993-3, e-ISBN (PDF) 978-3-11-049995-7,
e-ISBN (EPUB) 978-3-11-049724-3

Web Applications with Javascript or Java, Volume 2
G. Wagner, M. Diaconescu, 2018
ISBN 978-3-11-050024-0, e-ISBN (PDF) 978-3-11-050032-5,
e-ISBN (EPUB) 978-3-11-049756-4

Trusted Computing
D. Feng, 2017
ISBN 978-3-11-047604-0, e-ISBN (PDF) 978-3-11-047759-7,
e-ISBN (EPUB) 978-3-11-047609-5

Online Social Network Analysis

—

Volume 3: Information and Communication

Edited by
Binxing Fang, Yan Jia

 DE GRUYTER

 電子工業出版社·
PUBLISHING HOUSE OF ELECTRONICS INDUSTRY
http://www.phei.com.cn

Editors
Prof. Binxing Fang
Chinese Academy of Engineering
Building A, Tri-Tower
No. 66-1 Zhongguancun East Road
100190 Beijing, Haidian District
China

Prof. Yan Jia
National University of Defense Technology
No. 109 Deya Road, Kaifu Strict
410073 Changsha, China

ISBN 978-3-11-075630-2
e-ISBN (PDF) 978-3-11-059943-5
e-ISBN (EPUB) 978-3-11-059793-6

Library of Congress Control Number: 2018954393

Bibliographic information published by the Deutsche Nationalbibliothek
The Deutsche Nationalbibliothek lists this publication in the Deutsche Nationalbibliografie; detailed bibliographic data are available on the Internet at http://dnb.dnb.de.

© 2021 Walter de Gruyter GmbH, Berlin/Boston and Publishing House Electronics
This volume is text- and page-identical with the hardback published in 2019.
Typesetting: Integra Software Services Pvt. Ltd.
Printing and binding: CPI books GmbH, Leck
Cover image: Komjomo / iStock / Getty Images

www.degruyter.com

Preface: Information and Diffusion

Volume 3 of the book focuses on the third core factor, namely, "information and diffusion," which consists of four chapters. Chapter 1 is about the information retrieval for social networks, Chapter 2 is about the rules of information diffusion in social networks, Chapter 3 is the topic discovery and evolution, and Chapter 4 is about the influence maximization algorithms.

The following experts and scholars who participated in the data collection, content arrangement, and achievement contribution of this volume are sincerely appreciated: Zhaoyun Ding, Xiaomeng Wang, Bin Wang, Yezheng Liu, Xiaodong Liu, Shenghong Li, Aiping Li, Lei Li, Shiyu Du, Peng Wu, Xiuzhen Chen, Wei Chen, Yang Yang, Lumin Zhang, Peng Shi, and Yuanchun Jiang.

Thanks to Associate Professor Shudong Li for the careful coordination and arrangement for writing this volume, and also to Weihong Han and Shuqiang Yang for reviewing and proofreading.

https://doi.org/10.1515/9783110599435-201

Contents

List of Contributors

Prof. Xueqi Cheng
Institute of Computing Technology
Chinese Academy of Sciences
No. 6 Zhongguancun Kexueyuan South Road
100190 Beijing, China

Prof. Binxing Fang
Chinese Academy of Engineering
Building A, Tri-Tower
No. 66-1 Zhongguancun East Road
100190 Beijing, China

Prof. Li Guo
Institute of Information Engineering
Chinese Academy of Sciences
No. 89 Linzhuang Road
100093 Beijing, China

Prof. Changjun Hu
University of Science and Technology Beijing
No. 30 Xueyuan Road
100083 Beijing, China

Prof. Yan Jia
National University of Defense Technology
No. 109 Deya Road, Kaifu District
410073 Changsha, China

Prof. Jianhua Li
Prof. Shanghai Jiaotong University
Software Building
No. 800 Dongchuan Road
200240 Shanghai, China

Prof. Xiangke Liao
National University of Defense Technology
No. 109 Deya Road, Kaifu District
410073 Changsha, China

Prof. Jiayin Qi
Shanghai University of International Business
and Economics
Room 338, Bocui Building
No. 1900 Wenxiang Road
201620 Shanghai, China

Prof. Xindong Wu
Hefei University of Technology
No. 193, Tunxi Road
230009 Hefei, China

Prof. Jin Xu
Peking University
No. 5 Yiheyuan Road
100871 Beijing, China

Prof. Shanlin Yang
Hefei University of Technology
No. 193, Tunxi Road
230009 Hefei, China

Prof. Hongli Zhang
Harbin Institute of Technology
No. 92 Xidazhi Street
150001 Harbin, China

Prof. Bin Zhou
National University of Defense Technology
No. 109 Deya Road, Kaifu District
410073 Changsha, China

https://doi.org/10.1515/9783110599435-202

Li Guo

1 Information retrieval in social networks

Information retrieval (IR) is a process of retrieving information, which satisfies users' need, from massive unstructured datasets (such as natural language texts). IR is an important tool that helps users to rapidly and effectively derive useful information from massive data. With the drastic increase in the size of data and the increasingly growing user needs in search services, IR has evolved from a tool that was only designed for libraries into a network service indispensable in life, work, and study. In addition to the search systems represented by the popular Google search engine, some other common forms of IR systems include classification systems, recommendation systems, and Q&A systems.

With the rapid popularization and continual development of social networking services (SNS), IR not only has new resources and opportunities but is also confronted by new problems and challenges. Acquiring information from emerging resources such as social networks has gradually drawn attention from both industry and academics. Compared with the traditional webpages, social network texts have different characteristics, such as the limit of text length, special expression form (such as Hashtag[1] in microblogs), and existence of social relations between authors. These differences make it inappropriate to directly apply traditional IR technologies to an SNS environment. Social network-oriented IR technology still faces many problems and difficulties, and it is of great academic significance and application value to conduct research in this field.

This chapter mainly introduces IR for social networks, and aims to present the challenges faced by IR technology in its applications to new resources of social networks, and also introduces some possible solutions to these problems. Concretely, three most representative IR applications – search, classification, and recommendation are discussed in this chapter. This chapter is arranged as follows: Section 1.1 is the Introduction, which introduces the relevant concepts commonly used throughout the chapter, along with the challenges facing social network-oriented IR technology; Sections 1.2, 1.3, and 1.4, respectively, introduce the basic methods for content search, content classification, and recommendation in social networks, and the status quo of researches in these areas; Section 1.5 provides the summary of this chapter and future prospects. In Sections 1.2 and 1.3, relevant researches are introduced based on microblog data – one of the most representative SNSs, while Section 1.4 focusses on social networks developed from traditional

---

[1] Hashtag here refers to the tag bracketed with "#" in microblog text, also called theme tag, which can be regarded as a mark on a microblog made by the author. After development and evolution, it has been used by some social networking sites to represent topics.

https://doi.org/10.1515/9783110599435-001

e-commerce websites carrying social networking information, where commodities are recommended by integrating such online social networking information.

1.1 Introduction

IR is a process of retrieving information (generally documents), which satisfies users' need for information, from massive unstructured datasets (generally texts that are mostly stored in computers) [1].

Unstructured data refers to data without obvious structural markers which differs from structured traditional databases. Natural language texts are the most common unstructured data. User information need refers to an information theme that the user wants to find, while a query is usually a piece of text that the user submits to the retrieval system representing his information need or an object in any other form (such as one or several keywords in the text search engine or sample images in the image search engine).

The dataset being retrieved refers to a corpus or a collection. Each record in a collection is called a document. A document is the basic object to be retrieved such as a microblog message, a webpage, an image, or a sentence. It should be noted that the document here is different from a file. A file may contain a number of documents, and an IR document may be composed of several files.

During processing, a document is often converted into a format that can describe the key characteristics of its most important content, and such a characteristic is referred to as a "term" in IR, which is the basic retrieval unit in the retrieval system. Terms in texts are generally expressed by keywords. For example, in the sentence "social network oriented IR is very important," the terms can be "IR," "social," "networks," "very," and "important." In practical applications, the final selected terms depend on the applications.

The aim of IR is to return and search relevant documents from the document set, and the degree of relatedness is termed relevance between a document and the query. With respect to IR systems, it is usually necessary to rank documents based on the relevance between them and the query. To overcome the problem that an original query cannot precisely represent the user need, the original query can be modified, which is referred to as query expansion or query reformulation. After the retrieval results are returned, either the user or the system can apply explicit or implicit markers to some documents returned to determine whether they are relevant. The original query can be modified based on the marking results. This process is called relevance feedback. If we directly assume that the top k documents of the returned results are relevant and perform feedback based on this assumption, the feedback is referred to as pseudo-relevance feedback, and the top k documents are referred to as pseudo-relevant documents.

Evaluation is one of the important tasks in IR. On comparing the results returned by the system with the actual results, we can derive some evaluation metrics to measure the retrieval results. The most basic evaluation indicators for IR are "precision" and "recall," with the former referring to the proportion of actually relevant documents in the returned results, and the latter referring to the proportion of actually relevant documents that are returned. The two are used to measure the correctness of the results returned and the degree of coverage of returned results, respectively, on all correct results.

Example 1.1 Calculation of precision and recall. Provided that there are 100 documents relevant to a query, and a system returns 120 documents, in which 80 are actually relevant to the query, the precision of the system in terms of this query is 80/120 = 2/3, and the recall is 80/100 = 4/5.

Precision and recall are applicable for search and classification tasks in IR; the dedicated evaluation metrics for recommendation are introduced in Section 1.4. Precision and recall are extensively applied, however, in terms of search, the order of returned results, which is of vital importance to user experience, is not considered while calculating precision and recall. Therefore, in the application of information search, the following metrics that consider the order of returned results are usually used: $P@k$ and mean average precision (MAP).

Definition 1.1 $P@k$ (precision at k) refers to the precision of the top k results in the retrieval results; for example, $P@5$ and $P@10$, respectively, refer to the ratio of relevant documents to the top 5 and top 10 results. For a given query q, the $P@k$ is calculated based on the following equation:

$$P@k = \text{Number of relevant documents in the top } k \text{ results}/k \qquad (1.1)$$

Definition 1.2 Average precision (AP) is, given a query q, the average value of precisions at the positions of all relevant document in the returned result. AP is calculated based on the following equation:

$$AP(q) = \frac{1}{|\text{rel}(q)|} \sum_{i=1}^{|\text{ret}(q)|} \text{isrel}(d_i) \times P@i \qquad (1.2)$$

where rel(q) refers to the document collection actually relevant to q; ret(q) represents all returned document collection for q; di is the ith document in the documents returned; and isrel(di) is a Boolean function. If di is relevant to q, 1 will be returned; otherwise 0 will be returned.

Example 1.2 Calculation of AP. Provided that the size of the document collection (rel(q)) relevant to a query is 5, in which 4 documents appear at positions 1, 4, 5, and 10, respectively of the search result, the AP of the query will be:

$$(1/1+2/4+3/5+4/10+0)/5=0.5$$

It is clear that the higher the number the higher the relevant documents in the returned results and larger the AP.

Definition 1.3 MAP refers to the mean of the AP values of multiple queries. MAP is used to evaluate the quality of an IR system.

Different from traditional IR in many aspects, social network-oriented IR has its own characteristics, which has both challenges and opportunities for the traditional IR technology:

(1) SNS documents are normally very short and the contents are sparsely distributed to an extent, which makes it hard to calculate or accurately calculate the similarity because of scarce co-occurrence terms.

(2) The expressions of SNS documents are usually nonstandard, streaming, and dynamic. New terms mushroom from social networks which are extremely colloquial. The SNS contents of the same theme may shift over time, and hence, the original expressions and calculation models have to account for such a shift. This problem is particularly serious for classification.

(3) SNS documents have their own structures and interaction characteristics. They also have their specific ways of expression and structures. For example, a microblog document is likely to contain a Hashtag and an external URL link. In general, SNS documents contain information about the authors, while social relationships between authors can be formed by following or interacting. These characteristics can be used during IR.

(4) The time attribute can be found in most SNS queries and documents, for example, queries are always closely related to the current hot social events, and documents present different distribution characteristics with the passage of time. Using the time attribute to increase the effect of SNS IR is an important research objective.

The remaining parts of this chapter will introduce IR in social networks based on the three main IR applications or tasks. IR has an extremely wide coverage and is correlated with other fields. It is impossible to introduce all fields in this chapter due to the limitations of space. Readers interested in those topics can refer to social network related papers published in academic conferences (such as SIGIR and CIKM) in the field of IR.

1.2 Content search in social network

A content search task refers to the process of returning relevant information contents from a large amount of information in response to a given query. Content search is one of the most classical applications of IR. In SNS, content search is urgently needed. For example, a user enters "missing of MH370," with the aim of getting information about this event. Sometimes it is also possible to realize "Expert Location" based on social networks. For example, if you search "machine learning," some information about relevant experts can also be retrieved on SNS. This is a specific search application in SNS. Owing to space constraints, this topic is not discussed in this chapter. Interested readers can refer to Chapter 8 in the book "Social Network Data Analytics" [2]. The Text Retrieval Conference (TREC) added the sub-task of microblog search in 2011 to promote SNS search, in particular, microblog search, by providing standard queries and annotation data collections (Twitter).

The basic process of a traditional content search is as follows: Massive document data constitutes a corpus for the search; the user creates a query that can represent his information need; the query and documents are respectively processed and converted into certain representations; the relevance is calculated using the IR model; and the documents are returned to the user in an descending order (based on the calculation). It is clear from the above process, that in the IR process, the processed objects (documents and queries) should be converted into certain forms of representations first, following which the relevance between the objects can be calculated. The conversion of the retrieved objects into expressions and the calculation of the relevance between them fall into the scope of IR models. There are currently three classical IR models, including the vector space model, probabilistic model, and statistical language models. Now we briefly introduce these models and the corresponding feedback models.

1.2.1 Classical information retrieval and relevant feedback models

1. Vector space model

In the 1950s, the idea of converting texts into term vectors that bear weight information was proposed [3], which is the basis of the Vector Space Model (VSM). The modern VSM [4] proposed by Salton (1927–1995) et al. is one of the most extensively used retrieval models in the field of IR in the past few decades.

The basic concept of VSM: a query is considered a document; every document is converted into a vector in the same space; and the similarity between all vectors is used to measure the relevance between the query and documents. Each dimension of the vector corresponds to a term whose value represents the importance of the term in the document. This importance is referred to as weight, which is generally calculated using the TFIDF scheme: TF refers to the term frequency; namely, the number of times that a term appears in a document, denoting the representativeness of that term in the document; DF is the number of documents in the document set that contains the term, referred to as document frequency. DF is generally converted into inverse

DF (IDF) for calculation. The IDF of a term (t) is generally calculated based on the following equation[2]:

$$\text{IDF}_t = \log \frac{N}{\text{DF}_t} \qquad (1.3)$$

where N is the number of documents in the document set and IDF is the ability of the term to distinguish documents. The IDF of commonly used words, such as "of," "a," and "the," is small. That is to say, their ability to distinguish documents is very limited. In VSM, the weight of a term is the product of TF and IDF.

Example 1.3 Calculation of TFIDF. Assume that the TF of a term in a document is 2, and that it can be found in 10 out of 100 documents, the TFIDF of the term in the document will be:

$$2 \times \log(100/10) = 2$$

Similarly, the weight of the query and other terms in the document can be calculated to obtain the vector representations of the query and each document. The similarity is calculated at last. For VSM, the cosine similarity between vectors is used to calculate the relevance between a query and a document. The cosine similarity between a query (q) and a document (d) is calculated using the following equation:

$$\text{RSV}(d, q) = \frac{\sum_t \text{TF}_{t,d} \times \text{IDF}_t \times \text{TF}_{t,q} \times \text{IDF}_t}{\sqrt{\sum_t (\text{TF}_{t,q} \times \text{IDF}_t)^2} \sqrt{\sum_t (\text{TF}_{t,d} \times \text{IDF}_t)^2}} \qquad (1.4)$$

where $\text{TF}_{t,d}$ is the occurrence frequency (number of times) of the term (t) in the document (d).

Example 1.4 Cosine similarity calculation. Assume that the vector representation of a query is <2, 0, 1, 0> and that of a document is <1, 2, 2, 0>, the cosine similarity between them will be:

$$\text{RSV}(d, q) = \frac{2 \times 1 + 0 \times 2 + 1 \times 2 + 0 \times 0}{\sqrt{2^2 + 0^2 + 1^2 + 0^2} \times \sqrt{1^2 + 2^2 + 2^2 + 0^2}} = \frac{4}{\sqrt{45}}$$

In practice, there are several transformed calculation methods for TF and IDF. In addition, the document length is also considered in some VSM weighting representations. Details of the above methods are described in references [5] and [6].

VSM is very simple and intuitive and gives good practical results. The idea of vector representation is widely used in various fields. Its shortcoming is the "term independence assumption," i.e., terms in different dimensions are independent of each other; this assumption obviously does not hold in practice. For example, in an

---

2 For the purpose of unification, the log in this chapter refers to logarithm with 10 as the base.

article that contains the term "Yao Ming," the probability that "basketball" appears in that article obviously increases.

2. Probabilistic retrieval model and BM25 formula

The probabilistic retrieval model (PRM) was first proposed in 1960 [7]. It has developed from theoretical research to practical applications in the past decades. The PRM-based OKAPI[3] retrieval system [8] has made excellent contributions at TREC conferences. INQUERY [9], another probabilistic retrieval system, also has a good reputation. This section first introduces the classical binary independence retrieval (BIR) model and then describes the BM25 formula used in the OKAPI system that has evolved from the BIR model. PRMs are models of a category, and hence, there are many other PRMs in addition to those introduced here. The readers can refer to the reference [10] for more information on PRMs.

In the PRM, the relevance between a query and a document is measured by the probability that the document is relevant to the query. Formally, the model introduces three random variables, i.e., D, Q, and R, where D and Q, respectively, refer to the document and query, and R is a binary random variable, with a value of 1 or 0 (1 denotes that D is relevant to Q, and 0 otherwise). For a given query $Q = q$, when the document $D = d$, the probabilistic model is used to calculate the probability that the document is relevant to the query.

In the BIR model, the probability $P\,(R = 1|D,Q)$ is calculated using Bayes formula. In IR, the relevance between a query Q and each document is calculated, therefore, for the same query, we denote $P(R=1|D,Q)$ with $P(R=1|D)$, and get the following:

$$P(R = 1|D) = \frac{P(D|R = 1)P(R = 1)}{P(D)} \tag{1.5}$$

For the convenience of calculation, the BIR model uses the following log-odds to sort the documents[4]:

$$\log \frac{P(R = 1|D)}{P(R = 0|D)} = \log \frac{P(D|R = 1)P(R = 1)}{P(D|R = 0)P(R = 0)} \propto \log \frac{P(D|R = 1)}{P(D|R = 0)} \tag{1.6}$$

where $P(D|R=1)$ and $P(D|R=0)$ denote the probability of generating the document D, respectively, under the condition that $R=1$ (relevant) and $R=0$ (irrelevant). $\propto$ denotes order preserving, i.e., the order of the expression before $\propto$ is the same as that after $\propto$. In the BIR model, the document D is based on the term collection $\{ti|1 \le i \le M\}$ and is

---

3 http://www.soi.city.ac.uk/~andym/OKAPI-PACK/index.html.
4 Obviously, for the two documents D_1 and D_2, if $P(R=1|\,D_1) > P(R=1|\,D_2)$, will hold. That is to say, the log-odds function is order-preserving.

generated according to the multivariate Bernoulli distribution[5] (where, M is the number of terms). Consequently, the above formula is transformed into:

$$\log \frac{P(D|R=1)}{P(D|R=0)} = \log \frac{\prod_i p_i^{e_i(1-p_i)^{1-e_i}}}{\prod_i q_i^{e_i(1-q_i)^{1-e_i}}} = \sum_i \log \left(\frac{p_i}{q_i}\right)^{e_i} \left(\frac{1-p_i}{1-q_i}\right)^{1-e_i} \tag{1.7}$$

where p_i and q_i are the probabilities of occurrence of the term t_i in relevant and irrelevant documents, respectively. e_i is a variable with a value of 0 or 1 (if $t_i \in D$, $e_i=1$; otherwise, $e_i=0$) and denotes whether the term t_i exists in the document D. Parameters p_i and q_i can be estimated, and then the rank of each document can be obtained.

Example 1.5 BIR model calculation. Provided that the query is "Information Retrieval Textbook,"\a document D is "Retrieval Courseware," and the number of terms (M) is 5, the parameters p_i and q_i are shown in Table 1.1.

Table 1.1: A calculation example of BIR model

Term	Information	Retrieval	Textbook	Tutorial	Courseware
$R=1$, p_i	0.8	0.9	0.3	0.32	0.15
$R=0$, q_i	0.3	0.1	0.35	0.33	0.10

Consequently,

$P(D|R=1)=(1-0.8)\times0.9\times(1-0.3)\times(1-0.32)\times0.15$

$P(D|R=0)= (1-0.3)\times0.1\times(1-0.35)\times(1-0.33)\times0.10$

$\log(P(D|R=1)/P(D|R=0))=0.624$

The basic BIR model does not consider important factors such as TF and document length. Robertson et al. made improvements and proposed the well-known BM25 retrieval formula [8] as follows:

$$RSV(d, q) = \sum_{t \in q} In \frac{N - DF_t + 0.5}{DF_t + 0.5} \times \frac{(k_1 + 1)TF_{t,d}}{k_1((1-b) + b\frac{dl}{avdl}) + TF_{t,d}} \times \frac{(k_3 + 1)TF_{t,q}}{k_3 + TF_{t,q}} \tag{1.8}$$

where dl is the length of the document; avdl is the average length of documents in the document collection; $TF_{t,d}$ and $TF_{t,q}$ are the frequency of the term in the document and query, respectively; and b, k_1, and k_3 are empirical parameters. The formula can also be considered as a formula for calculating the inner product of vectors using different TF and IDF calculation methods.

---

5 Multivariate Bernoulli distribution can be considered as the process of flipping M coins, where each coin corresponds to a term. All terms that all upturned coins correspond to the document D.

The advantages of probabilistic models are that they are derived based on the probability theory and they are more interpretable than VSMs. However, in a calculation using probabilistic models, the assumption of term independence still exists. Moreover, the parameters in the models need to be precisely estimated.

3. Statistical language modeling-based retrieval models and query likelihood models

The statistical language modeling (SLM) technology attempts to build models for natural languages based on statistics and probability theory to obtain the law and features of natural languages and solve specific problems concerning language information processing. SLM technology dates back to the early 20th century. At that time, the intentions were to study the Russian reference and build models for sequences of Russian letters [11]. Since the 1980s, SLM has been widely applied in fields such as speech recognition, optical character recognition, and machine translation, and has become one of the mainstream technologies for language information processing [12].

Definition 1.4 Statistical language model. A language is essentially the result of certain probability distribution on its alphabet, which shows the possibility that any sequence of letters becomes a sentence (or any other language unit) of the language. The probability distribution is the SLM of the language. For any term sequence $S = w_1 w_2 \dots w_n$ in a language, probability can be determined based on the following equation:

$$P(S) = \prod_{i=1}^{n} P(w_i|w_1 w_2 \dots w_{i-1}) \tag{1.9}$$

To estimate the probability $P(w_i|w_1 w_2 \dots w_i{-}1)$ based on a given dataset (corpus) has become a key problem of SLM. It is impossible to obtain enough data to estimate $P(w_i| w_1 w_2 \dots w_i{-}1)$, hence, the n-gram model becomes relevant, according to which the occurrence of a term is only related to the n-1th term before it (the n-1th term is also called the history of the nth term), that is,

$$P(w_i|w_1 w_2 \dots w_{i-1}) \approx P(w_i|w_{i-n+1} \dots w_{i-1}) \tag{1.10}$$

When n=1, it is referred to as a unigram model, where the occurrence of any term is considered to independent of other terms, i.e., it is assumed that all terms are independent of each other. A model without regard to term sequence is also called a bag of words model (BOW model). When n=2, it is referred to as a bigram model, where the occurrence of the current term is considered to be only related to the previous term.

The basic idea of SLM-based IR models is considering relevance as the sampling probability in statistical models. The earliest model of this kind is the query likelihood model (QLM) proposed by Jay Ponte and Bruce Croft [13]. The model's basic idea: there is a language model M_d for each document d in the document set, while the query is a sampling result of the model, and documents can be ranked based on the sampling probability of the query based on different document models. The basic formula of the QLM is as follows:

$$RSV(d,q) = \log P(d|q) = \log \frac{P(q|d)P(d)}{P(q)}$$

$$\propto \log(P(q|d)P(d)) \propto \log P(q|d) \qquad (1.11)$$

$$= \sum_{t \in q} \log P(t|M_d) = \sum_{t \in q} TF_{t,q} \cdot \log P(t|M_d)$$

In the above derivation, QLM assumes that the prior probability $P(d)$ of the document follows a uniform distribution, i.e., $P(d)=1/N$ (N is the number of documents), hence this part can be removed. It should be noted that in some studies the prior probability can be reserved because other distributional hypotheses are adopted. $P(t|M_d)$ is the probability of considering the term t by the model M_d of the document d during sampling. This probability can be calculated by adopting the maximum likelihood estimation (MLE) as:

$$P_{ml}(t|M_d) = \frac{TF_{t,d}}{\sum_{t'} TF_{t',d}} \qquad (1.12)$$

The above estimation is likely to result in zero probability, i.e., the probability that the term t does not appear in the document is estimated to be 0. In this case, once a term in a query does not appear in the document, the score of the document will be zero. This is obviously inappropriate. Therefore, smoothing methods are commonly used for correction. At present, the main smoothing methods include Jelinek–Mercer (JM) smoothing method and Dirichlet prior smoothing method. The formula for the JM smoothing method is as follows:

$$P(t|M_d) = \lambda P_{ml}(t|M_d) + (1-\lambda)P_{ml}(t|C) \qquad (1.13)$$

where, $P_{ml}(t|C)$ is the MLE value of t in the entire document collection C. λ is the linear weighting coefficient between 0 and 1, which should be given beforehand. Consequently, for every term t in the document collection, it is necessary to calculate the $P_{ml}(t|C)$. For a document d, the retrieval status value $RSV(d,q)$ can be obtained by first calculating the $P_{ml}(t|M_d)$ of every term t in the document and then deriving the $P(t|M_d)$ of every term t in the query q by linear combination. The process is easy to understand, but owing to space constraints, the concrete calculation example is not presented here. Interested readers can try themselves.

A series of other statistical modeling-based IR models have been developed based on the QLM, including the KL divergence model [14] and the translation model [15]. With regard to the KL distance model, the KL divergence (relative entropy) between the two kinds of distributions, respectively, in the query language model and the document language model is calculated to rank the documents. The translation model introduces the translation probability between terms, and makes the conversion between terms in the query and those in the document possible.

The SLM-based retrieval model can be derived based on the probability statistical theory, which is highly interpretable and is the most popular retrieval model in the research field. In addition, the model, in essence, does not rely on the term independence assumption and is highly extendable. The shortcoming of the model also lies in parameter estimation.

As mentioned before, the query entered by a user might not accurately represent his information need, so it is necessary to expand (or reformulate) the user query in most cases. The most representative method is query expansion based on relevance feedback. The basic idea of the method is using partial documents returned during the first retrieval to modify the original query. The method that the system modifies the query by directly assuming that the top k documents returned for the first time are relevant is referred to as pseudo-relevance feedback (PRF). The following section introduces some classical query expansion methods based on relevance feedback and PRF.

4. Query expansion model based on vector space model

The most famous query expansion method in VSM is the Rocchio method [16]. The basic concept of the method is based on the assumption that "vector representations of relevant documents are similar to each other, while vector representations of relevant documents are dissimilar to those of irrelevant documents." Under this assumption, provided that all relevant documents and irrelevant documents in the document collection C composed of N documents are known, and they, respectively, constitute collection C_r and collection C_{nr}, the optimum query vector that distinguishes the two collections will be:

$$\vec{q}_{opt} = \frac{1}{|C_r|} \sum_{\forall d_j \in C_r} \vec{d}_j - \frac{1}{|C_{nr}|} \sum_{\forall d_j \in C_{nr}} \vec{d}_j \qquad (1.14)$$

where, $|C_r|$ and $|C_{nr}|$ represent the size of collection C_r and C_{nr}, respectively. The above formula indicates that when all relevant and irrelevant documents are known, the optimum query vector that distinguishes them is the vector difference between the average vector of all relevant documents (centroid vector) and that of all irrelevant documents [1].

However, in practice, for a given query, the collection of relevant documents and that of irrelevant documents are unknown beforehand. Although relevance feedback is performed, the relevance of only part of the documents can be obtained. RM is a method of gradually modifying the original query vector when the relevance of a part of the documents is known. Thus, assuming that $\vec{q}$ is the original query vector, and D_r and D_{nr} are, respectively, the collection of relevant documents and the collection of irrelevant documents in the returned documents, obtained through relevance feed-back or PRF, the query vector after modification will be:

$$\vec{q}_{opt} = \alpha\vec{q} + \frac{\beta}{|D_r|} \sum_{\forall d_j \in D_r} \vec{d}_j - \frac{\gamma}{|D_{nr}|} \sum_{\forall d_j \in D_{nr}} \vec{d}_j \qquad (1.15)$$

where, $|D_r|$ and $|D_{nr}|$ denote the sizes of document collections D_r and D_{nr}, respectively; $\vec{d}_j$ is the vector of document dj; obviously, $\frac{1}{|D_r|} \sum_{\forall d_j \in D_r} \vec{d}_j$ and $\frac{1}{|D_{nr}|} \sum_{\forall d_j \in D_{nr}} \vec{d}_j$, respectively, denote the average vector of all document vectors in the collection of relevant documents D_r and irrelevant documents D_{nr}; α, β, and y are constants and non-negative real numbers.

The above formula can be described as follows: The query vector after modification is the linear weighted sum of the initial query vector, the average document vector of the collection of relevant documents, and the average document vector of the collection of irrelevant documents, with the corresponding weighting coefficients being α, β, and $-y$. Essentially, the above formula makes the modified query continuously approach the centroid vector of the collection of relevant documents, but gradually deviates from the centroid vector of the collection of irrelevant documents. Due to the subtraction operation in the above formula, the components of the final result vector may be negative. In this case, the commonly used method is to set the value of the components to 0, i.e., remove the terms that these components correspond to.

In practical applications, there are many value assignment methods for α, β, and y, and a commonly used method is $\alpha = 1$, $\beta = 0.75$, and $y = 0.15$. When $y > 0$, the current Rocchio query expansion method allows negative feedback; when $y = 0$ and $\beta > 0$, the current method only allows positive feedback. In addition to the above-mentioned basic Rocchio formula, there are other transformed Rocchio formulas.

5. Query expansion based on probabilistic retrieval model

In the BIR model introduced above, the most important query-related parameters are the probability p_i of occurrence of a term t_i in relevant documents, and the probability q_i of occurrence of a term in irrelevant documents. The query expansion based on such a model mainly refers to the modification of the two parameters.

It is generally assumed that the top k documents in the results returned for the first retrieval are relevant, and form the collection V of relevant documents; except V, all other documents in the document collection C are irrelevant. Assume that the document collection in V that contains the query term t_i is V_i, $N=|C|$, $r_i=|V_i|$, and ni is the number of documents in C that contain ti, we derive the following formulas based on the definitions of p_i and q_i:

$$p_i = \frac{r_i}{|V|}, q_i = \frac{n_i - r_i}{N - |V|} \qquad (1.16)$$

In practice, it is necessary to smooth the above estimations, and a commonly-used smoothing method is adding $\frac{1}{2}$ to the numbers of documents that both contain and do not contain the term ti. Thus, we get the following formulas:

$$p_i = \frac{r_i + \frac{1}{2}}{|V| + 1}, q_i = \frac{n_i - r_i + \frac{1}{2}}{N - |V| + 1} \tag{1.17}$$

We can see that the original p_i and q_i in the above formulas do not appear in the query updating formula, which is obviously different from the Rocchio method introduced earlier. A query expansion method that uses the original p_i is as follows:

$$p_i^{(t+1)} = \frac{r_i + Kp_i^{(t)}}{|V| + K} \tag{1.18}$$

where, $p_i^{(t)}$ and $p_i^{(t+1)}$, respectively, denote the former p_i value and the p_i value after updating. Essentially, the former p_i value is introduced as the Bayes prior and is used together with the weight κ. Interested readers can refer to chapter 11 of "Introduction to Information Retrieval" [1].

6. Statistical language modeling-based retrieval model

A relevance model (RM) [17] is a query expansion model based on the SLM theory and the PRF concept. In the original SLM model, the information on the query's pseudo-relevant document collection is not used. However, research shows that this information is very effective in improving the retrieval performance.

The relevance model expands the query by estimating the generating probability $P(t|R)$ of terms in a given query. The formula for calculating $P(t|R)$ is as follows:

$$P(t|R) \approx \frac{P(t, q_1, q_2, \ldots)}{\sum_{t' \in V} P(t', q_1, q_2, \ldots)} \tag{1.19}$$

and

$$P(t, q_1, q_2, \cdots) = \sum_{d \in C_{prf}} P(d)P(t|M_d) \prod_i P(q_i|M_d)$$

where, $q_1, q_2, \ldots$ are terms in the query and $Cprf$ is the pseudo-relevant document collection.

According to the above formula, the relevance between each term in a term collection and the query q can be reckoned to select the term set, in terms of the value scale, which is most likely to be applied to the expansion, and get a new query by adopting the linear interpolation method in combination with both the original and extended terms. The conditional probability of the new term $P_{new}(t|Mq)$ is shown as follows:

$$P_{new}(t|M_q) = (1 - \lambda)P_{orgin}(t|M_q) + \lambda P(t|R) \tag{1.20}$$

The relevance model-based sorting function may adopt the KL divergence model [14] to calculate the KL divergence between P(t|Md) and P(t|Mq) and to obtain the final sorting result.

As mentioned earlier, documents and user queries are the basis for the input of the query model; therefore, in selecting the appropriate retrieval model, it is imperative to consider the documents used for retrieval and the characteristics of users' query input. However, the SNS content search is different from traditional text search in both the document and query. Consequently, corresponding modifications have to be made to query representation, document representation, and relevance computing models in the process of searching. In the following section, we will specifically introduce the SNS content search based on the above three aspects.

1.2.2 Query representation in microblog search

Query representation refers to the process of handling queries. In traditional methods, the longer the text, the more sufficient the data for estimating the model, and the more accurate the estimation will be. In general, if the query and document models are estimated more accurately, the calculation of the relevance will be more accurate and so will the retrieval effect. In the application of microblog search, microblog documents and queries are both extremely short, making query expansion more important. The research on query representation in microblog search focuses on query expansion.

In addition, as the real relevance feedback needs abundant user labeling information which is not easy to obtain in practice, the feedbacks are generally PRFs. The short length of microblog documents leads to the following issue: during the implementation of PRF, because the relevant microblog documents are short, when keywords are extracted according to methods similar to TFIDF, the probability that some occasional words are chosen is high; hence, the returned keywords will be noisy, greatly affecting the feedback model and the final retrieval effect. In such a case, how to propose a better query representation method and how to use feedback documents become more important.

1. Query expansion based on internal and external resources

According to different sources of expansion, query expansions can be divided into those expansions based on external resources and those based on internal resources. The latter refers to appropriate modification of the original query using the factors conducive to the performance of microblog retrieval (such as URL link, Hashtag, the author, etc.) based on the features of microblog itself after the first retrieval, as well as the performance of the second retrieval for the new query after the modification; the former generally refers to the expansion of the original query using query-related dictionaries, news, Wikipedia, and other knowledge bases or results from search engines after the first retrieval. For example, a generative model is used in reference [18] and the external resources are included in the model as variables, where the interdependency among queries, documents, and expanded documents is also considered. Specifically, two external resources including news and Wikipedia were used to carry out the experiment in this work, with good results.

In general, query expansion based on external resources is a commonly-used technology in ordinary searches, which appears basically the same when introduced to microblog searches, so we will not go into details about it here. The following section mainly introduces query expansion based on internal resources. Microblogs involve abundant information such as the author, Hashtag, URL, etc., which can be deemed as the resources of query expansion.

Example 1.6 Expansion of microblog queries using Hashtag. In reference [19], Hashtags in microblogs are mainly used to expand microblog queries. Specifically, first, in the paper, all Hashtags in the microblog corpus are extracted and a collection of Hashtags is obtained. Then, microblogs containing one certain Hashtag is used to construct the unigram language model of this Hashtag. By calculating the KL divergence between this language model and the QLM Mq, the best k Hashtags are selected for feedback. Finally, the original query model is expanded through the interpolation of the results obtained from the feedback. The final experiment shows that this method had improved in metrics such as the MAP and $P@10$.

1) Constructing a Hashtag model
Assuming that C is a data collection of n microblog posts and in this data collection there are m different Hashtags, denoted as t_i, we collected the microblogs bearing the same Hashtag and estimate the probability of occurrence of a word in each group of microblog posts. In fact, we also achieved m language models, where each language model corresponds to one Hashtag denoted as Θ_i.

Then, with a given query q (denoted as Θ_q in the model), k Hashtags most relevant to this query were found; the specific approach is sorting each tag t_i based on the following equation:

$$r(t_i, q) = -KL(\Theta_q \,\|\, \Theta_i)$$ (1.21)

After sorting, the top k Hashtags were selected.

2) Query expansion using Hashtag
Assuming that r_k is the collection of the top k Hashtags selected as above and Θ_r represents the corresponding language model, the formula of the post-feedback query model is as below:

$$\hat{\Theta}_{fb} = (1 - \lambda)\hat{\Theta}_q^{ML} + \lambda\hat{\Theta}_r \qquad (1.22)$$

where, $\hat{\Theta}_r$ can be estimated using the following two methods.

(1) HFB1: Nonzero elements in Θ_r are estimated based on uniform distribution.

(2) HFB2: Nonzero elements in $\hat{\Theta}_r$ are estimated based on the proportion of $\frac{IDF(t_i)}{\max IDF}$.

3) Improvements made using the relationship between Hashtags

Based on the aforementioned expansion models, the relationship between Hashtags will be further considered during feedback. Define X as the matrix of $k \times k$, with each element x_{ij} in the matrix representing the total co-occurrence number of Hashtags t_i and t_j. Then, carry out normalization for the matrix based on $x_{ii}=1$. Thus, the relevance between the Hashtag ti and the Hashtag collection r_k can be measured as below:

$$a(t_i, r_k) = \sum_j^k x_{ij} \qquad (1.23)$$

When a Hashtag co-occurs with more tags in the r_k, the relevance will be bigger. Introducing the relevance into the above-mentioned ranking formula, we get:

$$r_a(t_i, q) = r(t_i, q) + \log a(t_i, r_k) \qquad (1.24)$$

Conduct feedback (denoted as HFB1, HFB2, and HFB2a depending on different feedback methods) once more by using the new Hashtag collection calculated in this way. Table 1.2 gives the result of the final query feedback method.

Table 1.2: Experimental result [19] on microblog retrieval relevance feedback using Hashtags

Method	MAP	NDCG	P10
Baseline, no FB	0.4268	0.6110	0.7034
Baseline, FB	0.4381	0.6209	0.7138
HFB1	0.4605	0.6431 †	0.7483
HFB2	0.4617 †	0.6388 †	0.7414
HFB2a	0.4684 †	0.6488 †	0.7483

It is clear from Table 1.2, we can see that Hashtag can provide useful information for query relevance feedback, and feedback, with the consideration of the relationship between Hashtags further improving the retrieval performance.

Other applications where internal resources are used: According to reference [20], microblogs containing hyperlinks have more abundant information; therefore, increasing the weight of such microblogs during PRF will improve the retrieval result.

2. Query expansion based on time factor

The original query is the direct expression of users' query intent, where users often express their query intent with several query words. However, the expected results of queries from Web search and those from microblog search are different. In reference [21], a detailed analysis of queries in microblogs has been presented; the authors concluded that the main purpose of users' searching in microblogs is to query some time-sensitive news and social relationship information. The time-based news queries intend to find contents that users are interested in from the latest hot microblogs and are quite sensitive to time.

One typical manifestation of time-sensitive queries is that the distribution of the relevant collections changes significantly at every moment. In reference [22], the queries from No. 301, 156, and 165 TREC are taken as examples for detailed description. In addition, in reference [23], a similar analysis of microblog queries is carried out to verify similar characteristics of time response. Figure 1.1 shows the distributions of relevant documents of some randomly selected queries.

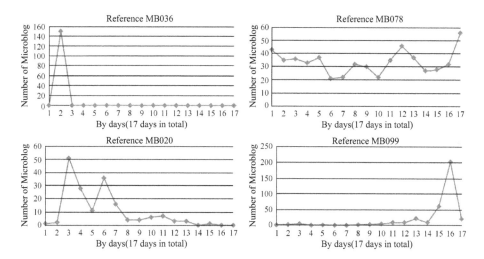

Figure 1.1: Distribution of relevant documents of TREC queries MB036, MB078, MB020, and MB099 over time [23]

From Figure 1.1, we can see that the distribution of relevant documents of microblog queries at each moment is far from even and shows obvious time sensitivity. During expansion of time-sensitive queries, the time factor should be considered; at present, some time-sensitive query expansion works have sprung up. These works can be divided into two categories based on different ways of time integration: one is to analyze the characteristics of the distribution of documents at certain time points to select the appropriate time point as the basis of document selection before query expansion; the other is to construct a graph using the time relationship between terms and obtain the relevance score of each candidate word corresponding to the given query through iterative computations, and finally, select the terms with high scores for expansion.

Example 1.7 Time-aware query expansion: In reference [24], it has been pointed out that there is a correlation between relevance and time to degree certain extent. The author verified this hypothesis by comparing the two kinds of time sequences (one is the time sequence formed by feedback documents consisting of the first retrieval results and the other is the time sequence formed by the really relevant documents). Then, the author counted the number of documents which appeared at each time frame t in the returned document collection at the first time, then selected the top k documents near the time frame when the largest number of documents appeared, and finally, used the Rocchio method to calculate the score of each term to select the expanded word. The experiment proved that this method can improve the retrieval effect.

1) Verifying the correlation between relevance and time
To construct the time sequence $Y=y_1, y_2, \dots, y_n$, the author collected all documents posted in the same time frame t; the computing method of y_t is as below:

$$y_t = \sum_{d \in D} f_t(d) \tag{1.25}$$

where, D is the document collection for constructing the sequence, and $f_t(d)$ is calculated as:

$$f_t(d) = \begin{cases} 1, & \text{if } d \text{ is posted in the time frame t} \\ 0, & \text{others} \end{cases}$$

The time frame can be 1 hour, 1 day, or 1 month, however in the experiment, the time unit was 1 day.

Using the above method, the author constructed two time sequences; sequence X represented the time sequence of real relevant documents whereas sequence Y represented the time sequence formed by the retrieval results. To determine whether the two sequences are related, the author introduced the cross correlation function (CCF) for calculation.

$$\rho_{xy}(\tau) = \frac{E\left[x_t - \mu_x\right]\left(y_{t+\tau} - \mu_y\right)}{\sigma_x \sigma_y} \tag{1.26}$$

where, μ_x and μ_y are the mean values of two time sequences, respectively, while σ_x and σ_y are the corresponding standard deviations. τ represents the delay time, $0 \le \tau \le 15$. Table 1.3 presents the CCF values of the two sequences.

From Table 1.3, it can be seen that the mean value of CCF is 0.7280 and its variance is 0.0393. Therefore, the retrieved and real relevant documents are highly related in terms of time distribution.

Table 1.3: Result of CCF values of two sequences from Giuseppe Amodeo [24]

	Full Time				Crawling Time			
	Min	**Max**	μ	σ_2	**Min**	**Max**	μ	σ_2
BL1	0.1216	0.9916	0.7459	0.0364	0.0635	0.9889	0.6122	0.0745
BL2	0.1688	0.9960	0.7145	0.0343	0.0087	0.9957	0.5363	0.0854
BL3	0.1313	0.9943	0.7204	0.0412	0.0586	0.9942	0.5805	0.0832
BL4	0.1577	0.9923	0.7496	0.0368	0.0471	0.9916	0.6043	0.0769
BL5	0.0914	0.9881	0.7094	0.0480	0.1461	0.9917	0.5935	0.0824
	0.1342	0.9925	0.7280	0.0393	0.0648	0.9924	0.5854	0.0805

2) Time-based query feedback

According to the above conclusion, the burst time frame of real relevant documents and their initial search results are highly related. Therefore, the author assumed that the pseudo-relevant documents at the burst peak period are more likely to be relevant to queries.

In this manner, the authors selected the documents at the peak period as pseudo-relevant documents and those at other time periods as irrelevant documents, and carried out feedback on queries using the Rocchio algorithm as:

$$q_m = \alpha q_0 + \beta \frac{1}{|D_r|} \sum_{d_j \in D_r} d_j - \gamma \frac{1}{|D_{nr}|} \sum_{d_j \in D_{nr}} d_j \tag{1.27}$$

The experiment shows that, after the queries are expanded using this method, the retrieval performance can be effectively improved.

Apart from the above work, there are other studies regarding query expansion using the time factor.

In reference [24], according to the time T of each document d and the specified rules, the burst collection B (one or more) can be obtained from the first search result collection R of queries, and the collection of bursts is denoted as bursts (R); then, the score of each term can be calculated according to the following formula:

$$P(t|q) = \frac{1}{|\text{bursts}(R)|} \sum_{B \in \text{bursts}(R)} \left(\frac{1}{N_B} \sum_{d \in B} P(t|d) e^{\gamma \left(\left| \max_{d' \in B} \text{Time}(d') - \text{Time}(d) \right| \right)} \right) \tag{1.28}$$

where, Time(d) represents the document time and NB the size of bursts (R) B. Finally, the top k terms with the largest probability are selected as the expanded query terms. The experimental result shows that this method can improve the retrieval effect.

In reference [25], in the context of blog retrieval, and based on the idea of the relevance model, a time-based $P(t|q)$ generation model is defined, and the expanded terms ranking ahead are selected through calculation. According to the paper, the generation process of $P(t|q)$ is: first, select a time moment T for the query q and then select a t under the conditions of T and q; thus, the formula of the query term generation model is:

$$P(t|q) = \sum_T P(t|T, q)P(T|q) \tag{1.29}$$

The experiment performed on the TREC data collection Blog08 indicates that this method improves the retrieval effect. Similar methods can also be applied to microblog search.

In reference [26], with the background of microblog retrieval, a PageRank-based query expansion method to calculate term weights was proposed. The method included the following steps: first, extract n-gram from the first returned results as the terms. Then, construct a directed graph for these terms, in which the terms are taken as the nodes and term TF is the prior value of the node. The edge represents the time correlation between terms while the weight represents the time-based relevance. Finally, use the PageRank random walk to calculate the final value of each term, and select some terms to expand the original query. The TREC Twitter data collection-based experiment indicates that good results can be ontained when $n = 1$ and $n = 2$ are selected for the n-gram.

1.2.3 Document representation in microblog search

The research on microblog document models mainly focuses on the scarcity of microblogs. On one hand, the short text is expanded through internal or external resources to make up for the inadequacy of information, improving the effect of microblog retrieval through document expansion; on the other hand, in terms of document representation, a representation method or model suitable for microblog texts is proposed.

1. Document expansion based on internal and external resources
Many studies have been conducted for the expansion of microblog documents, including expansion based on internal and external resources. For expansion based on external resources, Wikipedia, search engines, and other available external data are mainly used; for expansion based on internal resources, documents similar to the original one are retrieved for expansion in the context of current datasets and is based on the features of microblogs. Strictly speaking, some work mentioned in this section is not directly intended for microblogs. However, during microblog retrieval, the aforesaid method can be used to expand microblog documents, and then a re-ranking of those expanded documents is carried out, which might finally improve the retrieval performance. The method based on external resources is conceptually quite similar:

expanding the original document based on the external documents, which is not be repeated here. Next, we will introduce the research on the expansion of documents based on internal resources.

Example 1.8 Expansion of documents based on internal resources. According to reference [27], a short text only covers one topic in general. Therefore, in this paper, a short text is regarded as a pseudo-query, which is searched in some data collections, and the search results are taken as the object of document expansion.

1) Constructing pseudo-queries

First, assume document D as a pseudo-query which is denoted as QD. Then, execute query QD in collection C to get a ranking result of the top k documents: $RD=D_1, ..., D_k$, and their retrieval scores, and finally, calculate these scores $P(D|D1),...P(D|Dk)$ using the QLM.

2) Calculating the expansion document model D'

In a classical SLM, the distribution of documents and document collections in vocabularies (here, document collections are considered as the background to play a role in smoothing) is usually used to estimate the language model of documents. If the above ranking result RD is given, the following formula can be used to improve the estimation:

$$P(w|D') = P(w|d_1, ..., d_{|D|}) = \frac{P(w, d_1, ..., d_{|D|})}{P(d_1, ..., d_{|D|})} \tag{1.30}$$

The denominator $P(d_1, ..., d_{|D|})$ does not depend on w, so only the joint distribution needs to be retained; namely:

$$P\left(w, d_1, ..., d_{|D|}\right) = \sum_{D_i \in C} P(D_i)P\left(w, d_1, ..., d_{|D|}|D_i\right) \tag{1.31}$$

In which,

$$P(w, d_1, ..., d_{|D|}|D_i) = P(w|D_i) \prod_{j=1}^{|D|} P(d_j|D_i)$$

According to the above formula, we can get

$$P\left(w, d_1, ..., d_{|D|}\right) = \sum_{D_i \in C} P(D_i)P(w|D_i) \prod_{j=1}^{|D|} P(d_j|D_i) \tag{1.32}$$

The last factor in the aforesaid formula indicates that this joint distribution is, to a large degree, determined by the documents that are most similar to D. Therefore, the k most similar documents can be used to estimate the $P(w|D')$.

After the $P(w|D')$ is gained, the document model can be updated by interpolation:

$$P_\lambda(w|D') = (1-\lambda)P_{ml}(w|D) + \lambda P(w|D') \qquad (1.33)$$

In this paper, λ=0.5. It should be noted that the time factor is also used here to expand the documents at the same time.

Furthermore, other works related to expansion of the short-text documents have been reported. In reference [28], the URLs contained in microblogs have links to use for expanding the current microblogs. In some works, the translation model which is expanded based on the integration of microblog Hashtags, URLs, and other features is proposed, wherein various factors can be conveniently considered to expand the microblog document. The experimental result verifies that microblog documents can be effectively represented by these features.

In addition, it is also possible to realize microblog expansion using information about authors. In reference [29], an author-based modeling microblog retrieval method has been proposed. In the paper, information on authors is extracted from the corpus of the TREC microblog first, and all microblog documents posted by each author are sorted to form "new documents," and then user's language models are constructed based on these documents. In addition, smoothing is carried out using the information on authors to estimate the probability of new microblog document terms. The experimental result shows that properly using the author-related information can improve the microblog retrieval performance. In reference [30], the followers of the author of microblog documents as well as the microblog documents issued by the followers are used to expand the documents, which gave good effects.

2. Document representation based on microblog features

Example 1.9 Document representation based on microblog features. In reference [31], while constructing a language model for microblogs, the TF impacts were ignored; namely, the occurrence of terms was denoted as 1 and nonoccurrence as 0, while the frequency of the terms occurring in a document was not considered. In the paper, JM smoothing method was used to carry out smoothing for the documents: $P(t|\theta_d) = (1-\lambda)P(t|d) + \lambda P(t)$, where the $P(t|d)$ and $P(t)$ were calculated as follows, respectively:

$$P(t|d) = \frac{\hat{n}(t,d)}{\sum_{t' \in d} \hat{n}(t',d)}, \ P(t) = \frac{\sum_d \hat{n}(t,d)}{N}, \ \hat{n}(t,d) = \begin{cases} 0, n(t,d) = 0 \\ 1, n(t,d) > 0 \end{cases} \qquad (1.34)$$

The $n(t,d)$ is the term frequency of term t in document d and N is the total amount of microblog documents in data collection.

In the context of microblog search, reference [32] verified the impact of factors such as the TF which plays a promoting role in traditional retrieval and document length normalization (DLN) on microblog retrieval. The ranking model adopted in the paper is BM25 model, and the result indicated that the effect was only 0.0048 lower than the best-result $P@30$ when the document's TF was ignored; the effect was the best when the document's DLN factor was ignored. In conclusion, the paper points out that both TF and DLN are involved in the construction of the language model; therefore, how to reduce the negative impacts of these factors shall be considered during the construction of the language model.

Furthermore, the impact of the time factor can be considered in representing microblog documents. Relevant studies were mainly conducted in the context of statistical language retrieval models, where the key task is to calculate the term generation probability $P(t|M_d)$. There are currently two methods of adding the time factor in the $P(t|M_d)$: one is to define the time weight for the term t by introducing the time factor [33, 34]; the other is to introduce time during smoothing of the language model probability estimation [35].

Example 1.10 Temporal language model. In reference [34], the objective was to determine the document time through the Temporal Language Model (TLM). Although the study is not about microblog retrieval, the idea of introducing time for the term t can be used in the language model. It shall be noted that the data collection at this time will be divided into multiple blocks based on the time granularity, denoted as p, whose set will constitute P. The time granularity can be selected freely such as 1 month and 3 months. The author defined a time weight in allusion to the term t in the paper called the temporal entropy (TE), which can be calculated as follows:

$$TE(t_i) = 1 + \frac{1}{\log N_P} \sum_{p \in P} P(p|t_i) \times \log P(p|t_i) \tag{1.35}$$

where, $P(p|t_i) = \frac{\text{tf}(t_i, p)}{\sum_{k=1}^{N_P} \text{tf}(t_i, p_k)}$; N_P is the total number of data collection blocks, and $\text{tf}(t_i, p)$ is the number of t_i occurring in the block p. The time weights of terms can be used to modify the term probability of the language model, thus realizing the representation of microblog documents.

In reference [35], the improvement of the document language model lies in the smoothing part; the paper holds that the value of smoothing weights varies with the time of different documents; i.e., the newer the document, the smaller the λ value. Thus, priority shall be given to the document itself. According to this hypothesis, a new smoothing parameter λ_t is introduced in the smoothing formula and two calculation formulas are given:

$$\lambda_t^{\text{MLE}} = \frac{n(d, t < t_d)}{n(C)}, \ \lambda_t^{\text{MAP}} = \frac{n(d, t < t_d) + \alpha - 1}{n(C) + \beta - \alpha - 2} \tag{1.36}$$

where, $n(d, t < t_d)$ is the number of documents for which the time is smaller than that for document d in the entire dataset; $n(C)$ is the number of documents in the entire dataset; and α and β are the conjugate prior parameters of beta.

In addition, there are also many studies in allusion to short-text modeling: some studies [36–39] have focused on the classification and clustering and abstracting of microblog documents, while others concentrated on the recording training topic model of microblogs, where LDA [40] is adopted. In reference [40], the basic LDA and author topic model as well as the post-expansion LDA are compared, showing that the post-clustering retraining topic model has a better effect. All these studies can be used to reevaluate $P(t|d)$ to realize more sufficient representation of documents.

1.2.4 Microblog retrieval models

In the context of microblog search, the features of microblogs bring challenges to the retrieval models: first, the text is short and calculations in many models are carried out based on statistics, which cannot guarantee the sound effect in the case of super-sparse data. Second, the structures are richer; in the original retrieval models, the impacts of repost and reply (the network of microblog documents themselves) and the author's SNS on ranking were not considered. These two problems exist in the VSM, the BM25 retrieval model, and the current language models. Therefore, some changes in the original retrieval models should be made to guarantee retrieval quality.

1. Time prior method

The document prior method is a document processing method where different calculation formulas are defined by taking into consideration the corpus background due to different significances of documents in the corpus, and the calculation results in the retrieval model are used to achieve better retrieval effect. At present, studies concerning prior calculation of the document where time information has been considered can be divided into two kinds: one is defining changes in the relationship between the document and time; the other is modifying the PageRank method by adding the time relationship in it. Please note that the estimation of document prior here refers to the estimation of $P(d)$, whereas the document model estimation in the previous section is the estimation of $P(t|d)$.

According to reference [22], prior information varies with document time. From the perspective of time, the author assumed that the significance of new documents is higher than the old ones, and defined document significance as the temporal exponential distribution. The formula is as follows:

$$P(d) = P(d|T_d) = \gamma e^{-\gamma(T_c - T_d)} \tag{1.37}$$

where T_d stands for the time of the document; T_c is the latest time for document centralization; γ is the exponential distribution parameter, designated according to the human experience. This paper takes SLM as the basis, and regarding the document prior $P(d)$, the original constant is replaced by the exponential distribution (namely, the above calculation formula), modifying the original language model ranking function. This paper performed the experimental verification on the TREC's news corpus, and the result showed that the time-included ranking result is better than the no-time ranking result. This method can be used in microblog retrieval.

In reference [35], the method proposed in reference [22] is improved; this study pointed out that the significance of each document varies with different query conditions. Based on this hypothesis, the method of estimating the exponential distribution parameters using the pseudo-relevance feedback collection of queries is proposed; the given query information is introduced by changing the γ in the above formula into γ_q. The pseudo-relevance feedback collection of the query q is denoted as $C_{prf} = \{d_1, d_2, ..., d_k\}$, and $T_q = \{t_1, t_2, ..., t_k\}$ is used to represent the moment corresponding to each document in the collection C_{prf}; according to the maximum likelihood estimation, the calculation formula can be obtained as:

$$\gamma_q^{\mathrm{ML}} = 1/\overline{T_q} \tag{1.38}$$

where $\overline{T_q}$ stands for the average mean of the collection T_q, with the value being $\overline{T_q} = \sum_{i=1}^{k} t_i/k$.

In reference [35], in addition to the verification made on two TREC news corpora, a microblog corpus collection is constructed; the experiment is carried out in the microblog environment, which verifies that the retrieval result of this algorithm is better than that of the existing algorithms.

Example 1.11 Time-based SLM: In reference [33], a time-based New Temporal Language Model (NTLM) used for webpage searching is proposed, and the queries that this model faces include texts and obvious time information; for example, "earthquakes from 2000 to 2010." One of the major contributions of this paper is the proposed concept of time-based TF ("TTF" for short); wherein the time factor is added to the TF calculation formula to improve the retrieval effect through time information.

1) Time point extraction

It takes two steps to extract time points. One is the pre-processing stage, in which the paragraph segmentation and word segmentation are carried out. First, extract the main body and distribution time of webpages, and then segment each paragraph into sentences and classify words. Finally, remove the included verbs, conjunctions, and prepositions, and the rest of the words will be taken as the keywords.

The other is the extraction stage, which is mainly based on the similarity between sentences and retrospection. First, find the direct or hinted time information from the keywords defined in the previous step; if the time information is not found in the content, take the release time as the webpage's time; for each word w, if time $[ts, te]$ is included in w-covered sentences, we will construct a pair <w, $[ts, te]$> of the keyword and time quantum. If there is no information on time quantum, we will find the best-matching reference time using the retrospection method; that is, we will find the time of the sentence most similar to this one; the calculation method of the similarity is as follows:

$$\text{Sim}(S_1, S_2) = \frac{\sum_{i=1}^{n} k_i \times k_i'}{\sqrt{\sum_{i=1}^{n} k_i^2} \times \sqrt{\sum_{i=1}^{n} k_i'^2}} \tag{1.39}$$

where $S1$ and $S2$ stand for sentences to be matched, $K = \langle k_1, \ldots, k_n \rangle$ and $K' = \langle k_1', \ldots, k_n' \rangle$ stand for the frequencies of each keyword occurring in $S1$ and $S2$, respectively.

2) Time-aware term weight

In general, the distribution of a term in document d can be estimated with the frequency of this term, as follows:

$$P_{ml}(w|M_d) = \frac{\text{tf}_{w,d}}{\text{dl}_d} \tag{1.40}$$

$\text{tf}_{w,d}$ stands for the number of w occurring in document d while dl_d stands for the length of document d. At the same time, the author proposed a term frequency based on the time factor, and its specific definition is as follows:

$$\text{tf}_{w,d}^T = \frac{\text{num}(w, d, [T_s^q, T_e^q])}{\text{dl}_d} \tag{1.41}$$

$[T_s^q, T_e^q]$ represents the querying time; T_s^q the beginning time and T_e^q the ending time. $\text{num}(w, d, [T_s^q, T_e^q])$ represents that the word w occurs in document d and satisfies $[T_s^w, T_e^w] \in [T_s^q, T_e^q]$. The author defines $[T_s^w, T_e^w] \in [T_s^q, T_e^q]$ as in the four cases as below ($[T_s^w, T_e^w]$ is denoted as T^w and $[T_s^q, T_e^q]$ denoted as T^q).
(1) Contained: $T_s^q \le T_s^w$ and $T_e^q \ge T_e^w$.
(2) Contains: $T_s^q > T_s^w$ and $T_e^q < T_e^w$.
(3) Left overlapping: $T_s^q < T_s^w$ and $T_e^q \le T_e^w$.
(4) Right overlapping: $T_s^q \ge T_s^w$ and $T_e^q > T_e^w$.

The definition of the relationship between the two is shown in Figure 1.2.

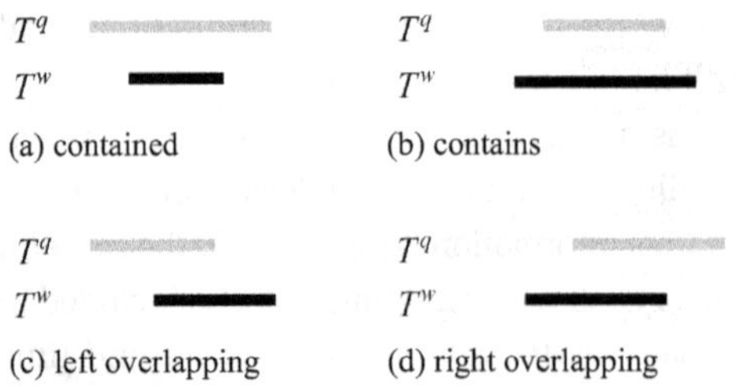

T^q T^q

T^w T^w

(a) contained   (b) contains

T^q T^q

T^w T^w

(c) left overlapping   (d) right overlapping

Figure 1.2: Schematic Diagram of $[T_s^w, T_e^w] \in [T_s^q, T_e^q]$

Finally, in allusion to the above term weight sensitive to time, several smoothing methods are proposed in the paper to improve the retrieval performance.

It is worth noting that TTF can be used in any TF-involved model, such as the language model and BM25, and the experimental result also indicates that TTF can help improve the retrieval effect.

During IR, PageRank (PR for short) indicates the significance of documents by virtue of the links between webpages. References [41–44] are a series of studies where time factor was added to the original PR algorithm.

In reference [42], it is mentioned that the time dimension information is ignored in the traditional PageRank or HITS algorithm in analyzing the webpage link, based on which the time factor is added in the original PR algorithm to obtain a new algorithm, called the Timed PageRank (TPR for short), and its formula is as follows:

$$\text{PR}^T(T) = (1-d) + d \sum_{T_i \in \text{InLinkT}} \frac{w_{T_i} \times \text{PR}^T(T_i)}{C(T_i)} \tag{1.42}$$

Where, $w_{T_i} = b^{(\max \text{time}(C) - \text{time}(T))}$.

In reference [43], the way of adding time is changed and the algorithm T-Rank is put forward. According to Berberich, when a user skips from the current webpage to a link-out page, the skipping probability will be different depending on different link-out webpages; meanwhile, the probability of the user selecting a page at random will vary with the current page, and thereby two probabilities (which can also be called the weight) are defined in the paper: one is the transmission probability of skipping from the page T to a page T_i where the link-out pages of the original page T are centralized, denoted as $t(T_i, T)$; the other is the random skipping weight of the current page, denoted as $s(T)$. The modified formula is as follows:

$$\text{T Rank}(T) = (1-d) \times s(T) + d \sum_{t_i \in \text{InLinkT}} t(T_i, T) \times \text{T Rank}(T_i) \tag{1.43}$$

The webpage time is used to define two kinds of freshness which shall be used in the calculation formula of the transmission probability and skipping probability. The experimental result indicates that the effect is improved. In a similar manner, in reference [41], the features of the last-modified tab of the webpage are added in the PageRank after being analyzed, to be taken as the weight of the edge between webpages.

In reference [44], the time weight of webpages is added in the score of webpages obtained through the original PageRank algorithm to adjust the PR. Jing Wan and Sixue Bai believe that a webpage has three properties: integrity, accuracy, and time-activity. Time-activity represents the freshness of the webpage content, while outdated information may bring negative impacts during IR, so the author proposed that time-activity shall become one of the factors influencing the PR degree. Assuming a webpage is T, four factors will be used to determine the activity of this page at a certain moment, and these four factors are: the activity of the domain name that this page belongs to, the activity of the creator of the domain that the page belongs to, the degree to which users are interested in this page, and the contents of the text that the page carries. The active scores of this page at different moments are calculated based on these four factors to form its time activity vector, denoted as $TR(T)$. The author classified the page into four categories: strong-temporal common quality, weak-temporal common quality, weak-temporal high quality, and no-temporal quality based on the active score at each moment, and gets the time vector $TR(T)$ of this page; meanwhile, the author gets the PageRank vector $PR(T)$ of this page according to different moments, and the final prior calculation formula of this webpage is $TR(T) \times PR(T)$.

2. Multi-feature integration method

In reference [45], microblog search is taken as the research content and the effect of multiple microblog features on microblog search are put forward and verified. The microblog features considered in this paper include: the number of microblogs posted by the microblog author, the number of followers and followees of the microblog author, the microblog length, and whether URL is included in the microblog. The numbers of followers and followees of a microblog author are taken as the in-degree and out-degree definition functions to indicate the author's weight. The selected verification method is re-ranking the top k results of special queries in the commercial search engine and determining whether the result after re-ranking is improved. The conclusion obtained finally is that the effect is the best when three features are combined.

Example 1.12 Ranking through integrating multiple features. The idea in reference [45] is simple, with the purpose of re-ranking the initial search results, and the effect of multiple factors on the results is considered.

1) Author score

If A is used to represent the collection of all authors, a mapping $A \rightarrow R+$ can be established, thus endowing each author a with a non-negative real number $g(a)$, which is called this author's score. First, the score can be estimated through the number of microblogs posted by the author thus far; the author whose underlying assumption is active may release more meaningful microblogs. Therefore, the author's TweetRank can be calculated through the following formula:

$$TR(a) = N(a) \qquad (1.44)$$

The $N(a)$ represents the number of microblogs posted by the author thus far. The score can be estimated according to the numbers of followers and followees of author a (FollowerRank), as follows:

$$FR(a) = \frac{i(a)}{i(a) + o(a)} \tag{1.45}$$

The $i(a)$ is the in-degree of the author a and $o(a)$ is the out-degree of the author a. Of course, more complicated algorithms similar to PageRank can also be used to calculate the author's score.

2) Microblog score

Assuming D represents all microblogs and Q represents the set of all queries, the retrieval is equivalent to making such a mapping as $D{\times}Q{\rightarrow}R+$; that is, to get a non-negative real number $f(d, q)$ for a given pair (d, q). In addition, use "auth" to stand for the author of a document; i.e., auth(d). Therefore, from the perspective of the author's influence, the microblog score can be estimated using the following two formulas:

$$\begin{cases} f_{TR}(d, q) &= \text{TR(auth}(d)) \\ f_{FR}(d, q) &= \text{FR(auth}(d)) \end{cases} \tag{1.46}$$

In addition, length may influence the microblog quality, hence, LengthRank is calculated as below:

$$f_{LR}(d, q) = \frac{l(t)}{\max_{s \in D_q^k} l(s)} \tag{1.47}$$

The D_q^K is the result of the top k queries returned in the first time, while $l(t)$ and $l(s)$ are the length of t and s, respectively. In addition, URLRank is calculated as below:

$$f_{UR}(d, q) = \begin{cases} c, & \text{if microblog } d \text{ contains URL} \\ 0, & \text{others} \end{cases} \tag{1.48}$$

The c is a positive constant.

3) Combination score

With the combination of the above factors, the follower length rank (FLR) score and follower length URLRank (FLUR) score can be obtained:

$$f_{FLR}(d, q) = f_{FR}(d, q) + f_{LR}(d, q) \tag{1.49}$$

$$f_{FLUR}(d, q) = f_{FLR}(d, q) + f_{UR}(d, q) \tag{1.50}$$

The experimental result of the paper indicates that FLUR method is the best; that is, to integrate the numbers of the author's followers and followees, the length of the author's microblog, and the factor that whether the microblog contains URLs.

In reference [46], how to use the "learning to rank" method to rank microblogs is introduced. It is also believed that the microblog search results shall be ranked according to some features rather than the time of the microblogs. To ensure an accurate model, the authors consider many features of microblogs, and then remove some useless ones through feature extraction, principal component analysis (PCA), among other methods, to obtain a conclusion similar to reference [45], which holds that the factor of whether the microblog containing URL, the author's authority and the microblog's length exert the most important impacts on the ranking.

In reference [47], it is believed that the difference between queries shall be considered for the "learning to rank" method in the microblog ranking, so they proposed a learning to rank pattern for query modeling; a semi-supervised Transductive Learning algorithm is used to train the model. The learning to rank scheme generally needs labelling. As the transductive learning algorithm is used, the ranking of new queries without any labeled examples is also attempted in this paper. The experiment indicates that this method can improve the current "learning to rank" method as well as improve the ranking effect.

1.3 Content classification

Classification refers to a process of classifying given objects into one or more given classes. The text-oriented classification is called text classification. Classification involves two stages: training and test. Simply put, training is a process of learning the classification rules or disciplines according to the labeled training data, whereas test is a process of applying the trained classifiers in the new test data. No matter whether it is training or test, characteristic representation shall be carried out for classification objects first, and then the classification algorithm will be used for learning or classification.

Classification can also be viewed as an application of IR. In this case, the documents to be classified can be taken as "inquiries," and the target category can be regarded as a "document" in the document set.

Several studies on the short text classification have been carried out at home and abroad. As one of the main features of SNS texts is also "being short," all the research work regarding short text classification can be used as reference for classifying SNS contents. Therefore, the conclusion of this section is not limited to the classification of SNS texts. It should be noted that, in the SNS research, according to different classification objects and classification systems, there are also the classification of users, communities, emotions, and high/low-quality contents in SNS. Due to space constraints, this section only focuses on topic-based SNS classification. Please refer to Chapter 6 of this book for the classification of emotions. Next, the research on classification of current short texts will be summarized from the dimensions of features and algorithms.

Another common content processing technology is clustering, which is also one of the main technologies for topic detection and tracking. Interested readers can refer to Chapter 11 of this book.

1.3.1 Feature processing in short text classification

Due to the scarcity of short texts, various resources shall be used to expand the features in classification of texts to expand the short text. In addition, in terms of the feature selection, most researchers will directly adopt the feature selection algorithm in text classification; also, some researchers will combine the features of short texts and modify the current feature selection algorithms or propose new feature selection algorithms, thus better reducing the short text feature dimension and removing the redundant or irrelevant features, with the hope of obtaining better classification results.

1. Feature expansion

Most microblog text contents are simple and concise, being only a sentence or a few phrases sometimes, and always depending on the context. If the microblog text is too short, the problem of serious data sparsity arises during text classification. To solve this problem, researchers may expand microblogs by introducing external resources; in addition to the WordNet and Wikipedia, external resources such as the search results, news, Mesh, and Open Directory Project (ODP) obtained through search engines are used to expand the contents of short texts. It should be noted that the expansion here is also applicable to the microblog document representation mentioned above, except that the final objective of feature expansion is classification.

Example 1.13 Short text classification based on Wikipedia feature expansion method. In reference [48], to overcome the sparsity problem in short text classification, the Wikipedia-based feature expansion method is used to carry out multi-class classification of texts.

(1) Each document d can be represented as the TFIDF form; namely, $\Phi_{\mathrm{TFIDF}}(d)=$ (TFIDF$_d(t_1)$, ... , TFIDF$_d(t_m)$), in which, m is the size of the term space.
(2) Each document maps the short text d into a collection of Wikipedia concepts defined in advance through explicit semantic analysis (ESA). Define the collection of Wikipedia articles as $W = \{a_1,\dots,a_n\}$, to obtain the ESA feature expression of document d: $\Phi\mathrm{ESA}(d)=(\mathrm{as}(d,a_1),\dots,\mathrm{as}(d,a_n))$, in which, the "as" function represents the association strength [49] between the document d and the concept, and is calculated as follows:

$$\mathrm{as}(d, a_i) = \sum_{t \in d} \mathrm{TF}_d(t) \cdot \mathrm{TFIDF}_{a_i}(t) \tag{1.51}$$

(3) Perform classification through two steps: first, search in the whole classification space by calculating the cosine similarity between the document and the class center to get k candidate classes. Then, use trained SVM in the k classes to carry out classification.

(4) The above processes can be carried out based on two feature representation methods, and at last, the two result probabilities, *P*TFIDF and *P*ESA calculated through the SVM classifier can be integrated. The integrated classification probability can be obtained as:

$$PEnsemble = PTFIDF + \alpha PESA \qquad (1.52)$$

α is the weighting coefficient, which can be determined in training.

The final experimental result shows that, when the Wikipedia features are integrated in the short texts, the classification effect can be improved significantly.

In reference [50], a method of conceptual expression of short texts based on Wikipedia is also proposed, and the experimental result indicates that this method can improve the classification effect.

Although effective words in short texts are limited, they contain plenty of latent semantic meanings; how to fully excavate the latent semantic meanings of short texts and the similarity of short texts has become one of the major directions of research on short text classification. In reference [51], a latent topics-based short text classification method is put forward; according to this method, latent topics are used to establish a general framework. The latent topics are trained from the "global data set;" Wikipedia and Medline are used in the experiments in this paper, following which the test of these two authoritative data sets is carried out. The experimental result shows that this framework can effectively enrich the information in short texts and improve the classification effect.

Under this framework, in reference [52], a method of using the multi-granularity latent topics to enrich short texts is proposed. According to this method, the granularities of topics are divided based on the original method, and these generated multi-granularity latent topics are used to enrich short texts for assisting the classification. Finally, both SVM and the maximum entropy model are used for classification, whose error rates of classification are reduced by 20.25% and 16.68%, respectively.

There are also many other researches that use external resources to expand short texts; for example, using meta-information in hyperlink targets to improve the classification of microblog topics, as discussed in reference [53]; using Wikipedia to carry out the text feature expansion, as proposedin reference [54]; and using other microblogs related to the microblog texts to be classified to enrich the contents of microblog texts for classification.

2. Feature selection

How to screen the most representative features is one of the focus and difficulty of research on short text classification at present.

In reference [56], the method of using eight features of Twitter to classify microblogs into five classes has been proposed. These five classes are news, events, opinions, deals, and personal messages; and the eight extracted features are: authorship, the presence of abbreviations and slangs, the presence of event related phrases, the presence of emotion words, the presence of emphasizing words (such as veeery, meaning the high degree of "very"), the presence of symbols of currency or percent, the presence of @ username at the beginning of the microblog, and the presence of @ username in the middle of the microblog.

The author represented each microblog with the above features, and designed a Naive Bayes classifier to classify the microblogs. The experimental result indicates that the above feature representation has significant improvements relative to the feature representation method for common bag of words, and that the classification has achieved an accuracy of more than 90%.

In reference [57], a simple, scalable, and non-parametric method has been proposed for the classification of short texts, and its main idea is as follows: first, select some guiding words representative to the topic as the query words, to query the texts to be classified; then, make full use of the information search technology to return the query result; finally, select 5~15 features by voting, to represent and classify the microblogs.

In reference [58], a feature selection method is proposed; first, select some words with rich part of speech as features, and then use Hownet to expand the semantic features of those words, as well as to improve the classification effect. In reference [59], short texts are classified according to features extracted based on the topic trend in Twitter, which achieved certain results.

1.3.2 Short text classification algorithm

1. Improved traditional algorithms

In reference [60], it is believed that in the context of microblog classification, classifiers that can realize incremental update are needed. Therefore, an in-depth analysis of the Bayesian classification method has been carried out in this paper and the test on the short text data sets to be classified has also been carried out; it is found that the classification effect can be signficantly boosted by using the effective smoothing method. In addition, the influences of the size and length of the training data collections on the classification effect are also analyzed in this paper.

In addition, the improvements in traditional algorithms are also embodied in the calculation of microblog similarity: the method of calculating microblog similarity is the special similarity calculation method to overcome the problem of large computations during the expansion of microblog contents when external resources are introduced. In reference [61], a "similar kernel function" dedicated to calculating the similarity of short texts is proposed, which can be used in any kernel-based machine learning algorithm; moreover, the information returned by the search engine can be used to measure the similarity of short texts. In addition, in reference

[62], a method of calculating the similarity of two documents that does not share any common terms is proposed, which can be used in microblog classification.

2. Improved algorithm based on concept drift

Another representative work is to classify microblogs by regarding them as the time-relevant streams. During the time-based microblog classification, the much-discussed problem is the drift of concepts; that is, as time goes on, the topic of classes will vary. Therefore, the original classification model has to be modified constantly.

Some representative work regarding concept drift: in reference [63], the idea of the "stability period" of a word is raised to overcome the concept drift problem in text classification; in reference [64], the microblog stream is deemed as the research content and a classification model has been proposed.

Example 1.14 Classification model of the microblog stream. In this model, to deal with the concept drift problem, the global occurrence probability and the recent occurrence probability of each word are estimated and the modeling for common words and some sudden words is carried out; the word changes in its ranking can be detected. Finally, use the word suffix array method to learn the time factor in the n-gram of the word, and present an effective n-gram realization scheme based on the full-text index method. The result of the three data collection-based experiment shows that the change of word probability is a very important factor and that this method can clearly boost the classification effect. In this paper, the exponentially weighted moving average (EWMA) method is used to estimate the word probability, using the following formula:

$$P_{\text{EWMA}}(w_i|c, t) = \sum_{j \in J_c(w_i)} (1-\lambda)^{|d_{c,t}|-j} \lambda \tag{1.53}$$

The $J_c(w_i)$ is the location collection of a word in d_c, t and λ is the smoothing parameter used in EWMA.

Using suffix arrays (SAs) to classify microblogs has been proposed in recent years. In reference [65], a character string method with good performance in both space and time is proposed based on SAs and the kernel technology in SVM. In reference [66], a new logistic regression model is presented by virtue of all valid string, and this model is also constructed based on the SAs technology.

3. Transfer learning for short text classification

Transfer learning is a framework of machine learning, by which a compact and effective representation can be learned from the labeled data samples in a source domain and unlabeled data samples or a few of labeled samples in the target domain, and then the learned feature representation method is applied in the target domain. The transfer learning technology has been successfully used in many fields, such as text mining [67, 68], image classification [69], named entity recognition [70], cross-language classification [71], and WiFi [72] positioning. In the field of microblog classification, to deal with such features as fast changes in microblog texts and the proneness to outdatedness of training data, a few scholars have introduced the transfer learning technology, which is briefly summarized as follows.

In reference [73], assisted learning for partial observation (ALPOS) has been proposed to solve the short-text problem in microblogs, which is a transfer learning method based on feature representation. According to this method, a microblog text is a part of an ordinary long text, and the reason why the text is short is that some characters have not been observed. In this method, long texts are used as the source data (assisted data) to improve the effect of microblog classification effect. This method expands the framework of the self-learning method, and requires that the source data and the target data have the same feature space and tag space; further, the labeled source data are also necessary.

Advantages of the transfer learning method lie in its simple operation and significant effect, whereas its disadvantages are that it is only applicable to situations where the source field and the target field are quite similar, and that it requires the source field and target field to have the same class space and feature space; the efficiency of the iteration-based training process is also not high. When some instances in the source field in the application scene conform to the distribution of the target field, the instance-based transfer learning method is applicable.

In reference [74], a transfer learning method is proposed to solve the problem of transfer classification of short and sparse text (TCSST); this method is an instance-based transfer learning method in the inductive transfer learning and expands the TrAdaBoost framework. To solve the problem of sparse labeled data in the source data, the semi-supervised learning method is adopted to carry out sampling for the original data. Based on the original labeled data, post-sampling original unlabeled data and target labeled data, and the TrAdaBoost's framework training classifier, the method performed experimental verification on the 20-Newsgroups data collection and a real seminar review datum.

1.4 Social network recommendation

Recommendation is the process of pushing relevant items or contents to users according to their preferences. It mainly includes content-based recommendation technology and collaborative filtering-based recommendation technology. The basic idea of content-based recommendation technology is to extract the characteristics of users from the personal information of users or to analyze the preferences of users to items according to the historical data of users, and then build a preference model of users by synthesizing these factors, and finally, calculate the degree of matching between the items to be recommended and users based on these characteristics. Another practice is to look for other users with similar preference or similar items from the score data of a large number of users, and then use such similarities to recommend items for current users; this practice is referred to as collaborative filtering.

Recommendation is a common application form of IR. In this application, a user can be taken as an "inquiry," an item as a "document;" therefore, it is a process to obtain a "document" best matching the "inquiry" from these "documents." Thus, the basic model and algorithms of IR can be applied in a recommendation system, especially a content-based recommendation system. A recommendation system based on collaborative filtering is somewhat different from an ordinary IR system. Therefore, in the presentation below, we will mainly present a recommendation system based on collaborative filtering.

In general, a recommendation system contains the following three elements.

User: the target of a recommendation system. The recommendation effect can vary greatly with the amount of user information mastered by the system. User information includes a user's personal attributes, such as age, gender, and occupation, as well as historical exchange data of the user with the system, which can more directly reflect user preference.

Item: the contents of a recommendation system. Here, item is a concept in a broad sense; it can be both commodities such as books, music, and films, as well as information content such as news, articles and microblog.

Rating of user preference for items: in websites such as Amazon or Netflix, scores are normally used to indicate user's preference for items. The commonly used scores are divided into five levels (1~5), with ratings from low to high. Depending on applications, the rating of preference degree can be in different forms, and sometimes two levels (like or dislike) are used for the rating.

Recommendation algorithm: given user u and item i, estimate the rating r of a user for the item. The recommendation algorithm can be abstracted as function $f(u, i) = r$. Essentially, the recommendation algorithm provides the estimation of matching degree of user and item; to obtain a precision recommendation result, it is necessary to tap in-depth characteristics of the user and the item, as well as the interactive relationship between them. The recommendation algorithm studies how to model various potential factors that may affect recommendation.

As mentioned above, recommendation algorithms can be classified into two major categories according to different types of information used.

(1) Content-based recommendation: the basic idea is to analyze the personal attributes of users and the attributes of item and to calculate the matching degree between the item to be recommended and the user in conjunction with the historical preference of the user for the item to recommend an item with high matching degree to the user. This technique allows directly completing recommendations based on information of users and items, and was used extensively in the early recommendation systems; although it can only push items similar to historical characteristics of items by establishing a direct relationship between

item characteristics and user preference, it cannot produce novel contents and its expandability is poor [75–80].

(2) Recommendation based on collaborative filtering: the evaluation of users on items constitutes the user-item matrix (see Table 1.4). Based on the basic assumption that "similar users have similar preferences," items preferred by users similar to the target user can be pushed to the latter. Collaborative filtering method does not take into account content and is entirely based on the historical information on interactions between users and items; therefore, it can solve the problem of lacking user and item description information in many cases. With its effectiveness in recommendation, collaborative filtering is now extensively applied in various commercial systems, such as, news recommendation in GroupLens, movie recommendation in MovieLens, and music recommendation in Ringo.

Table 1.4: User-item matrix

	Item 1	Item 2	Item 3	Item 4
User 1	1		2	
User 2		2		2
User 3	2	3	4	
User 4		2		5

In an actual system, to obtain better recommendation results, the two methods can be combined, such as the MatchBox recommendation system of Microsoft [81]. In the research circle, collaborative filtering has attracted extensive attention for two reasons: one is that the inputs (user-item matrix) of collaborative filtering is more accessible to many systems, while it is difficult to obtain users' personal attributes (except for a small number of social network websites); the other is that it has higher theoretical values to mine the user-item matrix by integrating multiple sources of information. Due to limitations of space, this section mainly focuses on how social network information is integrated in the collaborative filtering technology. In the following section, the meaning of social recommendation will be presented first, and then the memory-based social recommendation and model-based social recommendation methods will be presented.

1.4.1 Brief introduction to social recommendation

This section presents the differences between social recommendation and traditional recommendation technologies based on collaborative filtering to understand the basic issues of social recommendation.

1. Problems of Traditional Collaborative Filtering

For the given user-item matrix $R \in R^{m \times n}$, where m is the number of users, and n the number of items; the score of user u for item i is $r_{u,i}$ (or $R_{u,i}$), corresponding to the element in the uth line and ith row of R matrix. In the actual applications, most elements in matrix R are missing, so the target of collaborative filtering is to use the existing elements in R to predict the missing elements $\tilde{r}_{u,i}$ in R; i.e., to predict the rating of user u for item i.

The two main problems faced by collaborative filtering are:

(1) Data scarcity: in the user-item matrix R, all known elements come from user operation, but in real applications, both the number of users m and number of items n are huge, while items really scored by users are quite limited in number; for example, in Netflix data, only about 1% of the score values are known.

(2) The problem of cold start: collaborative filtering uses the historical score information of users to make recommendation; if a user uses the recommendation system for the first time, there is no historical information available at that time; therefore, it is quite difficult to recommend items to such users. Solutions to cold start include using the average value of existing user scores in the matrix to predict new users' scores for fore items, or forcing users to score some items to obtain available historical data from the users.

2. Problems with social recommendation

The ultimate goal of social recommendation is the same as that of collaborative filtering, i.e. to predict the missing items in the user-item matrix $R \in R^{m \times n}$; the available information includes two categories:

(1) User historical score information $R \in R^{m \times n}$;

(2) The social relation information of users.

Social relation is defined as a function on the user set; for example, in a social relation network $G = <V, E>$, V is a set of users, $<u, v> \in E$ indicates a connecting side of user u and user v, the social relation based on a social relation network can be expressed using user-user matrix $T \in R^{m \times m}$; i.e., if there is a relationship between user u and user v, then

$$\text{matrix element } T_{u,v} = 1; \text{ otherwise } T_{u,v} = 0.$$

Obviously, social network relation is just one of the social relations, and social relations extracted based on different applications are also different. For example, in the Epinions website [82], users can not only evaluate various items but also score the evaluations made by other users. In addition, the Epinions website uses the concept of "trust," and users can choose to directly "trust" or "screen" some users; in this manner, every user has his/her own trusted target user, and can be also possibly trusted by other users, thus forming a complicated trust network (see Figure 1.3).

Despite their diversified forms, social relations have the potential of improving the effect of collaborative filtering as long as they can reflect the similarities

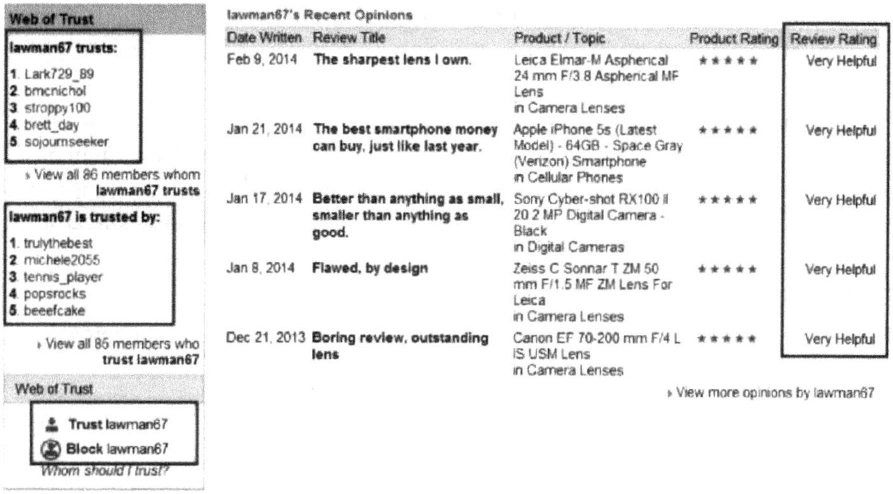

Web of Trust

lawman67 trusts:
1. Lark729_89
2. bmcnichol
3. stroppy100
4. brett_day
5. sojournseeker

‣ View all 86 members whom lawman67 trusts

lawman67 is trusted by:
1. trulythebest
2. michele2055
3. tennis_player
4. popsrocks
5. beeefcake

‣ View all 86 members who trust lawman67

Web of Trust

👤 Trust lawman67
🚫 Block lawman67
Whom should I trust?

lawman67's Recent Opinions

Date Written	Review Title	Product / Topic	Product Rating	Review Rating
Feb 9, 2014	The sharpest lens I own.	Leica Elmar-M Aspherical 24 mm F/3.8 Aspherical MF Lens in Camera Lenses	★★★★★	Very Helpful
Jan 21, 2014	The best smartphone money can buy, just like last year.	Apple iPhone 5s (Latest Model) - 64GB - Space Gray (Verizon) Smartphone in Cellular Phones	★★★★★	Very Helpful
Jan 17, 2014	Better than anything as small, smaller than anything as good.	Sony Cyber-shot RX100 II 20.2 MP Digital Camera - Black in Digital Cameras	★★★★★	Very Helpful
Jan 8, 2014	Flawed, by design	Zeiss C Sonnar T ZM 50 mm F/1.5 MF ZM Lens For Leica in Camera Lenses	★★★★★	Very Helpful
Dec 21, 2013	Boring review, outstanding lens	Canon EF 70-200 mm F/4 L IS USM Lens in Camera Lenses	★★★★★	Very Helpful

‣ View more opinions by lawman67

Figure 1.3: Direct trust relations between users in Epinions website

between users because the basic assumption of collaborative filtering is to make recommendation by making use of the preference of similar users. Social recommendation makes use of the social relations between users to improve the effect of collaborative filtering.

3. Evaluation for collaborative filtering

There are two commonly used evaluation metrics: mean absolute error (MAE) and root mean square error (RMSE). Both are used to measure the degree of difference between the predicted values and true values. The calculation formulas corresponding to the two metrics are as follows:

$$\begin{cases} \mathrm{MAE} = \frac{1}{T}\sum_{u,i}\left|\tilde{r}_{u,i} - r_{u,i}\right| \\ \mathrm{RMSE} = \sqrt{\frac{1}{T}\sum_{u,i}\left(\tilde{r}_{u,i} - r_{u,i}\right)^2} \end{cases} \tag{1.54}$$

where $\tilde{r}_{u,i}$ and $r_{u,i}$ represent respectively the predicted values and true values, and T the number of elements predicted.

1.4.2 Memory-based social recommendation

The memory-based collaborative filtering algorithm [40, 83–88] requires complete user-item matrix in calculation, and there are two basic assumptions:
(1) Similar users (based on historical record of users' scores for items) give similar scores for new items.

(2) Similar items (based on historical record of users' scores obtained) receive similar scores from new users.

Recommendation based on the first assumption is also referred to as user-based collaborative filtering, and that based on the second assumption is referred to as item-based collaborative filtering. Essentially, both assumptions filter off irrelevant score information, and use the most similar user-item score information to make prediction for $r_{u,i}$.

1. User-based collaborative filtering

The predicted score of user u for item i can be expressed as the formula below:

$$\tilde{r}_{u,i} = \overline{r}_u + \frac{\sum\limits_{v \in N(u)} \text{sim}(u,v)(r_{v,i} - \overline{r}_v)}{\sum\limits_{v \in N(u)} \text{sim}(u,v)} \tag{1.55}$$

where $N(u)$ indicates the set of users most similar to user u, and the number of set $|N(u)|$ should be designated in advance; $\overline{r}_u$ is the average value of user u's scores for all items; and $\text{sim}(u,v)$ gives the similarity between user u and user v. The similarity calculation $\text{sim}(u,v)$ is a critical step in the memory-based collaborative filtering algorithm, and commonly used similarity calculation methods are mainly Pearson's correlation coefficient [40] and cosine similarity [85].

Pearson's correlation coefficient is used to reflect the degree of linear correlation of two variables, and the calculation formula is as follows:

$$\text{sim}(u,v) = \frac{\sum_{i \in I}(r_{u,i} - \overline{r}_u)(r_{v,i} - \overline{r}_v)}{\sqrt{\sum_{i \in I}(r_{u,i} - \overline{r}_u)^2}\sqrt{\sum_{i \in I}(r_{v,i} - \overline{r}_v)^2}} \tag{1.56}$$

Calculation of $\text{sim}(u,v)$ also includes the limited Pearson's correlation coefficient [89], Spearman's ranking correlation coefficient [90], and so on. The following is a specific example of calculation.

Example 1.15 User-based collaborative filtering method. Suppose the user-item score matrix is as it is shown in Table 1.5, in which the scores given by users for items are integers of 1 to 5, we will use the user-based collaborative filtering algorithm to predict users' scores for items.

Suppose it is required to predict the score of user U_1 for item I_2, according to the user-based collaborative algorithm, we can use the above-mentioned score values to calculate the similarity of the other three users U_2, U_3, U_4 to user U_1:

$$\text{sim}(U_1, U_2) = \frac{(4-4.3)(4-3) + (5-4.3)(5-3) + (4-4.3)(1-3)}{\sqrt[2]{(4-4.3)^2 + (5-4.3)^2 + (4-4.3)^2} \cdot \sqrt[2]{(4-3)^2 + (5-3)^2 + (1-3)^2}} = 0.6923$$

Table 1.5: Example of user-based collaborative filtering

Item / User	I_1	I_2	I_3	I_4	I_5
U_1	4		5		4
U_2	4	2	5		1
U_3	2	4		2	2
U_4	1	5		3	3

In the same manner, we can obtain

$$\mathrm{sim}(U_1, U_3) = 0.5183$$

$$\mathrm{sim}(U_1, U_4) = 0.3$$

Therefore, the score value of user U_1 for item I_2 can be calculated as follows:

$$
\begin{aligned}
& r_{U_1, I_2} \\
&= \bar{r}_{U_1} + \frac{\mathrm{sim}(U_1, U_2) \cdot (r_{U_2, I_2} - \bar{r}_{U_2}) + \mathrm{sim}(U_1, U_3) \cdot (r_{U_3, I_2} - \bar{r}_{U_3}) + \mathrm{sim}(U_1, U_4) \cdot (r_{U_4, I_2} - \bar{r}_{U_4})}{\mathrm{sim}(U_1, U_2) + \mathrm{sim}(U_1, U_3) + \mathrm{sim}(U_1, U_4)} \\
&= 4.3 + \frac{0.6923 \cdot (2-3) + 0.5183 \cdot (4-2.5) + 0.3 \cdot (5-3)}{0.6923 + 0.5183 + 0.3} = 4.7535
\end{aligned}
$$

2. Item-based collaborative filtering

Similarly, the similarity between items can also be used to predict the score given by user u to item i, and in this case, the calculation formula is:

$$
\tilde{r}_{u,i} = \bar{r}_i + \frac{\sum_{j \in N(i)} \mathrm{sim}(i, j)(r_{u,j} - \bar{r}_j)}{\sum_{j \in N(i)} \mathrm{sim}(i, j)} \tag{1.57}
$$

In the same manner, $N(i)$ indicates the set of items most similar to i, and the number of set $|N(i)|$ should be designated in advance. $\bar{r}_j$ is the average value of scores obtained by item j from all users. The calculation of item similarity $\mathrm{sim}(i, j)$ is similar to that of user similarity $\mathrm{sim}(u, v)$, and similarity calculation methods, such as Pearson's correlation coefficient, can also be used.

3. Integrating social network information

User-based collaborative filtering transmits scores by estimating $\mathrm{sim}(u, v)$, and smoothens the scores of current users by using scores of neighbor users. However, in the real environment, as the score data of most users is limited and the problem of data sparsity is quite serious, it is very difficult to make similarity calculation for many users. Typical social network information includes association relationship between users, reflecting to a certain degree the similarity or trust between users. In fact, researches in social science show that trust diffusion exits extensively in social networks, as well as the trust-based socialized recommendation [91]; therefore, modeling the degree of user trust is an important task for social recommendation.

In references [76] and [83], the user trust relationship in Epinions is used to improve the calculation of user similarity. In references [92] and [93], the factor of trust relationship is introduced into the recommendation system to adjust the weight of scores with trust degree, and the experimental results have verified that user trust relationship can improve recommendation quality. Reference [90] proposed the trust relationship based semantic web recommendation system, which is based on intellectual entities, and connections are established between entities based on trust relationship.

Example 1.16 Recommendation based on user friend relations: reference [94] proposed a social relation diagram model constructed based on the friend relations of users and social tag information, and proposed a random walk model RWR to integrate user friend relations and social tags, thereby increasing the effect of recommendation (See Table 1.6).

Table 1.6: Example of user relations

User	U_1	U_2	U_3	U_4
U_1	0	3	0	5
U_2	2	0	7	0
U_3	5	2	0	7
U_4	0	3	6	0

The basic idea of memory-based social recommendation methods is that users and their friends share similar preferences; therefore, the trust degree between users is used directly to substitute the score similarity between users. Take the user trust relationship in Table 1.6 as an example, the user-based collaborative filtering integrated with user relations is calculated as follows:

$$r_{U_1,I_2} = \frac{\text{trust}(U_1, U_2) \cdot r_{U_2,I_2} + \text{trust}(U_1, U_4) \cdot r_{U_4,I_2}}{\text{trust}(U_1, U_2) + \text{trust}(U_1, U_4)} = \frac{3 \times 2 + 5 \times 5}{3 + 5} = 3.875$$

This method relies upon the trust relationship between users and their friends; however, it can be seen from the example above that, there is no direct trust value between user U_1 and user U_3, and when such relationship is seriously missing, the effect of this algorithm will be affected; therefore, researchers proposed establishing indirect trust relationship for users through trust transfer.

Reference [95] proposes a trust-based recommendation method to calculate user's authority scores through trust transfer and use the hierarchy of trust relationship to substitute the similarity calculation in traditional recommendations. Reference [96] proposed a recommendation method based on the random walk model, which can provide the credibility of score results.

In the recommendation methods based on trust relationship, it is most critical to obtain theset of trusting users, thereby avoiding the problem of data sparsity in the nearest neighbor based method. It is generally believed that trust between users is transferrable, as shown in Figure 1.4.

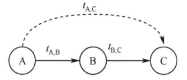

Figure 1.4: Transmissibility of trust relationship

If User A trusts B, and B trusts C, then it is believed that A also trusts C. In addition, trust relationship is one-way, if A trusts C, it does not mean that C also trusts A. Through the transfer of relationship, a user's range of trust relationship can be effectively expanded, even in a case of very sparse data; for example, user A only has one directly related trusting user B, however, through layers of transfer by the trusting users of B, a fairly big set of trusting users for user A can still be obtained, to effectively relax the data sparsity problem in score prediction.

A classical practice is to combine the maximum transfer distance with the minimum trust threshold [75], to limit by maximum transfer distance the levels of trust transfer in the calculable range, and then sieve out with minimum trust threshold the trusting friends that can be used. Reference [77] proposed a path-algebra-based trust transfer model; similarly, reference [78] proposed a method to express user trust relationship with trust transfer matrix, which can effectively integrate a number of trust transfer models. Reference [97] proposed the TidalTrust to make recommendations using the breadth-first search strategy in the trust relationship network. First, the shortest distance from all score users to target users is calculated and then the weight of scores is adjusted with the trust relationship between users on the shortest distance path. This approach only uses users on the shortest path and is very likely to lose a wealth of valuable information. On the basis of research in reference [97], reference [76] proposed the MoleTrust by introducing the concept of maximum trust depth; it requires that the integrated trust users are not only limited within the shortest distance but also within the maximum depth range, equivalent to a compromise between precision and coverage. Reference [98], based on the spreading activation model, proposerd the AppleSeed model, which states that the trust relationship of users has the cumulative effect. Even if the trust path between two users is very weak, it is also possible to obtain a very high trust weight as long as there are sufficient connection paths. In the following part, we will take TidalTrust as an example to introduce the trust transfer process.

Example 1.17 The method to adjust score weight with trust relations (TidalTrust).

Based on the trust relationships between users in Table 1.6, the trust diffusion path from user $U1$ to user $U3$ can be obtained, as shown in Figure 1.5.

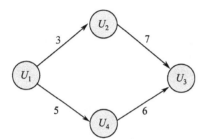

Figure 1.5: Trust diffusion path from user U_1 to user U_3

According to TidalTrust, it is necessary to first calculate the maximum value of trust at the nodes, and take this maximum value as the threshold to select a usable node, and the actual calculation method is as follows:

$$S_{ij} = \frac{\sum_{u_k \in F(i) \geq \max} S_{ik} S_{kj}}{\sum_{u_k \in F(i) \geq \max} S_{ik}} \tag{1.58}$$

where $u_k \in F(i)$ represents all neighboring friend of user i, and some neighboring friends with trust degree above the threshold are selected by as the nodes of diffusion.

It can be seen from Figure 1.5 that, in this example, U_2 and U_4 are the neighboring nodes of target user U_3; the trust value from user U_1 to U_2 is 3; the trust value from U_1 to U_4 is 5; only U_1 is connected to U_2 and U_4; therefore, U_2 and U_4 are respectively marked as 3 and 5. As for U_3, the threshold of trust degree for the node is 5; therefore, only U_4 satisfies the conditions. Thus, we can obtain the trust degree of users U_1 and U_3 as follows:

$$\text{trust}(U_1, U_3) = \frac{5 \times 6}{5} = 6$$

Apply this trust value in the above-mentioned user-based collaborative filtering formula, to achieve the score value of $U1$ for item $I2$ as follows:

$$r_{U_1, I_2} = \frac{\text{trust}(U_1, U_2) \cdot r_{U_2, I_2} + \text{trust}(U_1, U_3) \cdot r_{U_3, I_2} + \text{trust}(U_1, U_4) \cdot r_{U_4, I_2}}{\text{trust}(U_1, U_2) + \text{trust}(U_1, U_3) + \text{trust}(U_1, U_4)}$$

$$= \frac{3 \times 2 + 6 \times 2 + 5 \times 5}{3 + 6 + 5} \approx 3$$

All the above-mentioned researches are memory-based methods, in which recommendations are made by using user relations based on the heuristic rules, which cannot optimize the effect. To solve this problem, researchers have proposed many model-based methods, to obtain parameters of models through machine learning.

1.4.3 Model-based social recommendation

The model-based recommendation algorithm models the user-item matrix, to learn from it the corresponding model parameters, so recommendation results can be obtained by just loading the model, without the need to analyze the original user-item matrix. Common recommendation models include the neighborhood model and the matrix decomposition model.

1. Neighborhood model

The neighborhood model was an improvement on the memory-based recommendation method; it was proposed in reference [99], with the basic idea to obtain similar users on the basis of the score similarity between users, and then to predict users' scores for items by using the scores given by similar users. The calculation formula is as follows:

$$\tilde{r}_{u, i} = \sum_{v \in V} r_{v, i} w_{u, v} \tag{1.59}$$

where $w_{u, v}$ is the interpolation weight, which is used to integrate the score values of different users. This idea is basically the same as that of the memory-based collaborative filtering algorithm, except that after selecting similar users, it does not use similarity as the weight to integrate the score values of users; instead, a regression model is used to obtain the values of these weights through learning and training, and the optimized target function is expressed as follows:

$$\min \sum_{v \in V} \left(r_{v, i} \sum_{j=1}^{n} r_{v, j} w_{u, v} \right)^2 \tag{1.60}$$

The interpolation weight parameters obtained through learning can better fit the data deviation and improve the recommendation effect.

Some scholars introduced the bias information on the basis of this job [100, 101]:

$$\tilde{r}_{u,i} = \mu + b_u + b_i + \sum_{j \in R(u)} (r_{u,i} - b_{u,j}) w_{i,j} + \sum_{j \in N(u)} C_{i,j} \tag{1.61}$$

In this model, u is the global average score, b_u the bias of user, b_i the bias of item, $R(u)$ the set of items already scored by user u; the parameter w is the tightness between items; $N(u)$ is the set of items for which user u has made implicit feedback; $c_{i,j}$ represents the bias based on implicit feedback item j on item i.

2. Matrix decomposition model

The basic idea of this model is to decompose the user-item score matrix. After the decomposition, both users and items can be expressed with k-dimension implicit characteristics. Matrix decomposition can reduce the dimensions of users' score data on items to build the characteristic models of users and items with less dimensions, thereby effectively solving problems resulting from data sparsity. Many recommendation models based on matrix decomposition are now available [83, 92, 93, 97, 102].

The RSVD model [103] is one of the classical matrix decomposition methods. Specifically, the user-item matrix R can be decomposed into a form of user matrix U multiplied by item matrix V, as shown by the following equation:

$$R = U^T V$$

where $U \in R_{k \times m}$ and $V \in R_{k \times n}$ respectively express the k-dimension implicit characteristic vectors of users and items; by minimizing the residual differential square, the expression of users and items in implicit space is obtained:

$$U, V = \arg\min_{P,Q} O(U, V) = \arg\min_{P,Q} \frac{1}{2} \| R - U^T V \|_F^2 + \lambda (\| U \|_F^2 + \| V \|_F^2) \tag{1.62}$$

where λ is the coefficient of a regular term, which can prevent overfitting of the model. This formula can be solved using the gradient descent method [83, 93]. The RSVD model is actually the basic frame of matrix decomposition, which has room for improvement. To better fit a user-item matrix, reference [104] introduced global bias, user bias, and item bias, hence, the scoring term can be expressed as

$$R_{u,i} = \bar{r} + b_u + b_i + \sum_{k=1}^{K} U_{u,k}^T V_{i,k} \tag{1.63}$$

where $\bar{r}$ is the global average score, b_u is the user bias, and b_i the item bias. The corresponding optimizing target function is expressed as:

$$O(P, Q) = \frac{1}{2} \sum_{u=1}^{m} \sum_{i=1}^{n} (\tilde{r}_{u,i} - r_{u,i})^2 + \lambda_1 (\| U \|_F^2 + \| V \|_F^2) + \lambda_2 (b_u + b_i)^2 \tag{1.64}$$

where $\|U\|F$ and $\|V\|F$ are respectively F norms of matrixes U and V, i.e., the squares and square roots of all elements of the matrixes. λ_1 and λ_2 are combinatorial coefficients. Paterek has very good universality for expanding ideas of the model. There may be many potential factors influencing the recommendation result, such as the information about time and geographic locations, which can all be added into formula (1.60) as bias terms to better fit the user-item score value. Reference [105] considered the matrix decomposition from the perspective of probability, and proposed the probability matrix decomposition model PMF, which assumes that user' score R for items conforms to the normal distribution with the mean value $P^{\mathrm{T}}Q$ and variance $\sigma R2$, and that a set of users with similar scores have similar preferences.

3. Integrating social network information

Essentially, two assumptions are associated with the influence of social networks on recommendation:
(1) User scores are subject to the influence of the user's friends.
(2) The related user implicit vector expressions should be similar.

Recommendation methods integrated with the social relations of users can make effective use of user relations, and the currently prevailing methods can be classified into three types.
(1) Common factorization model: methods of this type factorize the user-to-item score matrix and user relation matrix at the same time, and both matrixes share the same user bias vector. The basic assumption is that users have the same bias vector in the score matrix space and relation matrix space, and this method is used to merge the score data with user relation data. Representative models include SoRec and LOCABAL.
(2) Integration models: methods of this type make weighed merging of the friend-to-term score matrix decomposition term with the user score matrix decomposition term. The basic assumption is that users have similar preferences as their friends; therefore, the bias term of users is smoothened with bias term of friends. Representative models include STE and mTrust.
(3) Regular model: methods of this type introduce regular terms of user relations in the matrix decomposition model, and in the optimizing process, the distance between user-and friend's bias terms is also one of the optimizing targets. Its basic assumption is similar to that of integration models, and users have similar bias as their friends. The representative models include SocialMF and Social Regularization.

Example 1.18 The graphic model method SoRec integrating social relations and score records. Reference [99] proposed SoRec, which integrates the social relations and score records of users by mapping the user social relations and user

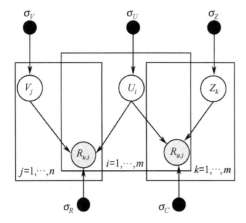

Figure 1.6: Graphic model expression of SoRec

score records on the same implicit characteristic space, thus mitigating data sparsity and improving precision. The graphic model of SoRec is as shown in Figure 1.6.

As shown in Figure 1.6, the SoRec model factorizes the user score matrix into two terms U_i and V_j, and the user relation matrix into two terms U_i and Z_k; U_i, as the common term, links the two matrixes, thus realizing the integration of user relations. Its optimizing target function is as follows:

$$\min \| R - U^T V \|^2 + \alpha \sum_{i=1}^{n} \sum_{uk \in N_i} \left(S_{ik} - u_I^T z_k \right)^2 + \lambda \left(\| U \|^2 + \| V \|^2 | \| Z \|^2 \right) \quad (1.65)$$

Based on assumption 1, if two users have a friend relationship, their scores for items should be close to each other. Reference [106] proposed the STE model, which performs linear combination of the basic matrix factorizing model with social networks, and makes final score prediction by weighted summation of basic score matrix and trust score matrix. Its graphic model expression is as shown in Figure 1.7.

As shown in Figure 1.7, the STE model first factorizes the user-to-item score matrix, and then makes weighted merging of user's bias term on an item and the bias term of friend on the same item, with the weight value being the weight of user's relation with friend.

$$R_{u,i} = g \left(\alpha U_u^T V_i + (1 - \alpha) \sum_{v \in N_u} T_{u,v} U_u^T V_i \right) \quad (1.66)$$

The corresponding $R_{u,i}$ is the normalized user scores, and g (g)is a logistic function. Obviously, reference [106] is only a linear combination model of a superficial level, and has not tapped the bonding role of friend relations. For reference [106] and reference [99], the characteristic space of neighbors affects the user's score, rather

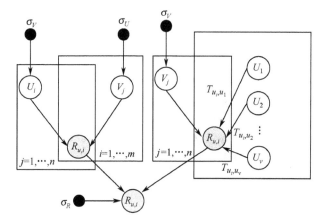

Figure 1.7: Graphic model expression of STE

than its characteristic space; therefore, it is not possible to solve the issue of trust transfer.

Based on assumption 2, if the two users have relations in social network, the user vector expressions after matrix decomposition should have some similarities. Assumption 2 can be taken as a restriction on the matrix decomposition, equivalent to adding an extra regular term into the previous optimizing target, as indicated below:

$$O(U, V) = \frac{1}{2}\left\|R - U^T V\right\|_F^2 + \lambda\left(\|U\|_F^2 + \|V\|_F^2\right) + \sigma L(U) \tag{1.67}$$

where $L(U)$ is the regular term of social networks to user implicit vector. The relevant work can better fit the recommendation result by designing the mathematical form of $L(U)$. Specifically, reference [107] has proposed two forms of regularization as follows:

$$L(U) = \sum_{i=1}^{m}\left\| U_i \frac{\sum\limits_{f \in F^+(i)} \mathrm{sim}(i,f)U_f}{\sum\limits_{f \in F^+(i)} \mathrm{sim}(i,f)} \right\|_F^2 \tag{1.68}$$

$$L(U) = \sum_{i=1}^{m} \sum_{f \in F^+(i)} \mathrm{sim}(i,f)\left\| U_i - U_f \right\|_F^2 \tag{1.69}$$

where $F^+(i)$ is the collection of friends of user i, $\mathrm{sim}(i,f)$ is the similarity between user i and user f. The experiment indicates that regularization based on the second formula produces better effect.

In the PLSF model proposed by Shen [108], the regular term used is as follows:

$$L(U) = \sum_{i,j \in E} \text{Loss}\left(e_{i,j}, \log\left(1 + \exp\left(-U_i^T U_j\right)\right)\right) \tag{1.70}$$

If there is social relation between user i and user j, then $e_{i,j} = 1$; otherwise $e_{i,j} = 0$. The implicit vector similarity between users i and j is calculated using cosine similarity $U_i^T U_j$, and $Loss(x, y)$ reflects the variance of the discrete binomial variable x and continuous variable y, and a loss function of the corresponding form can be used, such as square loss. The above formula requires that the user implicit vector obtained by matrix decomposition be consistent as much as possible with the actual relations existing between users.

Example 1.19 Matrix decomposition model SocialMF. Reference [91] proposes the SocialMF model, and the regular term is defined as the calculation result of the following formula:

$$L(U) = \sum_i \left\| U_i - \sum_{j \in N_i}^m T_{i,j} U_j \right\|_F^2 \tag{1.71}$$

Where, if user u and user v have relations, then matrix element $T_{u,v} = 1$; otherwise $T_{u,v} = 0$. The formula above requires that the vector expression obtained by neighbor users be as close as possible to the vector expression of the user itself.

To make the matrix decomposition model significant in probability, references [91] and [108] presented the corresponding probability generation model to model the user-item score matrix.

Take referee [91] as an example; suppose the implicit vectors of both users and items comply with Gaussian distribution, and the implicit vector expression of each user is influenced by its neighbor, then the posterior probability of the characteristic vectors of users and items can be expressed as the product of the likelihood probability function of score matrix and the priori probability function of the characteristic vectors, as indicated by the formula below:

$$p\left(U, V | R, T, \sigma_R^2, \sigma_T^2, \sigma_U^2 \sigma_V^2\right) \propto p\left(R | U, V, \sigma_R^2\right) p\left(U | T, \sigma_U^2, \sigma_T^2\right) p\left(V | \sigma_V^2\right)$$

$$= \prod_{u=1}^N \prod_{i=1}^M \left[N\left(R_{u,i} | g\left(U_u^T V_i\right), \sigma_r^2\right)\right]^{I_{u,i}^R} \times \prod_{u=1}^N N\left(U_u \Big| \sum_{v \in N_u} T_{u,v} U_v, \sigma_T^2 I\right)$$

$$\times \prod_{u=1}^N N\left(U_u | 0, \sigma_U^2 I\right) \times \prod_{i=1}^N N\left(V_i | 0, \sigma_V^2 I\right) \tag{1.72}$$

$N(x|\mu,\sigma2)$ represents the Gaussian distribution with expectation as μ and variance as σ. The generation process is expressed using a probabilistic graphical model, as shown in Figure 1.8.

In addition, some other studies also tried to perform social recommendation by establishing models. Reference [84] proposed a new matrix decomposition method to

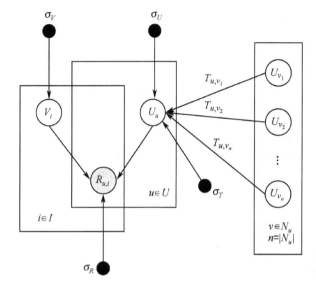

Figure 1.8: Graphical expression of Social MF model

solve the issue of social influence at the item level. Reference [109] has built a user interest spreading model based on friend relation to explain the user friend relations and interaction relations through random walking on the interest network of users, and thereby combining the issues of recommendation and linking prediction into one.

All the above studies use the known social network relations; however, under many circumstances, the relations between users cannot be directly observed. To solve this problem, many researchers have used the score similarity of users to simulate user relations. Reference [110] directly used the user score similarity as degree of trust, and used the trust transfer method to expand the closest neighbors.

Example 1.20 Metering of trust degree based on user score variance: references [111 and 112] proposed the metering method of trust degree based on user score variance, as shown by the following formula:

$$u(a, b) = \frac{1}{|R_a \cap R_b|} \sum_{i \in (R_a \cap R_b)} \left(\frac{|r_{a,i} - r_{b,i}|}{\max(r)} \right) \tag{1.73}$$

This method calculates the degree of trust between users by summing up the absolute values of errors of user a and user b on all score sets.

Reference [93] proposed the method to calculate according to score error proportions, which first defines the correctness evaluation method for scores between users, to classify the scores of users for the same item into a binary issue of being correct and incorrect by setting the threshold of errors. Reference [113] expanded this method and proposed the non-binary judging method to adjust the effect of score variance on user relations by introducing error penalizing factor. Reference [114] proposed the model of merging trust degree and similarity, which has the advantage of trust transfer and most neighboring methods.

In addition, references [89] and [115] proposed to improve the recommendation effect by using the user similarity and item similarity as the implicit social relations, use the Pearson's correlation coefficient to calculate user and item similarity, and add the similarity into the matrix decomposition model as a regularized parameter.

Reference [116] proposed the MCCRF model based on the condition random field, to establish links for user's scores; the conditional probability between different scores is estimated by using the user score similarity and item similarity, and the parameters of the model are trained using the MCMC method.

1.5 Summary

This chapter presented the research development of IR in social networks based on the three typical applications of search, classification, and recommendation. In terms of search, we mainly summarize the current work from three aspects: query representation, document representation, and similarity calculation. In terms of classification, we mainly summarize the progress of short text classification based on the two dimensions of features and algorithms. In terms of recommendation, we mainly present how to add social information into traditional recommendation from the memory-based and model-based perspectives to increase the effect of collaborative recommendation.

As shown in this chapter, IR in social networks mainly involves short text representation and calculation. As the texts are short, it is an extensive practice to expand texts when they are expressed. The fact that social networks are rich in information makes it is an interesting topic to explore the ways of using such information, especially social networking information, to improve the effect of text representation. In terms of calculation models, usually a model that can merge multiple features is used to introduce the features of microblogs.

We believe that the future development trend of IR can be summarized as follows:

(1) Integrating more social network-specific information: for example, information such as age, gender and geographic location of users in social networks has been proved useful in auto-completion query tasks [117]. Such information can be used

to retrieve social network information, and thereby realize personalized precise retrieval. Another example is that the dialogue context, social relations, and even communities in the social network content can be very helpful for retrieval.

(2) Precise representations and computing models: as stated in this chapter, representation and calculation of short texts is the core content of IR in the context of social network texts; therefore, in-depth study of such a core content is undoubtedly an important direction in the research of social network text retrieval.

(3) In-depth understanding of short text: researches on short text matching under the semantic space have been carried out recently [118]; therefore, how to mine the profound meanings of short texts will be a direction worth our attention.

(4) Novelty and diversity: in addition to correlation, novelty and diversity should also be taken into account in social network IR to find diversified new information.

References

[1] Christopher Manning, Prabhakar Raghavan, and Hinrich Schütze. Introduction to Information Retrieval. Cambridge University Press. 2008.

[2] Charu Aggarwal. Social Network Data Analytics. Springer, March, 2011.

[3] Peters Han Luhn. A statistical approach to mechanized encoding and searching of literary information. IBM Journal, 1957: 309–317.

[4] Gerard Salton, Andrew Wong, ChungShu Yang. A vector space model for automatic indexing. Communications of ACM, 1975: 613–620.

[5] Gerard Salton, Christopher Buckley. Term-weighting approaches in automatic text retrieval. Information Processing & Management, 1988, 24(5): 513–523.

[6] Amit Singhal, Christopher Buckley, Mandar Mitra. Pivoted document length normalization. In Proceedings of the 34th Annual International ACM SIGIR Conference on Research and Development in Information Retrieval (SIGIR), 1996: 21–29.

[7] Melvin Earl Maron, John L Kuhns. On relevance, probabilistic indexing and information retrieval. Journal of the ACM, 1960: 216–244.

[8] Stephen Robertson, Steve Walker, Susan Jones, Micheline Hancock-Beaulieu, Mike Gatford. Okapi at TREC-3. In Proceedings of the Third Text REtrieval Conference (TREC). Gaithersburg, USA, November 1994.

[9] James Callan, Bruce Croft, Stephen Harding. The INQUERY retrieval system. In Proceedings of 3th international conference on Database and Expert Systems Applications, 1992: 78–83.

[10] Fabio Crestani, Mounia Lalmas, Cornelis J. Van Rijsbergen, I Campbell. Is this document relevant?... probably: A survey of probabilistic models in information retrieval. ACM Computing Surveys (CSUR), 1998, 30 (4): 528–552.

[11] Christopher D. Manning, Hinrich Schütze. Foundations of Statistical Natural Language Processing. MIT Press, 1999.

[12] Huang Changning. What is the main Chinese language information processing technology. China Computer, 2002, 24.

[13] Jay M.Ponte, Bruce Croft. A language modeling approach to information retrieval. In Proceedings of the 21st annual international ACM SIGIR conference on Research and Development in Information Retrieval, New York, USA. 1998.

[14] Chengxiang Zhai, John Lafferty. Model-based feedback in the language modeling approach to information retrieval. In Proceedings of the 10th ACM international conference on Information and Knowledge Management (CIKM), pages 403–410, 2001. Atlanta, Georgia, USA.

[15] Adam Berger, John Lafferty. Information retrieval as statistical translation. In Proceeding of the 22rd international ACM SIGIR conference on Research and Development in Information Retrieval (SIGIR), 1999: 222–229.

[16] Rocchio JJ, Relevance Feedback in Information Retrieval. Prentice-Hall, 1975: 313–323.

[17] Victor Lavrenko, Bruce Croft. Relevance based language models. In Proceedings of the 24th international ACM SIGIR conference on Research and Development in Information Retrieval (SIGIR), pages 120–127, 2001. New Orleans, Louisiana, USA.

[18] Wouter Weerkamp, Krisztian Balog, Maarten de Rijke. A Generative Blog Post Retrieval Model that Uses Query Expansion based on External Collections. In Proceedings of the Joint Conference of the 47th Annual Meeting of the ACL and the 4th International Joint Conference on Natural Language Processing (ACL-IJCNLP), 2009.

[19] Miles Efron. Hashtag Retrieval in a Microblogging Environment. In Proceeding of the 33rd international ACM SIGIR conference on Research and Development in Information Retrieval (SIGIR), 2010.

[20] Cunhui Shi, Kejiang Ren, Hongfei Lin, Shaowu Zhang. DUTIR at TREC 2011 Microblog Track.

[21] Jaime Teevan, Daniel Ramage, Meredith Ringel Morris. #TwitterSearch: A Comparison of Microblog Search and Web Search. In Proceedings of Web Search and Data Mining (WSDM), 2011: 9–12.

[22] Xiaoyan Li W. Bruce Croft. Time-based language models. In Proceedings of the 12th ACM international conference on Information and Knowledge Management (CIKM), 2003: 469–475.

[23] Wei Bingjie, Wang Bin. Combing Cluster and Temporal Information for Microblog Search [J]. Journal of Chinese Information Processing, 2013.

[24] Giuseppe Amodeo, Giambattista Amati, Giorgio Gambosi. On relevance, time and query expansion. In Proceedings of the 20th ACM international conference on Information and Knowledge Management (CIKM), pages 1973–1976, 2011, Glasgow, Scotland, UK.

[25] Mostafa Keikha, Shima Gerani, Fabio Crestani. Time-based relevance models. In Proceedings of the 34th international ACM SIGIR conference on Research and Development in Information Retrieval (SIGIR), 2011: 1087–1088.

[26] Stewart Whiting, Iraklis Klampanos, Joemon Jose. Temporal pseudo-relevance feedback in microblog retrieval. In Proceedings of the 34th European conference on Advances in Information Retrieval (ECIR), 2012.

[27] Miles Efron, Peter Organisciak, Katrina Fenlon. Improving retrieval of short texts through document expansion. In Proceedings of the 35th international ACM SIGIR conference on Research and Development in Information Retrieval (SIGIR), 2012: 911–920.

[28] Yubin Kim, Reyyan Yeniterzi, Jamie Callan. Overcoming Vocabulary Limitations in Twitter Microblogs. In Proceedings of the Twenty-First Text REtrieval Conference (TREC), 2012.

[29] Li Rui, Wang Bin. Microblog Retrieval via Author Based Microblog Expansion. Journal of Chinese Information Processing, 2014.

[30] Alexander Kotov, Eugene Agichtein. The importance of being socially-savvy: quantifying the influence of social networks on microblog retrieval. In Proceedings of the 22nd ACM international conference on Information and Knowledge Management (CIKM), 2013: 1905–1908.

[31] Kamran Massoudi, Manos Tsagkias, Maarten Rijke, Wouter Weerkamp. Incorporating Query Expansion and Quality Indicators in Searching Microblog Posts. in Advances in Information Retrieval, P. Clough, et al., Editors, 2011: 362–367.

[32] Paul Ferguson, Neil O'Hare, James Lanagan, Owen Phelan, Kevin McCarthy. An Investigation of Term Weighting Approaches for Microblog Retrieval. in Advances in Information Retrieval, R. Baeza-Yates, et al., Editors, 2012: 552–555.

[33] Xiaowen Li, Peiquan Jin, Xujian Zhao, Hong Chen, Lihua Yue. NTLM: A Time-Enhanced Language Model Based Ranking Approach for Web Search Web Information Systems Engineering. WISE 2010 Workshops, D. Chiu, et al., Editors, 2011: 156–170.

[34] Nattiya Kanhabua, Kjetil Nørvåg. Using Temporal Language Models for Document Dating Machine Learning and Knowledge Discovery in Databases. W. Buntine, et al., Editors, 2009: 738–741.

[35] Miles Efron, Gene Golovchinsky. Estimation methods for ranking recent information. In Proceedings of the 34th international ACM SIGIR conference on Research and Development in Information Retrieval (SIGIR), 2011: 495–504.

[36] BP Sharifi. Automatic Microblog Classification and Summarization. University of Colorado, 2010.

[37] Carter Simon, Tsagkias Manos and Weerkamp Wouter (2011) Twitter Hashtags: Joint Translation and Clustering. In Proceedings of the ACM WebSci'11, 2011:14–17.

[38] Beaux Sharifi, Hutton MA, Kalita JK. Experiments in Microblog Summarization. In Proceedings of IEEE Second International conference on Social Computing (SocialCom), 2010.

[39] Gustavo Laboreiro, Luís Sarmento, Jorge Teixeira, Eugénio Oliveira. Tokenizing micro-blogging messages using a text classification approach. In Proceedings of the fourth workshop on Analytics for noisy unstructured text data, 2010.

[40] Daniel Ramage, Susan Dumais, Daniel Liebling. Characterizing Microblogs with Topic Models. In Proceedings of ICWSM, 2010.

[41] Einat Amitay, David Carmel, Michael Herscovici, Ronny Lempel, Aya Soffer. Trend detection through temporal link analysis[J]. Journal of the American Society for Information Science and Technology (JASIST), 2004, 55(14): 1270–1281.

[42] Philip Yu, Xin Li, Bing Liu. On the temporal dimension of search. In Proceedings of the 13th international World Wide Web conference on Alternate track papers posters, 2004: 448–449.

[43] Klaus Berberich, Michalis Vazirgiannis, Gerhard Weikum. Time-Aware Authority Ranking[J]. Internet Mathematics, 2005, 2(3): 301–332.

[44] Jing Wan, Sixue Bai. An improvement of PageRank algorithm based on the time-activity- curve. In Proceedings of IEEE International conference on Granular Computing(GRC), 2009.

[45] Rinkesh Nagmoti, Ankur Teredesai, Martine De Cock. Ranking Approaches for Microblog Search. In Proceedings of 2010 IEEE/WIC/ACM International conference on Web Intelligence and Intelligent Agent Technology (WI-IAT), 2010.

[46] Yajuan Duan, Long Jiang, Tao Qin, Ming Zhou, Heung-Yeung Shum. An empirical study on learning to rank of tweets. In the 23th International Conference on Computational Linguistics (COLING), 2010: 295–303.

[47] Xin Zhang Ben He, Tiejian Luo, Baobin Li. Query-biased learning to rank for real-time Twitter search. In Proceedings of the 21st ACM international conference on Information and Knowledge Management (CIKM), 2012:1915–1919.

[48] Xinruo Sun, Haofen Wang, Yong Yu. Towards effective short text deep classification. In Proceedings of the 34th international ACM SIGIR conference on Research and development in Information Retrieval, 2011: 1143–1144.

[49] Evgeniy Gabrilovich, Shaul Markovitch. Computing semantic relatedness using Wikipedia-based explicit semantic analysis. In Proceedings of 22nd AAAI Conference on Artificial Intelligence (AAAI), 2007: 6–12.

[50] Xiang Wang, Ruhua Chen, Yan Jia, Bin Zhou. Short Text Classification using Wikipedia Concept based Document Representation. In Proceedings of International conference on Information Technology and Applications (ITA), 2013.

[51] Xuan-Hieu Phan, Le-Minh Nguyen, Susumu Horiguchi. Learning to classify short and sparse text & web with hidden topics from large-scale data collections. In Proceedings of the 17th International World Wide Web Conference (WWW), 2008: 91–100.

[52] Mengen Chen, Xiaoming Jin, Dou Shen. Short text classification improved by learning multi-granularity topics. In Proceedings of the 21st International Joint Conference on Artificial Intelligence (IJCAI), 2011: 1776–1781.

[53] Sheila Kinsella, Alexandre Passant, John G. Breslin. Topic classification in social media using metadata from hyperlinked objects. In Proceedings of the 33th European conference on Advances in Information Retrieval (ECIR), 2011: 201–206.

[54] Evgeniy Gabrilovich, Shaul Markovitch. Overcoming the Brittleness Bottleneck using Wikipedia: Enhancing Text Categorization with Encyclopedic Knowledge. In Proceedings of the 21st National Conference on Artificial Intelligence (NCAI), 2006: 1301–1306.

[55] Duan Yajuan, Wei Furu, Zhou Ming. Graph-based collective classification for tweets. Proceedings of the 21st ACM international conference on Information and Knowledge Management (CIKM), 2012: 2323–2326.

[56] Bharath Sriram, Dave Fuhry, Engin Demir, Hakan Ferhatosmanoglu, Murat Demirbas. Short text classification in Twitter to improve information filtering. In Proceedings of SIGIR, 2010: 841–842.

[57] Aixi Sun. Short Text Classification Using Very Few Words. In Proceedings of SIGIR2012, 2012: 1145–1146.

[58] Zitao Liu, Wenchao Yu, Wei Chen, Shuran Wang, Fengyi Wu. (2010). Short Text Feature Selection for Micro-Blog Mining. In Proceedings of the International conference on Computational Intelligence and Software Engineering, 2010: 1–4.

[59] Danesh Irani, Steve Webb. Study of Trend-Stuffing on Twitter through Text Classification. In Proceedings of CEAS 2010, July 13–14: 114–123.

[60] Quan Yuan, Gao Cong, Nadia Magnenat Thalmann. Enhancing naive bayes with various smoothing methods for short text classification. In Proceedings of the 21st International World Wide Web Conference (WWW), 2012: 645–646.

[61] Mehran Sahami, Timothy D. Heilman. A web-based kernel function for measuring the similarity of short text snippets. In Proceedings of the 15th International World Wide Web Conference (WWW), May 23–26, pages 377–386, 2006.

[62] Sarah Zelikovitz, Haym Hirsh. Improving short-text classification using unlabeled background knowledge to assess document similarity. In Proceedings of the 17th International conference on Machine Learning (ICML), 2000: 1191–1198.

[63] Thiago Salles, Leonardo Rocha, Gisele Pappa, et al. Temporally-aware algorithms for document classification. In Proceedings of the 33rd international ACM SIGIR conference on Research and Development in Information Retrieval (SIGIR), 2010: 307–314.

[64] Kyosuke Nishida, Takahide Hoshide Ko Fujimura. Improving Tweet Stream Classification by Detecting Changes in Word Probability. In Proceedings of SIGIR2012, 2012: 971–980.

[65] Choon Hui Teo S. V. N. Vishwanathan. Fast and space efficient string kernels using suffix arrays. In Proceedings of the 23rd International conference on Machine Learning (ICML), 2006: 929–936.

[66] D. Okanohara, J. ichi Tsujii. Text categorization with all substring features. In Proceedings of SDM, 2009: 838–846.

[67] Wenyuan Dai, Gui-Rong Xue, Qiang Yang, Yong Yu, Co-Clustering Based Classification for Out- of-Domain Documents. In Proceedings 13th ACM SIGKDD international conference Knowledge Discovery and Data Mining (SIGKDD), Aug. 2007.

[68] Rajat Raina, Andrew Y. Ng, Daphne Koller. Constructing Informative Priors Using Transfer Learning. In Proceedings of the 23rd International conference on Machine Learning (ICML), 2006: 713–720.

[69] Pengcheng Wu, Thomas Dietterich. Improving SVM Accuracy by Training on Auxiliary Data Sources. In Proceedings 21st International conference Machine Learning (ICML), July 2004.

[70] Andrew Arnold, Ramesh Nallapati, William W. Cohen, A Comparative Study of Methods for Transductive Transfer Learning. In Proceedings of the Seventh IEEE International conference on Data Mining Workshops, 2007: 77–82.

[71] Xiao Ling, Gui-Rong Xue, Wenyuan Dai, Yun Jiang, Qiang Yang, Yong Yu. Can Chinese Web Pages be Classified with English Data Source. In Proceedings of the 17th International conference on World Wide Web (WWW), 2008: 969–978.

[72] Sinno Jialin Pan, Vincent Wenchen Zheng, Qiang Yang, Derek Hao Hu. Transfer Learning for WiFi-Based Indoor Localization. in Workshop Transfer Learning for Complex Task of the 23rd Assoc. for the Advancement of Artificial Intelligence (AAAI) Conf. Artificial Intelligence, July 2008.

[73] Dan Zhang, Yan Liu, Richard D. Lawrence, Vijil Chenthamarakshan. Transfer Latent Semantic Learning?: Microblog Mining with Less Supervision. In Proceedings of the 25th AAAI Conference on Artificial Intelligence (AAAI), 2011: 561–566.

[74] Guodong Long, Ling Chen, Xingquan Zhu, Chengqi Zhang. TCSST: Transfer Classification of Short & Sparse Text Using External Data Categories and Subject Descriptors. In Proceedings of the 21st ACM international conference on Information and Knowledge Management (CIKM), 2012: 764–772.

[75] Paolo Avesani, Paolo Massa, Roberto Tiella. A trust-enhanced recommender system application: Moleskiing. In Proceedings of the 2005 ACM symposium on applied computing (SAC), 2005.

[76] Paolo Massa, Paolo Avesani. Trust-aware recommender systems. In Proceedings of the 2007 ACM conference on recommender systems(RecSys2007), 2007.

[77] Matthew Richardson, Rakesh Agrawal, Pedro Domingos. Trust management for the semantic web. The Semantic Web-ISWC 2003. Springer Berlin Heidelberg, 2003: 351–368.

[78] R. Guha, Ravi Kumar, Prabhakar Raghavan, Andrew Tomkins. Propagation of trust and distrust. In Proceedings of the 13th international conference on World Wide Web (WWW), 2004: 403–412.

[79] Kailong Chen, Tianqi Chen, Guoqing Zheng, et al. Collaborative personalized tweet recommendation. In Proceedings of the 35th international ACM SIGIR conference on Research and Development in Information Retrieval (SIGIR), 2012: 661–670.

[80] Jilin Chen, Rowan Nairn, Les Nelson, et al. Short and tweet: experiments on recommending content from information streams. In Proceedings of the SIGCHI Conference on Human Factors in Computing Systems, 2010: 1185–1194.

[81] David Stern, Ralf Herbrich, Thore Graepel Matchbox. . Large Scale Online Bayesian Recommendations. In Proceedings of the 18th International World Wide Web Conference (WWW), 2009.

[82] http://www.epinions.com/.

[83] Paolo Massa, Bobby Bhattacharjee. Using trust in recommender systems: an experimental analysis[J]. Trust Management. Springer Berlin Heidelberg, 2004: 221-235.

[84] Peng Cui, Fei Wang, Shaowei Liu, et al. Who should share what?: item-level social influence prediction for users and posts ranking. In Proceedings of the 34th international ACM SIGIR conference on Research and Development in Information Retrieval (SIGIR), 2011: 185–194.

[85] Ibrahim Uysal, Bruce Croft. User oriented tweet ranking: a filtering approach to microblogs. In Proceedings of the 20th ACM international conference on Information and Knowledge Management (CIKM), 2011: 2261–2264.

[86] Zi Yang, Jingyi Guo, Keke Cai, et al. Understanding retweeting behaviors in social networks. In Proceedings of the 19th ACM international conference on Information and Knowledge Management (CIKM), 2010: 1633–1636.

[87] Maksims Volkovs, Richard Zemel. Collaborative Ranking With 17 Parameters. In Proceedings of the 26th Neural Information Processing Systems (NIPS), 2012: 2303–2311.

[88] Suhrid Balakrishnan, Sumit Chopra. Collaborative ranking. In Proceedings of the fifth ACM international conference on Web Search and Data Mining(WSDM), 2012: 143–152.

[89] Hao Ma. An experimental study on implicit social recommendation. In Proceedings of the 36th international ACM SIGIR conference on Research and Development in Information Retrieval (SIGIR), 2013: 73–82.

[90] Punam Bedi, Harmeet Kaur, Sudeep Marwaha. Trust Based Recommender System for Semantic Web. In Proceedings of the 17th International Joint Conference on Artificial Intelligence (IJCAI), 2007: 2677–2682.

[91] Mohsen Jamali, Martin Ester. A matrix factorization technique with trust propagation for recommendation in social networks. In Proceedings of the fourth ACM conference on Recommender systems (RecSys), 2010: 135–142.

[92] Sherrie Xiao, Izak Benbasat. The formation of trust and distrust in recommendation agents in repeated interactions: a process-tracing analysis. In Proceedings of the 5th international conference on Electronic commerce, 2003: 287–293.

[93] John O'Donovan, Barry Smyth. Trust in recommender systems. In Proceedings of the 10th international conference on Intelligent user interfaces. ACM, 2005: 167–174.

[94] Ioannis Konstas, Vassilios Stathopoulos, Joemon M Jose. On social networks and collaborative recommendation. In Proceedings of the 32nd international ACM SIGIR conference on Research and Development in Information Retrieval (SIGIR), 2009: 195–202.

[95] Paolo Massa, Paolo Avesani. Trust-aware collaborative filtering for recommender systems.On the Move to Meaningful Internet Systems 2004 : CoopIS, DOA, and ODBASE. Springer Berlin Heidelberg, 2004: 492–508.

[96] Mohsen Jamali, Martin Ester. TrustWalker: A random walk model for combining trust-based and item-based recommendation. In Proceedings of the 15th ACM SIGKDD international conference on Knowledge Discovery and Data mining (SIGKDD), 2009: 397–406.

[97] Jennifer Ann Golbeck. Computing and Applying Trust in Web-based Social Networks[D]. University of Maryland College Park, 2005.

[98] Cai-Nicolas Ziegler. Towards decentralized recommender systems[D]. University of Freiburg, 2005.

[99] Hao Ma, Haixuan Yang, Michael R. Lyu, Irwin King. Sorec: Social recommendation using probabilistic matrix factorization. In Proceedings of the 17th ACM conference on Information and Knowledge Management (CIKM). ACM, 2008: 931–940.

[100] Yehuda Koren. Factorization meets the neighborhood: A multifaceted collaborative filtering model. In Proceedings of the 14th ACM SIGKDD international conference on Knowledge Discovery and Data mining (SIGKDD), 2008: 426–434.

[101] Yehuda Koren. Factor in the neighbors: Scalable and accurate collaborative filtering[J]. ACM Transactions on Knowledge Discovery from Data (TKDD), 2010, 4(1): 1.

[102] Quan Yuan, Li Chen, Shiwan Zhao. Factorization vs. regularization: Fusing heterogeneous social relationships in top-n recommendation. In Proceedings of the fifth ACM conference on Recommender systems (RecSYS), 2011, 245–252.

[103] Simon Funk. Netflix update: Try this at home[EB/OL]. http://sifter.org/ simon/journal/ 20061211.html, 2006.

[104] Arkadiusz Paterek. Improving regularized singular value decomposition for collaborative filtering. In Proceedings of KDD cup and workshop. 2007: 5–8.

[105] Ruslan Salakhutdinov, Andriy Mnih. Probabilistic Matrix Factorization. In Proceedings of the 21st Neural Information Processing Systems (NIPS), 2007, 1(1): 1–2.

[106] Hao Ma, Irwin King, Michael R. Lyu. Learning to recommend with social trust ensemble. In Proceedings of the 32nd international ACM SIGIR conference on Research and Development in Information Retrieval (SIGIR), 2009: 203–210.

[107] Hao Ma, Dengyong Zhou, Chao Liu, et al. Recommender systems with social regularization. In Proceedings of the fourth ACM international conference on Web Search and Data Mining (WSDM). ACM, 2011: 287–296.

[108] Yelong Shen, Ruoming Jin. Learning personal+ social latent factor model for social recommendation. In Proceedings of the 18th ACM SIGKDD international conference on Knowledge discovery and data mining. ACM, 2012: 1303–1311.

[109] Shuang-Hong Yang, Bo Long, Alexander J Smola., et al. Like like alike: Joint friendship and interest propagation in social networks. In Proceedings of the 20th international conference on World Wide Web (WWW), 2011: 537–546.

[110] Manos Papagelis, Dimitris Plexousakis, Themistoklis Kutsuras. Alleviating the sparsity problem of collaborative filtering using trust inferences[J]. Trust Management. Springer Berlin Heidelberg, 2005: 224–239.

[111] Georgios Pitsilis, Lindsay Marshall. A Model of Trust Derivation from Evidence for Use in Recommendation Systems[R]. In Technical Report Series, CS-TR-874. University of Newcastle Upon Tyne, 2004.

[112] Georgios Pitsilis, Lindsay Marshall. Trust as a Key to Improving Recommendation Systems[J]. Trust Management, pages 210–223. Springer Berlin/ Heidelberg, 2005.

[113] Neal Lathia, Stephen Hailes, Licia Capra. Trust-Based Collaborative Filtering. In Joint iTrust and PST Conferences on Privacy, Trust Management and Security (IFIPTM), Trondheim, Norway, 2008.

[114] Chein-Shung Hwang, Yu-Pin Chen. Using trust in collaborative filtering recommendation. New Trends in Applied Artificial Intelligence. Springer Berlin Heidelberg, 2007: 1052–1060.

[115] Hao Ma, Irwin King, Michael R. Lyu. Learning to recommend with explicit and implicit social relations. ACM Transactions on Intelligent Systems and Technology (TIST), 2011, 2(3): 29.

[116] Xin Xin, Irwin King, Hongbo Deng, Michael R. Lyu. A social recommendation framework based on multi-scale continuous conditional random fields. In Proceedings of the 18th ACM conference on Information and Knowledge Management (CIKM), 2009: 1247–1256.

[117] Milad Shokouhi, Learning to personalize query auto-completion. In Proceedings of the 36th international ACM SIGIR conference on Research and Development in Information Retrieval (SIGIR): 103–112.

[118] Zhengdong Lu, Hang Li: A Deep Architecture for Matching Short Texts. In Proceedings of the 27th Neural Information Processing Systems (NIPS), 2013: 1367–1375.

Hu Changjun

2 The rules of information diffusion in social networks

Owing to their inherent liberality and openness, online social networks have gradually become an important information distributing center in contemporary society. Information diffusion in social networks has also become unprecedentedly active. Studying the rules of information diffusion in social networks can help us to better understand the structure and attributes of online social networks as well as the rules associated with sudden events from the perspective of information diffusion. These results have a wide range of applications in marketing, information pushing in shopping websites, public opinion monitoring and guidance, etc. From the viewpoint of social benefits, social groups and government agencies can not only carry out information dissemination and improve the efficiency and transparency of management by drawing on the characteristics and laws of information diffusion but also rationally guide public opinions by screening and filtering information based on such characteristics and laws. From the viewpoint of economic benefits, enterprises can optimize the allocation of resources according to the characteristics and laws of information diffusion in social networks, facilitating the promotion and sales of products. Therefore, it is of great theoretical and practical significance to study the rules of information diffusion in social networks.

2.1 Introduction

Information diffusion is a process where people transmit, receive, and feedback information using symbols and signals for achieving mutual understanding and influence by exchanging opinions, ideas, and emotions. Information diffusion in online social networks specifically refers to the diffusion of information realized via online social networks.

Information diffusion in online social networks has the following characteristics: first, the release and reception of information is extremely simple and fast; users are able to release and receive information through mobile phones and other mobile devices anytime and anywhere; second, information diffuses as "nuclear fission;" as long as a message is released, it will be pushed by the system to all the followers, and once forwarded, it will spread out instantly among another group of followers. third, everyone has the opportunity to become an opinion leader; each internet user is allowed to play an important role in the occurrence, fermentation, dissemination, and sensationalization of a sudden event; finally, it takes on the form of "We Media;" from super stars to grassroots, everyone can build

https://doi.org/10.1515/9783110599435-002

their own "media," where they can express themselves freely, create messages for the public, and communicate ideas, while receiving information from all directions on the platform. In general, social networks have sped up the process and expanded the breadth of information diffusion. As a result, people are able to access richer information through social networks.

Studying the law of information diffusion in social networks can help us deepen our understanding of social networking systems and social phenomena, and thereby furthering the understand the topologies, communication capabilities, and dynamic behaviors of complex networks. In addition, the study of information diffusion is also conducive to researches in other aspects such as the discovery of models, identification of more influential nodes, and personalized recommendations.

The vigorous development of social networks provides a rich database for researchers to carry out relevant researches, allowing them to study the mechanism of information diffusion and understand the law of information diffusion based on massive real data, and have achieved phasic results. Information diffusion in social networks mainly involves the base network structure, network users, diffusing information, among other factors; relevant researches have been carried out on these factors. Research results based on the network structure mainly include the independent cascade model, linear threshold model, and their extended versions. Research based on the state of the users mainly include the epidemic model and the influence diffusion model. Research based on the characteristics of information mainly include the multi-source information diffusion model and competitive diffusion model. Consdering that explicit diffusion models cannot explain certain phenomena of information diffusion, some researchers studied the method of information diffusion prediction based on certain given data to predict the effect of information diffusion such as the popularity of hot topics in social networks. Considering numerous and jumbled sources of information in social networks, some researchers studied the method of information source location to look for the original sources of information and track their diffusion paths based on the distribution status of the existing information, thereby providing support for such applications as network security.

This chapter is organized as follows: Section 10.2 analyzes the main factors that affect the diffusion of information in social networks. Section 10.3, 10.4, and 10.5 describe the diffusion models and application examples based on network structure, group status, and information characteristics, respectively. Section 10.6 introduces the method as well as the application examples of predicting the state of information diffusion based on certain given data. Section 10.7 describes the information source location method and analyzes few cases. Finally, the challenges and prospects faced by the research work of information diffusion in social networks are proposed.

2.2 Influencing factors related to information diffusion in social networks

Based on mutual understanding, hobbies, personal worship, or other factors, individuals in social networks connect with others to form a complex "structure of relationship." Based on such a structure, connected individuals gather together and form a "networking group" with common behavioral characteristics through mutual influence and interdependence. Based on the relational structure and social networking groups, all kinds of information is published and diffused. Therefore, the relational structure of online social networks provides a base platform for information diffusion. The social groups directly promote information diffusion, and the rich information serves as the necessary resource for information diffusion.

2.2.1 Structure of social networks

A social network is a social structure comprising a set of social actors and a set of ties between these actors. From a macro perspective, different types of social networks can have different modes of information diffusion. For example, information in forums and blogs is mainly diffused in the "one-to-many" or "point-to-plane" mode. In such cases, after a disseminator releases a message, who will view it and how the viewers will react to it are unknown factors. There is an indefinite connection between the transmitter and receiver. In contrast, instant messaging services such as QQ and MSN adopt the "point-to-point" communications methodology, where one can initiate a chat session with a particular individual whenever someone on their private list is online, and recipients are often defaulted to respond to this particular information; micro-blogging allows disseminators to disseminate information to their followers, and followers can choose to forward or comment on the information or unfollow the object they use to follow and reject his information. Consequently, one "node" can have connections with countless other nodes in the network, which ultimately brings forward a combination of various diffusion modes, such as "one-to-multiple," "one-to-one," "multiple-to-multiple," and "multiple-to-one."

In essence, it is the different strengths of the ties between nodes and the different densities of networking that results in diversified modes of information diffusion in online social networks. The strength of a tie is a combination of the connection time, emotional intensity, the intimacy, and reciprocal services characterizing the tie [1]. It is usually defined as the relative overlap of the neighborhood of two nodes in the network. The greater the proportion of the two nodes' common neighborhood is, the greater the strength of the tie between the two nodes. Strong ties can lead to a closely tied and clustered community structure [2], with higher trust between nodes, which plays an important role in promoting individuals to reach a consensus [3, 4], whereas weak ties are usually formed between individuals who are not connected closely or frequently, and these individuals are usually dissimilar from one another; therefore, weak ties can provide new information, serving as sources of diverse information; thus, weak ties play a more important role in a wide range of information diffusion than strong ties [1, 3, 5, 6]. The density of networking indicates the degree to which participants in the social network are interconnected. The closeness between individuals in a network reduces uncertainty and generates a sense of belonging, which may enhance trust between the members and facilitate the diffusion of information [3, 7].

2.2.2 Groups in social networks

From the perspective of network users, information diffusion is more or less influenced by different characteristics of users' behaviors. Naaman et al. categorized network users into nine groups by analyzing the contents of the status information from users on Twitter, of which information sharing (IS), options/complaints (O), random thoughts (RT), and about the user him/herself (ME) categories are main [8]. Java et al. divided users into the following four categories according to their intentions of using a social network: daily chatting, conversation, sharing information, and news reporting. Based on this, according to the role of users in information diffusion, they are divided into the following three categories: information sources, information collection, and friends [9].

Normally, "celebrities" who have rich knowledge in certain areas or a wealth of personal experience may greatly enhance the trust of viewers in the information. Such people always receive higher attention than ordinary people. Their messages usually spread very fast and easily form an orientation of topics. These people are regarded as "information sources;" that is, the information released by them is of high credibility and has a value for dissemination. In information diffusion, if the disseminator is an "information source," the information sent from him/her will be far more significantly diffused in terms of both strength and breadth than those of ordinary users.

Individuals in social networks grow into groups in the networks through aggregation and mutual influence. Compared with communication groups, in reality, groups in online social networks are more interactive, open, cross-regional, and extensive. The tendencies of such groups are closely related to information diffusion. Thelwall et al. evaluated the relationship between the development of popular topics and the emotional intensity of groups on Twitter using the SetiStrength algorithm. The results show that popular events on Twitter are usually associated with an increase in the intensity of negative emotions. The intensity of positive emotions during the peak period is higher than that before the peak [10].

2.2.3 Information

Different from social networks in the actual world which are formed based on factors such as geographical location, common activities, and kinship, users in online social networks communicate with each other and establish connections mainly through releasing, sharing, commenting, and forwarding information. Therefore, information in online social networks carries all the records of users' online activities. The information itself has distinctive characteristics such as timeliness, multi-source concurrency, and subject diversity, which plays an indispensable role in the analysis of information diffusion.

Multi-source information implies that users in a network acquire information not only through links in the online social network but also through factors outside the network. For many traditional media or online media, online social networks can allow more users to access high-quality information, which is an effective way for them to test new models of news report and explore new channels of communication; for online social networks, participation of traditional media and online media leads to massive external information, which, coupled with the real social networks of their own, safeguards the quality and scope of information diffusion.

Some messages, especially those in the same category, can have mutual influence when diffused simultaneously in social networks, which distinguishes its rule of diffusion from those of independent information [11]. In fact, the simultaneous diffusion of multiple inherently related messages is widely seen in social networks; for example, "Evergrande winning championship" and "Wang Feng's confession," "Red Cross" and "Guo Mei Mei," "flu," and "Banlangen," and so on. Studying the multi-message diffusion mechanism in social networks holds great significance.

2.3 Diffusion model based on network structure

This method is modeled based on the structure of the network where information is diffused and the interaction between neighbor nodes. It is assumed that each node in the network has only two states: active or inactive. The active state indicates that the user receives a message; otherwise it is inactive. Only one-way change of state is considered; i.e., from "inactive" to "active." This book introduces the linear threshold model, independent cascade model, and extended model.

2.3.1 Linear threshold model

In 1978, Mark Granovetter investigated the potential resistance of individuals whose participation in a collective activity was ascribed to the influence of their neighbors who had also participated in the same activity. He proposed a threshold model regarding collective behaviors [12]. Drawing upon the ideas of such a threshold, researchers have conducted extensive researches. Among them, the linear threshold model is universally recognized.

In the linear threshold model, each node v is assigned with a threshold $\theta(v) \in [0, 1]$, representing its susceptibility to infections. Node w, which is adjacent to node v, influences node v with a non-negative weight of $b_{v,w}$, and the sum of the $b_{v,w}$ values of all the w nodes neighboring node v is less than or equal to 1.

An inactive node v is activated only if the sum of the influence of its active neighbor nodes is greater than or equal to its threshold, as shown in Equation 2.1; i.e., the decision of an individual in the network is subject to the decisions of all its neighbor nodes, and the active neighbor nodes of node v can participate in the activation of v multiple times. Algorithm 2.1 shows the implementation of the linear threshold model.

$$\sum_{w\,:\,\text{active neighbor of }v} b_{v,w} \geq \theta v \tag{2.1}$$

Algorithm 2.1 Linear Threshold Model Propagation Algorithm
(1) Initial active node set A.
(2) At time t, all the active neighbor nodes of node v attempt to activate v. If the sum of the influence of all active neighbor nodes exceeds the activation threshold of θv, node v is transitioned to the active state at time $t + 1$.
(3) The above process is repeated until the sum of the influence of any active nodes already present in the network cannot activate the neighbor node in the inactive state. Thus, the propagation process ends.

Example 2.1 Example of a linear threshold model application

In the network shown in Figure 2.1, we know that node a is the initial active node, and the thresholds of nodes b, c, d, e, and f are 0.2,0.4,0.5,0.6, and 0.2, respectively. The direction of the edge represents "being followed;" for example, $b \to c$ represents that b is followed by c; that is, the message posted on the social network by b can be viewed by c and b will impact c. The weight of the edge indicates the size of the influence, where the influence of b on c is 0.3 and the range of influence is [0,1].

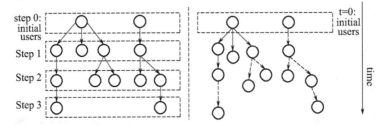

Figure 2.1: Example of a linear threshold model

The diffusion process based on linear threshold model is shown in Figure 2.1:

Time Step 0: node a is activated.

Time Step 1: node a's influence on node b is 0.5; node a's influence on node c is 0.2. At this point, the influence on node b is 0.5, greater than its threshold of 0.2; thus node b is activated.

Time Step 2: node b's influence on node c is 0.3; node b's influence on node d is 0.5; node a's influence on node c is 0.2. At this point, node c is subject to the influence of 0.3 + 0.2 = 0.5, greater than its threshold of 0.4; thus, node c is activated.

Time Step 3: node c's influence on node d is 0.1; node c's influence on node e is 0.2; node b's influence on node d is 0.5. At this point, node d is subject to the influence of 0.5 + 0.1 = 0.6, greater than its threshold of 0.5; thus, node d is activated.

Time Step 4: node d's influence on node e is 0.2, node c's influence on node e is 0.2. At this point node e is subject to the influence of 0.2 + 0.2 = 0.4, less than its threshold of 0.6. In this time step, no new node is activated; thus, the diffusion stops.

2.3.2 Independent cascades model

The independent cascades model (IC) is a probabilistic model [13, 14] initially proposed by Goldenberg et al. in the research of a marketing model. The basic assumption of the model is that whether node u trying to activate its neighbor node v is successful is an event with a probability of pu,v. The probability that a node in an inactive state is activated by a neighbor node that has just entered an active state is independent of the activity of the neighbor who had previously tried to activate the node. In addition, the model also assumes that any node u in the network has only one chance to attempt to activate its neighbor node v, whether it succeeds and that even though node u itself is still active at a later time, it does not have influence any more. Such a node is called noninfluential active node. The implementation of the independent cascade model is described in Algorithm 2.2.

Algorithm 2.2 Independent Cascade Model Diffusion Algorithm

(1) The initial active node set A.

(2) At time t, when the newly activated node u attempts to influence its adjacent node v, the probability of success is pu,v. If node v has multiple neighbor nodes that are newly activated, then these nodes will attempt to activate node v in any order.

(3) If node v is activated successfully, then at time $t + 1$, node v becomes active and will have an effect on its adjacent nonactive nodes; otherwise, node v has no change at time $t + 1$.

(4) The process repeats until there is no influential active node exists in the network; thus, the diffusion process ends.

Example 2.2 Example of an independent cascade model application

The direction of the edge in Figure 2.2 represents "being followed," and the weight of the node represents the probability of activation of the node. For example, the weight of $b \rightarrow c$ is 0.3, indicating that the probability of node b activating node c is 0.3.

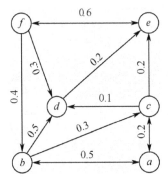

Figure 2.2: Example of an independent cascade model

The diffusion process of the independent cascade model based on Figure 2.2 is as follows:

Time Step 0: node a is activated.

Time Step 1: node a attempts to activate b with a probability of 0.5, and attempts to activate c with a probability of 0.2, assuming that node b is successfully activated within this time step.

Time Step 2: node b attempts to activate c with a probability of 0.3 and attempts to activate d with a probability of 0.5, assuming that node c and node d are successfully activated within this time step.

Time Step 3: node c attempts to activate e with a probability of 0.2, node d attempts to activate e with a probability of 0.2, assuming that all the attempts within this time step have failed, and no new nodes are activated; thus, the diffusion ends.

2.3.3 Related extended models

No matter whether it is a linear threshold model or an independent cascade model, the diffusion process is simulated in a synchronous manner based on a discrete time axis, whereas in real social networks, the information diffuses along a continuous time axis and an asynchronous delay occurs in diffusion. Many researchers have improved the linear threshold and independent cascade models [15–19]. Gruhl et al., by giving an algorithm for calculating the reading probabilities and replication probabilities between nodes, provided each edge with an occurrence probability of diffusion, allowing the independent cascade model to be applied to environments with potentially delayed diffusion [15]. Saito et al. used a continuous time and added a time delay parameter to each edge in the graph, extending the independent cascade model and the linear threshold model to the AsIC (asynchronous independent cascades) and the AsLT (asynchronous linear threshold) models [18].

The above methods focus on the reasoning of diffusion behaviors, without taking into account the influence of content on diffusion. Information diffusion is a complex social and psychological activity, and the content of diffusion inevitably affects the action between neighbor nodes. Galuba et al. analyzed the diffusion characteristics of URL in Twitter, starting from the attractiveness of URL, user's influence and the rate of diffusion, and constructed the linear threshold diffusion model of URL using these parameters to predict which users would mention which URLs. This model can be used for personalized URL referrals, spam detection, etc. [20]. Guille et al. proposed the T-BaSIC model (time-based asynchronous independent cascades) using the Bayesian logistic regression method on the basis of the AsIC model from three dimensions: semantic meaning of topics, network structure and time, and to predict the probability of diffusion over time between nodes on Twitter. The experimental results show that the model has a good effect in predicting the dynamics of diffusion [21].

To analyze and model the action between neighbor nodes by extracting the network structure based on the diffusion model of network topology is characteristic of simple model and easy expansion, which has certain advantages in the case of large social networks or limited information. In addition, such methods cross a number of disciplines such as graph theory, probability statistics, sociology, and physics, and have a solid theoretical basis. The model is suitable for the study of diffusion cascade behavior, predict the diffusion path, and provide personalized recommendations based on the degree of the user accepting the information.

However, the topology-based diffusion model also has some drawbacks: first, from the perspective of timeliness, the social network topology that researchers achieved is static, which is equivalent to a snapshot of the original network, on which all explicit social relations before acquisition are recorded; that is to say, all connections established 10 years ago and those established 1 second ago are collected at the same time; the connection that received just one notice and the connection of intimate communications between two friends are treated equally in the calculation model; second, in such a network topology, the weights of the connections are generally equal or identically distributed, implying that the connected users have the same influence on each other, or that the influence among the users in the social network satisfy the simple probability function; third, the role of other factors outside the network is ignored; users in the social network are affected not only by neighbor nodes but also by the traditional media and the like in the external world, thus participating in information diffusion. The next step should be focused on improving existing methods based on the topology characteristics of dynamic networks, user influence analysis, external factors under consideration, and the introduction of corresponding parameters.

2.4 Diffusion model based on the states of groups

There are two types of diffusion models based on group states. One of these models is based on groups. By drawing upon the idea of the epidemic model, this model categorizes nodes in a social network into several states, and depicts the process of information diffusion through changes of states. The other is based on individuals, where a diffusion model based on the influences of individuals is established by taking into consideration the different roles of different individuals on information diffusion.

2.4.1 Classical epidemic models

The most well-known theoretical model in the field of information diffusion is the epidemic model developed based on the spread of infectious diseases in reality. The epidemic model has a long history. As early as 1760, Daniel Bernoulli used mathematical methods to study the spread of smallpox. At the beginning of the 20th century, some scholars began to study the deterministic epidemic model. W.H. Hamer and Ross et al. made great contributions to the establishment of a mathematical model of infectious diseases. In 1927, William O. Kermack and Anderson G. McKendrick proposed the SIR model [22] for studying the black death in London and the plague in Mumbai. Taking into consideration the situation of repeated infection, they established the SIS model [23] in 1932. Based on these models, the "threshold theory" was proposed to distinguish the epidemic nature of diseases, which laid the foundation for the development of infectious disease dynamics. Girvan et al. added the concepts of immunity and mutation to explain the evolution of diseases [24].

In the epidemic model, the individuals in a system are divided into several types; each type of individual is in the same state. The basic states includes the susceptible state (S); namely, healthy but susceptible to infection; infected state (I), implying that it is infectious; the recovered state (R), indicating that the infected body was cured and acquired immunity or was dead after the infection. Different diffusion models are named after the transitions between such states. For example, if an individual shifts from the susceptible state into the infected state, such a diffusion model is named SI model; if a susceptible individual is infected, and becomes susceptible state again, such a diffusion model is called SIS model; if a susceptible individual is infected, but recovered and developed immunity afterwards, such a diffusion model is named SIR model. The above-mentioned models are introduced below.

1. SI model
The SI model is used to describe diseases that cannot be cured after the infection, or infectious diseases that cannot be effectively controlled due to the emergent outbreak; for example, black death, SARS, etc. We may also say that, in the SI model,

once an individual is infected, it will remain in the infected state permanently. $S(i)$ and $I(j)$ are used to express the susceptible population and the infected population, respectively. Assuming that the individual becomes infected at the mean probability β, the infection mechanism can be expressed by Equation 2.2:

$$S(i) + I(j) \xrightarrow{\beta} I(i) + I(j) \tag{2.2}$$

At time t, the proportion of S-state individuals in the system is $s(t)$, and that of the I-state individuals is $i(t)$. Based on this assumption, each infected individual can infect $\beta s(t)$ susceptible individuals. As the infected individuals have a proportion of $i(t)$, a total of $\beta i(t)s(t)$ susceptible individuals are infected. The dynamical model of the SI model can be described by the differential equations, as shown in Equation 2.3:

$$\begin{cases} \frac{ds(t)}{dt} = -\beta i(t)s(t) \\ \frac{di(t)}{dt} = \beta i(t)s(t) \end{cases} \tag{2.3}$$

2. SIS model

The SIS model is suitable for describing diseases such as colds and ulcers, which cannot be effectively immunized after cure. In the SIS diffusion model, the infected individuals, as the source of infection, transmit the infectious disease to susceptible individuals with a certain probability β, while the infected individuals return to the susceptible state with a certain probability y. On the other hand, the susceptible individuals, once infected, become a new source of infection. The infection mechanism can be described by Equation 2.4:

$$\begin{cases} S(i) + I(j) \xrightarrow{\beta} I(i) + I(j) \\ I(i) \xrightarrow{y} S(i) \end{cases} \tag{2.4}$$

Assuming that the proportion of S-state individuals in the system at time t is $s(t)$ and that of I-state individuals is $i(t)$, and that the growth rate of the infected individuals is $\beta i(t)s(t) - yi(t)$ when susceptible individuals are fully mixed with infected individuals, the dynamic behavior of the SIS model can be expressed by the differential equations shown in Equation 2.5:

$$\begin{cases} \frac{ds(t)}{dt} = -\beta i(t)s(t) + yi(t) \\ \frac{di(t)}{dt} = \beta i(t)s(t) - yi(t) \end{cases} \tag{2.5}$$

3. SIR model

The SIR model is suitable for diseases that, once being caught, can give the patients lifelong immunity, such as smallpox and measles. Assuming that in unit time the infected individuals are in contact with some randomly selected individuals in all states at the average probability β, and recover and obtain the immunity at an average probability y, the mechanism of the infection is described in Equation 2.6:

$$\begin{cases} S(i) + I(j) \xrightarrow{\beta} I(i) + I(j) \\ I(i) \xrightarrow{\gamma} R(i) \end{cases} \tag{2.6}$$

Assuming that the proportions of individuals in the susceptible, the infected and the recovered states at time t in the system are $s(t)$, $i(t)$ and $r(t)$, respectively, and in the condition that the susceptible individuals are well mixed with the infected individuals, the growth rate of the infected individuals is $\beta i(t)s(t) - \gamma i(t)$, the decline rate of the susceptible individuals is $\beta i(t)s(t)$, and the growth rate of the recovered individuals is $\gamma i(t)$, then the dynamic behavior of the SIR model can be described as Equation 2.7.

$$\begin{cases} \frac{ds(t)}{dt} = -\beta i(t)s(t) \\ \frac{di(t)}{dt} = \beta i(t)s(t) - \gamma i(t) \\ \frac{dr(t)}{dt} = \gamma i(t) \end{cases} \tag{2.7}$$

2.4.2 Infected diffusion models in social networks

The ideas of epidemic disease models are borrowed to divide nodes in a social network into the "susceptible" (S) group, to whom the information is still unknown, the "infected" (I) group, who have already received and keep transmitting the information, and the "recovered" (R) group, who have received the information but lost interest in transmitting it. The information diffusion is analyzed based on the change of these different states [25–27].

Example 2.3 Example of epidemic information diffusion model in social networks

Saeed Abdullah and Xindong Wu studied the diffusion of information on Twitter using the SIR model [25]. They believed that, similar to traditional epidemiology which takes into account the birth rate, when the nodes in the infected state (Class I) in a social network tweet about something, the fans will become a new susceptible

Table 2.1: Comparison of parameters in the epidemiology and Twitter dissemination model

	Epidemiology	Information dissemination on Twitter
$S(t)$	Susceptible individual set at time t	Set of users who can receive tweets from infected individuals at time t
$I(t)$	Infected individual set at time t	Set of individuals who tweet about certain topics at time t
$R(t)$	Recovered individual set at time t	Set of infected individuals who stopped tweeting about certain topics in a specific period of time
β	Infection rate	Diffusion rate
μ	Birth rate	The number of new fans that each infected individual gained in unit time
γ	Recovery rate	1/average infection time

population, and their total number keeps growing (Table 2.1). Assuming that the new susceptible population is introduced by the infected individual, they will establish a dynamic equation, as shown in Equation 2.8.

$$\begin{cases} \frac{dS}{dt} = -\beta \cdot S(t) \cdot I(t) + I(t) \cdot \mu \\ \frac{dI}{dt} = \beta \cdot S(t) \cdot I(t) - \gamma \cdot I(t) \\ \frac{dR}{dt} = \gamma \cdot I(t) \end{cases} \tag{2.8}$$

The article focuses on three types of events:
(1) Twitter's internal events; i.e., the events appear and disappear on Twitter whose external impact is limited. The "Follow Friday" event was selected.
(2) Real-time news; the "World Cup soccer match between the United States and Ghana on June 26, 2010" was selected.
(3) Social events; the "Memorial Day of the United States" was selected.

The experimental process of Abdullah et al. [25] is as follows:
(1) Prepare the dataset. For each event, a set of infected state $I(t)$, susceptible state S (t), and recovered state $R(t)$ are maintained. Specific keywords are searched using Twitter's API at an internal of Δt. Users who tweeted about a certain topic within $[t-;\Delta t, t]$ are retrieved to update the infected state set $I(t)$. The fans of each infected individual are retrieved; users already included in $I(t)$ are filtered out and the remaining are added to the susceptible state set $S(t)$. Users who did not tweet about the topic in $[t-2\Delta t, t]$ are removed from $I(t)$ and added to the recovered state set $R(t)$.
(2) Computer simulation; three kinds of events are simulated using the proposed model. The experimental results show that the model can effectively simulate the diffusion trend of events on Twitter.

2.4.3 Diffusion models based on influence

Different individuals have different effects on information diffusion. For instance, authoritative users or users at a central position will have greater influence to promote information diffusion.

Yang et al. proposed a linear influence model (LIM) [28] based on a large number of empirical studies on user behaviors on Twitter. The model assumes that information diffusion is subject to the influence of certain individual nodes, and the trend of information diffusion can be predicted by evaluating the influence of these nodes.

The influence function $Iu(l)$ of node u represents the number of fans referring to its message in a period of l after it was influenced. The function $v(t)$ represents the number of nodes in the system that refer to a message at time t. The LIM model assumes that $v(t)$ is the sum of the influence functions of all influenced nodes, as shown in Equation 2.9:

$$v(t+1) = \sum_{u \in A(t)} I_u(t-t_u) \tag{2.9}$$

where $A(t)$ represents the set of influenced nodes, and node u is influenced at time t_u ($t_u \leq t$).

This model can be described as follows: nodes u, v, and w are influenced at time t_u, t_v and t_w, respectively, after which each generates an influence function $I_u(t-t_u), I_v(t-t_v)$ and $I_w(t-t_w)$. The quantity of a message being referred to in the system at time t, represented by $v(t)$, is the sum of these three influence functions.

Yang et al. present the influence function of a node in a nonparametric manner and estimate it by using the non-negative least squares problem of the mapping Newton method [29]. This model can effectively evaluate the influence of nodes and can be used to predict the dynamic changes of information diffusion over time.

The population-based diffusion model describes the dynamic changes in information diffusion by describing the state of acceptance of information by users in the network and the redistribution of individuals between these states. Such models are widely used in viral marketing, rumor spread analysis, information source location, among others.

However, there are still some problems with the population-based diffusion model. In the epidemic diffusion model, the individuals are only classified in three states: infected, susceptible, and immune, and each state will continue for some time until the infection of the virus. However, in social networks, an individual's status after receiving a message is highly susceptible to the influence of the surrounding environment or other information, and such status also changes very fast. Based on the model of individual influence, because of the enormous scale and the large number of nodes in a social network, and the fact that different opinion leaders can appear in different scenarios, it remains a major challenge to establish an influence-based diffusion model by identifying the key nodes and estimating the influences of these nodes.

2.5 Diffusion model based on information characteristics

Information in online social networks carries all the records of users' online activities. The information itself has such distinctive characteristics as timeliness, multi-source concurrency, subject diversity, etc., which plays an indispensable role in the analysis of information diffusion. Different models can be created based on such characteristics.

2.5.1 Diffusion analysis for multiple source information

Most existing social network information diffusion models assume that information is not affected by factors outside the networks, and that it is only diffused among nodes along the edges of social networks. However, in the real world, users in social networks can access information through multiple channels.

When a node u in a social network releases information k and if none of its neighbor nodes have released information related to k, it indicates that u is influenced by some unobservable external factors, causing the unprecedented emergence of information k; however, if its neighbor node has released the related information, then the fact that u releases information k may be the result of being influenced by its neighbors or some external factors.

Based on the above idea, Myers et al. believe that, in addition to acquiring information through network links, nodes in social networks also acquire information through external influences. Thereby, they created model [30], as shown in Figure 2.3, in which function $\lambda_{ext}(t)$ is used to describe the amount of information that a user receives through external influences. If its neighboring nodes have posted relevant information, the user will have a link-based internal influence $\lambda_{int}(t)$ from them. Function $\eta(x)$ describes the probability that the user will post microblog after being exposed to the information. Eventually, the user will either post a relevant microblog under the influence or cease reacting to the information.

The total influence on node i is shown in Equation 2.10:

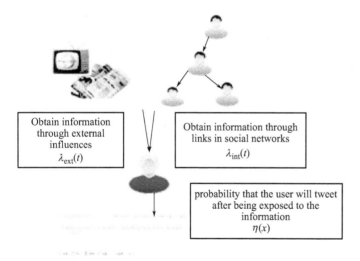

Figure 2.3: Schematic diagram of multi-source information influence

$$P_{\exp}^{(i)}(n;t) \approx \binom{t/dt}{n}\left(\frac{\Lambda_{\text{int}}^{(i)}(t)\Lambda_{\text{ext}}(t)}{t}\cdot dt\right)^{n}$$
$$\times \left(1 - \frac{\Lambda_{\text{int}}^{(i)}(t)+\Lambda_{\text{ext}}(t)}{t}\cdot dt\right)^{t/dt-n} \tag{2.10}$$

where $\Lambda_{\text{int}}^{(i)}(t)$ is the expected value of the node obtaining information through internal influence, and $\Lambda_{\text{ext}}(t)$ is the expected value of the node obtaining information through external influence.

Finally, the probability that user i will post microblogs after being exposed to the information is as shown in Equation 2.11:

$$F^{(i)}(t) = \sum_{n=1}^{\infty} P[i \text{ has } n \text{ exp.}] \times P[i \text{ inf } .|i \text{ has } n \text{ exp.}]$$
$$= \sum_{n=1}^{\infty} P_{\exp}^{(i)}(n;t) \times \left[1 - \Pi_{k=1}^{n}[1 - \eta(k)]\right] \tag{2.11}$$

where function $\eta(x)$ describes the possibility that the user will post a microblog after having read a message.

Myers et al. estimated the parameters of the model by using artificial networks and the infection time of some nodes. After applying this model to Twitter, they found that 71% of the information on Twitter was diffused based on the internal influence of the network, and the remaining 29% was triggered by factors outside the network.

2.5.2 Competitive diffusion of information

Some information, especially those in the same domain, can have mutual influence when spreading in a social network simultaneously; therefore, the diffusion rule of such information is different from that of independent information. To address multi-source information diffusion, Beutel et al. introduced the interaction factor to describe the intensity of interaction between two messages. The SI1|2S model [31] featuring the mutual influence of information was proposed based on the expansion of the SIS epidemic model.

The model assumes that the nodes have four states: I_{12} indicates that the node is infected with both virus 1 and virus 2; $I1$ indicates that the node is only infected with virus 1; I_2 indicates that the node is only infected with virus 2; S indicates that the node is not infected. The cure rate is δ, representing the probability of recovery from the infected state. The cure rates of virus 1 and virus 2 are δ_1 and δ_2, respectively. The infection rate is β; the node in the S state is infected with virus 1 at the probability of β_1, and infected with virus 2 at the probability of β_2. The node infected with virus 1 has a probability of $\in \beta_2$ to be infected with virtue 2, and the node infected with virus 2 has a probability of $\in \beta_1$ to be infected with virtue 1, as shown in Figure 2.4.

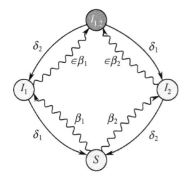

Figure 2.4: SI1|2S model's four states transition diagram from Alex Beutel [31]

Assuming that I_1, I_2, and I_{12} indicate the number of nodes in each of the three states, the number of nodes in each state changes with time as follows:

$$\frac{dI_1}{dt} = \beta_1 S(I_1 + I_{12}) + \delta_2 I_{12} - \delta_1 I_1 - \in \beta_2 I_1 (I_2 + I_{12}) \tag{2.12}$$

$$\frac{dI_2}{dt} = \beta_2 S(I_2 + I_{12}) + \delta_1 I_{12} - \delta_2 I_2 - \in \beta_1 I_2 (I_1 + I_{12}) \tag{2.13}$$

$$\frac{dI_{12}}{dt} = \in \beta_1 S_2(I_1 + I_{12}) + \in \delta_2 I_1 (I_2 + I_{12}) - (\delta_1 + \delta_2)I_{12} \tag{2.14}$$

If N is the total number of nodes, then the number of nodes in the S state is:

$$S = N - I_1 - I_2 - I_{12} \tag{2.15}$$

Threshold $\in_{\text{critical}}$ satisfies Equation 2.16:

$$\in_{\text{critical}} = \begin{cases} \frac{\sigma_1 - \sigma_2}{\sigma_2(\sigma_1 - 1)}, & \sigma_1 + \sigma_2 \geq 2 \\ \frac{2(1 + \sqrt{1 - \sigma_1\sigma_2})}{\sigma_1\sigma_2}, & \sigma_1 + \sigma_2 < 2 \end{cases} \tag{2.16}$$

Where $\in$ reflects the interaction between the two viruses: when $\in > \in_{\text{critical}}$, both viruses can coexist; when $\in = 0$, both viruses are immune to each other; when $0 < \in < 1$, both viruses compete with each other; when $\in = 1$, both viruses do not affect each other; when $\in > 1$, both viruses promote each other's diffusion.

Beutel et al. selected two video service websites, Hulu and Blockbuster, and two browsers, Firefox and Google Chrome, as the cases for study. The search volume of the relevant information is obtained from Google Insights, and the data is fitted with SI1|2S model. This model can fit the data well, which shows the applicability of the model.

Multi-source information diffusion analysis, through information modelling sources, helps us understand the mechanism of action between the real world and online social networks. In real scenarios, different information spreads through social networks at the same time; the research on the competitive diffusion of information helps to establish a model that can better reflect information diffusion in the real world, and thus improve our understanding of the law of diffusion.

The existing researches mainly start from the scope, time, and other factors of information diffusion. In addition to these factors, other properties of information such as time, content, and source constitute the inherent attribute of its diffusion. In what manner is the role of information combined with the role of users when it is diffused in a social network? Investigating this problem will help people to better understand the mechanism of diffusion.

2.6 Popularity prediction method

An information diffusion model describes the law of information diffusion; however, how to express and measure the overall effect of information diffusion in social networks is also a question worthy of study. Some tweets posted by celebrities are quickly forwarded and commented by their fans, leading to hot discussions in society; for example, the message about the "divorce of Faye Wong and Li Yapeng" on Weibo was forwarded for more than a hundred thousand times in just half an hour, while messages posted by some users are rarely viewed. The number and frequency of certain behaviors of users in social networks are associated with a significant difference between the spreading of online contents in terms of pace and scope. In this book, popularity is used to measure the overall degree and effect of information diffusion.

Popularity in different forms of media is reflected differently. For example, the popularity of a BBS post can be the number of replies to the posts. The popularity curve of the post about the "missing of Malaysia Airlines flight" on Tianya Forum is shown in Figure 2.5; for a video clip, its popularity can be the number of views; the popularity of a message on Weibo can be the sum of forwards and responses. In general, the greater the popularity value of an online content is, the more "popular" the online content is; i. e., the more widely or deeper it is spread. In this section, we introduce a couple of ways to predict the popularity of information diffused in social networks.

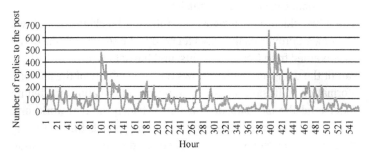

Figure 2.5: Popularity curve of the post about the "missing of Malaysia Airlines flight"

2.6.1 Prediction models based on historical popularity

Some researchers believe that there is a correlation between historical popularity and future popularity. A regression model that shows the correlation between historical and future popularities is established by considering the popularity at a particular point in the early stage or at a series of time points. The classical model is the SH model proposed by Gabor Szabo and Bernardo Huberman in 2008 [32]. The results were verified by posts on Digg and videos on YouTube.

To better observe the relationship between early popularity and late popularity, Gabor Szabo and Bernardo Huberman pretreated the data, and found that if the popularity is logarithm transformed (ln), early popularity and late popularity show a strong linear correlation, and the random fluctuations can be expressed in the form of additive noise. They also built a scatter plot to describe the early popularity and late popularity of the dataset by means of mathematical statistics. As far as the Digg posts are concerned, each scattered point represents a post sample, and the abscissa value that each point represents the number of "likes" for the post 1 hour after it was released, while the ordinate value represents the number of "likes" 30 days later. In the case of videos on Youtube, each scattered point represents a video sample, and the abscissa value that each point corresponds to represents the number of views 7 days after the video was posted, whereas the ordinate value represents the number of views 30 days later. According to the scatter plot, the specific relationship between the early popularity and late popularity of Digg posts and that of Youtube videos can be discovered using the least squares method: $\ln y = \ln x + 5.92$, $\ln y = \ln x + 2.13$.

The SH model established according to the above process is as follows:

$$\ln N_s(t_2) = \ln r(t_1, t_2) + \ln N_s(t_1) + \varepsilon_s(t_1, t_2) \tag{2.17}$$

where $N_s(t_2)$ represents the popularity of an online content s at time t_2, whereas $\ln N_s(t_2)$ is the dependent variable, indicating late popularity. $\ln r(t_1,t_2)$ is the intercept. $\ln N_s(t_1)$ is an independent variable, indicating early popularity. ε_s is the additive noise, i.e., the error term.

As far as linear regression fitting is concerned, if the error is subject to the normal distribution, then the fitting is correct. Therefore, the normality of the residual is detected by the quantile-quantile plot (QQ plot). It is found that the effect of the SH model for fitting the early popularity and the late popularity is acceptable. The QQ plot is used to visually verify whether a set of data is from a certain distribution, and is often used to check whether it is subject to the normal distribution.

2.6.2 Prediction models based on network structure

Bao et al. [33] improved the SH model by taking into account the effect of the structural characteristics of a network on popularity. Using Sina Weibo as the study object, they found that the structural characteristics of early microblog forwarders could reflect the final popularity of an online content.

The researchers first measured the correlation between the final popularity and the link density, and that between the final popularity and the diffusion depth of microblogs, and discovered a strong negative correlation between the final popularity and the link density, and a strong positive correlation between the final popularity and diffusion depth. This shows that groups of low link density and high diffusion depth are more conducive to enhance the popularity of microblogs. Based on the above findings, the researchers improved the SH model.

The improved model is shown in Equation 2.18:

$$\text{In}\hat{p}_k(t_r) = \alpha_1 \text{In}p_k(t_i) + \alpha_2 \text{In}\rho_k(t_i) + \alpha_3 \tag{2.18}$$

where $\hat{p}_k(t_r)$ is the popularity at time t_r, i.e., the late popularity; $p_k(t_i)$ is the popularity at time t_i, i.e., the early popularity; $\rho_k(t_i)$ is the link density at time t_i. $\alpha1, \alpha2, \alpha3$ are the parameters trained from the dataset.

$$\text{In}\hat{p}_k(t_r) = \beta_1 \text{In}p_k(t_i) + \beta_2 \text{In}d_k(t_i) + \beta_3 \tag{2.19}$$

where $\hat{p}_k(t_r)$ is the popularity at time t_r, i.e., the late popularity; $\text{In}p_k(t_i)$ is the popularity at time t_i, i.e., the early popularity; $d_k(t_i)$ is the diffusion depth at time t_i. $\beta_1, \beta_2, \beta_3$ are the parameters trained from the dataset (Table 2.2).

Table 2.2: Comparison of network structure based model and SH model

Model	RMSE	MAE
SH model	0.77	0.57
Link density model	0.63	0.45
Diffusion depth model	0.61	0.43

The comparison of network structure-based models and SH model is shown in Table 2.2. It can be seen from the table that the root mean squared error (RMSE) and the mean absolute error (MAE) of the improved model are significantly reduced compared with the SH model.

2.6.3 Prediction models based on user behaviors

Some researchers believe that the promotion of the popularity of online contents is closely related to the behaviors of social network users. Kristina Lerman and Tad Hogg argued that user's social behavior, such as registering a website, reading a message, "liking" a message, and becoming friends or fans of the message poster. Such behaviors can be represented with the state transition in the stochastic process [34]. At the same time, user behaviors can also determine the visibility of online contents. Take Digg for example. After having sufficient "likes," a post will be pushed to the home page where its visibility is elevated. The higher the visibility of a post is, the more likely its popularity is enhanced, whereas the more hidden a post is, the more likely it stays invisible.

The model established by Kristina Lerman and Tad Hogg is as follows:

$$\frac{dN_{\text{vote}}(t)}{dt} = r(v_f(t) + v_u(t) + v_{\text{friends}}(t)) \tag{2.20}$$

where N vote(t) represents the number of "likes" a post receives at time t, i.e., the popularity. r represents the fun factor of the post, i.e., the probability of users liking it once after being viewed. v_f, v_u, v_{friends}, respectively, represent the rates of users seeing the post via the front page, the "upcoming" section, and the "friends" interface.

The researchers assume that all users will first browse the front page after visiting the Digg website, and then enter the "upcoming" section at a certain probability. The posts posted by all users on Digg are grouped, with every 15 in one group. The latest 15 posts will be on the first page, the next 15 on the second page, and so on. Researchers use the function $f$page(p) to indicate the visibility of a post. If p has a value of 1.5, it implies that the post is in the middle of the second page. $f$page(p) decreases as p increases, whereas p increases as time increases. Researchers use the Gaussian inverse function to represent the distribution of the number of pages viewed by users. Finally, measure the $v$friends, i.e., the rate of a post being viewed via the "friends" interface. Users can see the posts both submitted and liked by friends. Researchers use the function $s(t)$ to represent the number of friends who have not seen the post, out of the total number of the friends of the liker. Suppose a friend of the liker finally sees the post at the rate of w, then $v$friends=$ws(t)$.

So here we have:

$$v_f = vf_{\text{page}}(p(t))\Theta(N_{\text{vote}}(t) - h) \tag{2.21}$$

$$v_u = cvf_{\text{page}}(q(t))\Theta(h - N_{\text{vote}}(t)\Theta(24hr - r)) \tag{2.22}$$

$$v_{\text{friends}} = ws(t) \tag{2.23}$$

where t is the length of time after the post was submitted, and v is the rate at which the user visits Digg.

Where the rate of users visiting Digg, the probability of browsing the "upcoming" section, the rate of liker's fans visiting Digg, the distribution of page views and some other parameters are the empirical values trained from the train set; the fun factors, and the number of fans of the poster vary with different posts (Table 2.3).

Table 2.3: Values of the parameters in the model

Parameter	Value
The frequency of users visiting Digg	$v = 10$ users/min
The probability of browsing the "upcoming" section	$C = 0.3$
The rate of liker's fans visiting Digg	$\omega = 0.002$/min
Distribution of page views	$\mu = 0.6, \lambda = 0.6$
The number of the liker' fans	$a = 51, b = 0.62$
The number of likes required for pushing a content	$h = 40$
The update rate of posts in the "upcoming" section	$ku = 0.06$ pages/min
The update rate of posts on the front page	$kf = 0.003$ pages/min
Posts feature parameters	
Fan factor	r
Number of the poster's fans	S

2.6.4 Prediction models based on time series

Many methods for predicting the popularity of the online contents are based on sample set; that is, to establish a mathematical model that describes the relationship between different factors and future popularity, the model parameters are trained from the sample set. These methods based on the sample set can accurately predict the long-term popularity of common online contents, however, the accuracy of predicting the popularity of hot online contents is low. However, it is difficult to find a suitable sample set for hot online content, which will be verified at the end of this section. What makes a hotspot content hot is that it has some characteristics that distinguish it from the ordinary ones. It is neither appropriate to collect ordinary contents into a sample set nor to select hotspot contents to create a sample set because the popularity of each hotspot content has its own status. If the samples in a sample set do not share any common characters, it is a failure. Therefore, in this section, we will describe a method for predicting the popularity of online contents using a time series based model [35]. This method does not require a sample set but simply the historical data of the online content. It allows analyzing the statistical laws and characteristics of the historical data.

1. Time series method
Time series is the series of the different values of an observed variable at different points in time arranged in the sequence of time. The basic assumption of the time series method is the notion of continuity in the development of things; that is, history provides a means to predict the future.

The time series consists of four constituent components: level, trend, seasonality, and noise, where "level" reflects the average level of the observed variables in this group; "trend" indicates the increases or decreases of the time series in a period of time; "seasonality" refers to the repeated fluctuations of the time series in a period of time, i.e., the aforementioned periodicity. The "level," "trend," and "seasonality" are called the systematic part, whereas "noise" is the nonsystematic part. Time series is aimed to make predications on the systematic part.

These different components together constitute the entire time series. The compound modes of different components are divided into addition and multiplication.

Addition mode: Yt = level + trend + seasonality + noise

Multiplication mode: Yt = level × trend × seasonality × noise

The seasonality components of a time series are subdivided into additive season and multiplicative season. The behavior of the additive season is that the seasonal fluctuation does not change with the overall trend and level of the time series. The behavior of the multiplicative season is that the seasonal fluctuation changes with the overall trend and level of the time series. The type of season selected for analysis determines whether to choose an additive model or a multiplication model. For time series of additive seasons, the additive model is usually selected for fitting, whereas for time series of multiplicative seasons, the multiplicative model is usually selected for fitting.

The basic steps of prediction using the time series method are as follows:

(1) access to data;
(2) visual analysis: analyze data characteristics, select the data granularity, and develop the time series plot;
(3) data preprocessing: deal with missing values, extreme values, etc.;
(4) data division: division of train set and validation set;
(5) application of prediction methods: select the appropriate model;
(6) evaluation of the prediction performance: use mean absolute percentage error (MAPE), relative absolute error (RAE), mean square error (MSE) and other methods for performance evaluation.

2. Time series models

There are some classical methods for prediction in time series, such as regression and smoothing. This section chooses the typical additive Multiple Linear Regression (MLR) model in the regression method and the typical multiplication model HW (Holt-Winters) model in the smoothing method.

The time series in the MLR model is presented as follows:

$$Y_t = P_t + (a_1x_1 + a_2x_2 + \ldots + a_{m-1}x_{m-1}) + E_t \tag{2.24}$$

where t represents time; Y represents the actual value of the time series; P_t is a polynomial, representing the trend and the level terms; m is the length of season, x_1, $x_2, \ldots x_{m-1}$ are the dummy variables; in the case of m periods, there are m-1 dummy variables; the period without a corresponding dummy variable is the reference value. The dummy variable is either 0 or 1. If time falls within a specific period, the dummy variable in this period is 1, and the others are 0. $a1, a2, \ldots a_{m-1}$ are the coefficients corresponding to the dummy variables respectively. Et represents noise.

The time series in the HW model is presented as follows:

$$Y_t = (L + tT)S_t + E_t \qquad (2.25)$$

where t presents time, Y is the fitted value of the time series, L is the level component, T is the linear trend component, S is the seasonal factor, and E is the noise component

$$L_t = \alpha y_t / S_{t-m} + (1-\alpha)(L_{t-1} + T_{t-1}) \qquad (2.26)$$

$$T_t = \beta(L_t - L_{t-1}) + (1-\beta)T_{t-1} \qquad (2.27)$$

$$S_t = \gamma(y_t / L_t) + (1-\gamma)S_{t-m} \qquad (2.28)$$

where y_t represents the observed value at time t, m is the length of the season, and α, β, and y are called smoothing parameters, which can be calculated with the least MSE of the train set.

The multiplicative HW model performs exponential smoothing for level, trend, and seasonality components. The smoothing parameters determine the rate of the latest information. The more approximate to 1 the value is, the more recent new information is used.

Thus, the k-step ahead-of-time prediction can be achieved in Equation 2.29.

$$Y_{t+k} = (L_t - 1 + kT_{t-1})S_{t+k-m} \qquad (2.29)$$

Example 2.4 Example of online content popularity prediction based on time series

The above sections depicted the basic idea of time series and two time series models. In the following section, we will describe the specific application of the time series approach in predicting the popularity of online contents: predicting the popularity of topics on Tianya Forum. Two types of hot topics were selected for analysis and prediction: one is the long-term, nonemergent type, such as Christmas and the US general election; the other is the short-term, emergent type, such as H7N9 and Beijing haze.

1) Dataset collection
Source: Sina News Center (http://news.sina.com.cn) and Tianya Forum (http://www.tianya.cn). Sina News Center is one of the major channels of Sina, with 24-hour rolling coverage of domestic, international, and social news, and more than 10,000 pieces of news issued daily. Tianya Forum is the largest forum website in China, founded in 1999, with registered users up to 85 million and daily visits of about 30 million. The Forum consists of politics, entertainment, economy, emotion, fashion, and other sections. As of June 2013, the posts in the entertainment section had exceeded 3.2 million, and the replies exceeded 170 million; the posts in the economy section exceeded 1.4 million, and the replies exceeded 17 million.

The dataset was collected into two steps:
(1) select hot topics from Sina News Center;
(2) search on Tianya Forum for the hot topics screened out in the first step.

Here, the popularity of hot topics is defined as the quantity of all posts and replies related to the topic within a certain period of time.

Hot topics in Sina News Center starting from July 5, 2004 were collected. Topics on a specific date can be searched by date. A total of 10,000 topics were collected from the international, social, entertainment, sports, science and technology, and other sections, which were then artificially divided into two types: emergent and nonemergent, with 6,000 emergent-type topics and 4,000 nonemergent-type topics. Then, the topics collected in the first step were used as keywords, which were searched in Tianya Forum using its internal searching section. There are multiple searching methods including searching by relevance, searching by posting time, searching from the full text, searching titles, and so on. We chose the relevance and the title searching methods. After further screening, we selected 7,000 hot topics, of which 3,000 were nonemergent and 4,000 were emergent topics. The nonemergent topics collected were data from January 2001 to December 2012, and the popularity of each topic was higher than 15,000; the emergent topics collected were data from January 2011 to December 2013, and the popularity of each topic in the first 15 days was higher than 18,000.

2) Analysis of characters of time series

Seasonality is also known as periodicity. Nonemergent topics tend to show seasonality when periodic events occur or are about to occur. Take the US general election for example, whenever the season of election arrives, the popularity of such a topic begins to rise, and the length of season stretches for 4 years, as shown in Figure 2.6. As for emergent topics, they are discussed by numerous people every day in a short period of time. In a day, the amount of discussions reaches a climax between 21:00 and 23:00, but drops to the lowest point between 2:00 and 4:00, which is in line with the habits of people. Therefore, the length of season is 24 hours. A topic goes through a process of emerging, climaxing, and declining. Hot topics show smaller fluctuations in the decline period than in the peak period. Therefore, the seasonality of the time series of the topic's popularity is multiplicative, which will be proved in the next experiment.

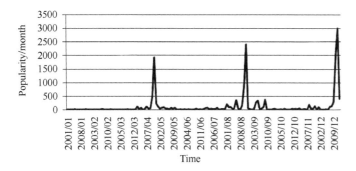

Figure 2.6: Popularity of the "US general election" topic from January 2001 to December 2012

If the data is too fine-grained, many values would result in 0. For example, nonemergent topics are not discussed much, and if the granularity is set at the level of "hour," the popularity is calculated once an hour. As a result, many of the values might be 0, and it is not easy to identify seasonal characteristics. Therefore, it is better to select "month" as the granularity. Take the topic "Christmas" for example, the value reaches its peak in December every year, while it is quite lower in other months. This shows a strong seasonality and the season length is 12 months; however, if the data granularity is too rough, some seasonal characteristics of a time series are likely to be overlooked. For example, an emergent topic becomes a hot topic among many people. If "day" is selected as the granularity, it is not easy to observe the period, but if "hour" is used as the granularity, the law of the hourly quantity of replies in every 24 hours is found to coincide with the habits of people, which is the characteristic of seasonality, with a season length of 24 hours. Figure 2.7 shows the frequency of replies on Tianya Forum in each time period of a day. The statistics is based on 35,619,985 replies to 10,000 posts on Tianya Forum.

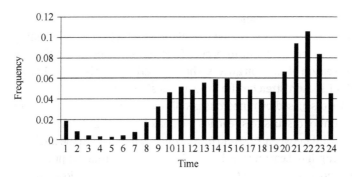

Figure 2.7: Frequency distribution of replies to hot posts on Tianya BBS during different periods of a day

3) Prediction experiment and the results

We chose "Beijing haze" as an example of emergent type topics and "Christmas" as an example of nonemergent topics.

Figure 2.8 shows the time series of the popularity of the "Beijing haze" topic. The topic's popularities on the 5th, 6th, and 7th day after the occurrence were chosen to form a train set to predict the popularity on the 8th day, i.e., the peak day, which served as a validation set. In the MLR model here, a quadratic polynomial with one variable is used as the trend; because the data in the train set is limited, a polynomial of higher order may lead to over-fitting. The multiplicative HW model minimizes the MSE of the train set. α, β, y are determined, where $\alpha = 0.98$, $\beta = 0.54$, $y = 0.01$. The results are shown in Figure 2.9. The time series predicted by the MLR model train set is negative in the location of lower trend because MLR is an additive model. The seasonal fluctuation is stable perhaps because the selected

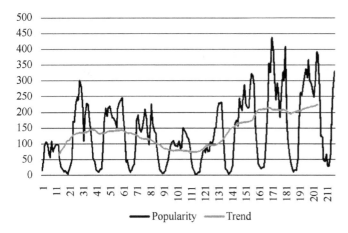

Figure 2.8: The blue line indicates the time series of "Beijing haze" topic in the first 9 days. The red line indicates the trend of the time series. The trend line is drawn with a moving average of a window size of 24

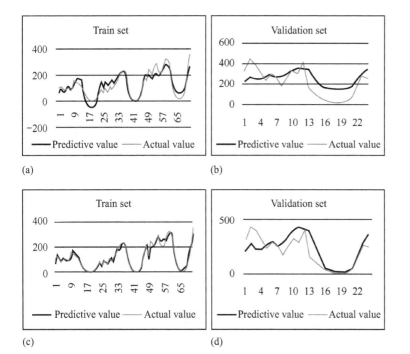

Figure 2.9: Results of "Beijing haze" popularity prediction from the MLR model and the multiplicative HW model

trend terms are lower than the actual ones. The accuracy rate of the MLR model in predicting the popularity on the 8th day is 79.1%, and the accuracy rate of the HW model is 88.3%.

Take the topic of "Christmas" as an example. As shown in Figure 2.10, the peak arises in December each year; the trend line is drawn with the move smoothing method using a window size of 12. The data from January 2008 to December 2009 were used as the train set, and the data from January to December of 2010 were used as the validation set. The results are shown in Figure 2.11.

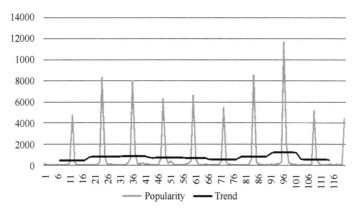

Figure 2.10: The grey line indicates the time series of the "Christmas" topic from January 2003 to December 2012. The black line indicates the trend of the time series. The trend line is drawn with a moving average of a window size of 24. The popularity reaches its peak in December each year

A total of 3,000 samples were collected for the nonemergent topics and 4,000 samples for the emergent topics. The historical data of both have a time span of 3 periods. The multiplicative HW model shows an average accuracy rate of 80.4% in predicting the trend of nonemergent topics, and an average accuracy rate of 84.7% in predicting the trend of emergent topics, whereas those of the MLR model are 63.7% and 71.4%, respectively.

The HW model is much more accurate than the MLR. In addition, it also validates that the seasonality of the hot topics is multiplicative season. The experimental results also show that the smoothing parameters usually remain stable in a certain range in both cases: $\alpha < 0.5, \beta < 0.5, y < 0.07$ (non-emergent), $\alpha > 0.55, \beta > 0.5, y < 0.07$ (emergent), which indicates that short-term emergent topics have more unstable level and trend terms, and more severe ups and downs, and therefore, they require frequent collection of the latest information; in other words, the dependence of its future popularity on historical data is weaker than long-term type topics, whereas the historical data of long-term topics has stronger impact on the future popularity of these topics.

3. Minimum historical data

For achieving accurate predictions, we conducted a study to determine the minimum periods of historical data required for making the most accurate prediction as far as the multiplicative HW model is concerned. For each topic, the last period of data was

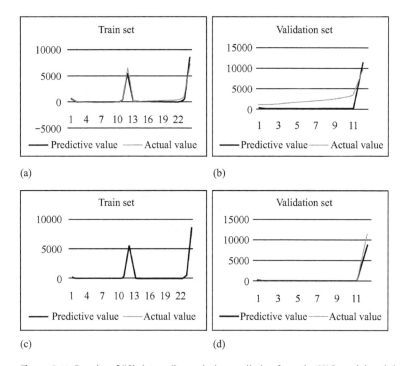

(a) (b) (c) (d)

Figure 2.11: Results of "Christmas" popularity prediction from the MLR model and the multiplicative HW model

used to form the validation set. The results are shown in Figure 2.12. According to the results, the prediction for long-term nonemergent topics is the most accurate when three periods of historical data are collected, with an average accuracy rate of 0.813; the prediction for short-term emergent topics is the most accurate when two periods of historical data are collected, with an average accuracy rate of 0.858. This also re-verified the fact that the historical data of long-term topics has a stronger impact on the future popularity, whereas the dependence of short-term nonemergent topics'

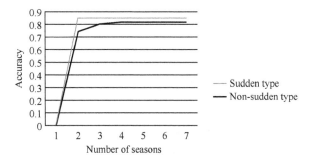

Figure 2.12: Average accuracy rates resulting from different season numbers used as train sets examined on two types of topics

popularity on historical data is weaker. When the number of historical data periods exceeds three, the accuracy cannot be significantly improved because data in one period can reflect the seasonal information, data in two periods can reflect the trend information. As the levels and trends are constantly changing, earlier historical data cannot reflect the current popularity. Therefore, the accuracy reaches saturation after a time length of 3 periods.

4. Comparative analysis

To validate the time series method, the SH Model based on the sample set is used for comparative analysis. Gabor Szabo and Bernardo Huberman found that the early popularity and late popularity exhibit linear relationship in logarithmic form: $\ln y = \ln x + b$, where x is the early popularity, a known data; y is the late popularity, to be predicted; b is a parameter trained from the sample set.

The multiplicative HW and SH models are used for comparison. Four thousand emergent-type hot topics serve as the sample set of the SH model; the trained parameter $b = 0.267$, and "Beijing haze" is the topic of prediction. Data in the first 7 days are used for early popularity, and data on the 8th day are used for late popularity. The popularity on the 8th day predicted by the SH model is 9154, that predicted by the time series is 5488, and the actual popularity is 4913. The error rates of the two models as to the two topics are shown in Table 2.4.

Table 2.4: Average accuracies of SH and HW models in calculating the two topics

	Emergent	Non-Emergent
SH	29.5%	23.0%
HW	85.1%	80.4%

The reason why the SH model is not ideal to predict the popularity of hot topics is that it relies on the sample set, and the development law of each hot topic has its own characteristics. For example, each has different peak and base values, making it difficult to find the right sample set. However, the time series method does not depend on the sample set but on analyzing the historical data of the hot topic to be predicted.

It is easy to obtain historical data for a historical popularity-based prediction model, which is suitable for predicting the long-term popularity of online contents. It can also be applied to predict the popularity of various online contents because all posts, news, video, and microblogs have the historical data of popularity. However, predicting long-term popularity with premature historical data can lead to inaccurate predictions, whereas the use of late historical data can lead to delayed predictions.

The advantage of a model based on the network structure is that the network structure factor is taken into consideration, which is more accurate than the prediction model based on the historical popularity, while its limitation is the same as that of the

historical data-based predication; i.e., predicting long-term popularity using premature historical data and network structure information can lead to inaccurate predictions, while using late historical data and network structure information can lead to
late predictions. Therefore, it is not suitable for social networks having vague features
of network hierarchy structure, such as video sharing websites and forum websites.

The predication model based on user behaviors takes into consideration the
direct factors that enhance the popularity of online contents while analyzing user
behaviors and the status of online contents; therefore, the predictions are timely.
However, this model assumes that all users have the same habits and behaviors,
while individuals on social networks are actually different from one to another.

In contrast, a prediction model based on time series predicts the future popularity of certain online content using the historical data of the contents themselves,
which is more suitable for online content with more complex popularity evolution
patterns. In general, the more popular the online content is the more complex the
popularity evolution pattern is. Of course, the time series method also has its drawbacks; i.e., it is only suitable for short-term prediction and is not accurate for
predicting future trends farther beyond.

2.7 Information source location

2.7.1 Concept of information source location

In the study of diffusion process, how to determine the source of the diffusion based
on the observed results of diffusion is a fundamental problem. Research results on
this issue can usually be applied to spam management, computer virus prevention,
rumour prevention, and control on social networks and other areas.

Because of the conveniency and strong interactivity of social networks, information on social networks can spread very fast and widely, which also lead to the
uncontrolled diffusion and spread of enormous false and illegal information. To
identify the source of malicious information by means of the information source
location technology and other effective methods is the key to control the diffusion of
false and illegal information on social networks. The basic goal of information source
location is to determine the initial source of information diffusion.

According to the existing researches on information source location, information
source location is defined as follows: to determine the initial source node of information diffusion on a network in the condition of knowing the observed result, given the
attributes of the underlying network structure, the mode of information diffusion,
etc. Oftentimes, our observations of the results of diffusion are not complete as we
can only observe a part of the overall result, which adds difficulty to the source
location of the information. In addition, due to the diversity and uncertainty of the

underlying network structure and the different characteristics of various diffusion modes themselves, the research of information source location technology faces many challenges.

The following section will introduce the main research results of information source location. In the model proposed by Fioriti et al. [36], the dynamic importance of each node is calculated to sort the nodes. Given the diffusion result, the undirected contact graph, it is possible to identify multiple source nodes or neighbors near these source nodes. This method behaves very well when the diffusion result exhibits a graph structure similar to a tree structure but is poorly behaved in other cases.

In their studies on identifying the starting point of a diffusion process in complex networks [37], Comin et al. mainly analyzed the characteristics of the centrality of the source node and identified it by using an improved centrality measurement method. This method has a high success rate in ER networks and scale-free networks. The method was experimented in three different diffusion modes. The results show that the effect is the best when the diffusion mode approximates the Snowball.

In the model [38] proposed by Lokhov et al., information diffusion is assumed to fit the SIR model. A reasoning algorithm based on the dynamic message transfer equation is used for source location, and with each node serving as the source node, the probabilities of the other nodes in the three states of SIR are calculated. The algorithm is also effective in the case where only a part of the diffusion result is observed, however, the complexity is relatively high in the case where the number of nodes is high in the network.

Nino et al. proposed a statistical reasoning framework based on maximum likelihood estimation [39] for source location. The study assumes that the diffusion process fits the SIR model and obtains a sorted list of possible nodes by likelihood estimation based on the observed diffusion result on any network. The study performs well on different network structures.

Each of the above methods has its own different applicable conditions. The basic ideas of these methods can be divided into two categories: one is the measurement (grading) of node attributes, and the other is source location based on statistical reasoning. In the following sections, we will first introduce two representative methods, the source location method based on centrality measurement and the source location method based on a statistical reasoning framework, and then we will introduce a multi-source information source location method [41] based on the reverse diffusion and node partitioning targeted for the conditions of multi-source concurrency and incomplete observation.

2.7.2 Source location methods based on centrality

For identifying the starting point of the diffusion process in complex networks, Comin et al. analyzed the characteristics of the centrality of the source node and identified the source node using an improved centrality measurement method. The study mainly examined two different networks: the ER network and the scale-free network, and experiments were conducted on both networks.

In reality, information diffusion exhibits different modes. For example, in a computer virus diffusion network, when a new virus appears, the node that is infected with the virus will diffuse it to all its neighbors; almost all of the neighbors will be infected, and the process keeps on; however, in the information diffusion process on social networks, there is a certain probability that an infected node infects its neighbors. Normally not all of them are infected, and only a part of the nodes are infected due to their interest in the information. Obviously, the performance of the information source location method will be affected by the different characteristics of different modes of diffusion. The study mainly considered the following three types of diffusion modes and the conducted experiments:

1. Snowball (also known as Dilation)
This diffusion method is similar to the classic breadth-first search algorithm, which corresponds to spam diffusion in the real world, i.e., information is sent from one node to all contacts.

2. Diffusion
The random walk algorithm can be referred to in this diffusion method. A node chooses one of its neighbor nodes for diffusion. Each neighbor node has a probability of being diffused.

3. Contact process
This diffusion method can be viewed as a classic virus diffusion. Each node has a certain probability to infect its neighbors.

The source location method proposed in this study mainly deals with calculating the centrality of each node. In previous studies, the four major centrality measuring methods are "Degree," "Closeness," "Betweenness," and "Eignvector."

The first measurement method, i.e., degree, uses the classical definition of degree given in the graph theory; that is, the number of edges associated with a node. d_{ij} represents the length of the shortest path between nodes i and j, so the average shortest distance passing node i l_i is:

$$l_i = \frac{1}{n-1}\sum_{j, j \neq i} d_{ij} \tag{2.30}$$

The second measurement method is closeness. In the following equation, the closeness of node i C_i is the reciprocal of the average shortest distance of node i:

$$C_i = \frac{1}{l_i} \tag{2.31}$$

We can see that in the "closeness" method, the distance between one node and the other nodes is used to measure the centrality of the node. Obviously, if the average distance between the node and the other nodes is small, it approximates the "center" of the network; in other words, it has higher centrality.

The third measurement method is "betweenness." As shown in the following equation, the "betweenness" of node i is:

$$B_i = \sum_{s,t,s \neq t, s \neq i, t \neq i} \frac{n_{st}^i}{n_{st}} \tag{2.32}$$

where n_{st}^i is the number of the shortest paths between node s and node t via node i, and n_{st} is the number of shortest paths between node s and node t. It can be seen that the betweenness method measures the centrality of a node by testing whether the node is on the shortest path between other nodes. If a node is on the shortest path between many other nodes, it is more like a "hub" which has higher centrality.

The fourth measurement method is "eignvector." Eignvector centrality follows the principle that when a node is connected to other high-level nodes, its importance becomes higher. Let s_i represent the score of the i-th node, and A denote the adjacency matrix of the network, the score obtained by the i-th node is the sum of the scores of all its neighbor nodes. Therefore,

$$s_i = \frac{1}{\lambda} \sum_{j=1}^{N} A_{ij} s_j \tag{2.33}$$

where λ is a constant. The above equation can be rewritten as:

$$As = \lambda s \tag{2.34}$$

The eigenvector of the largest eigenvalue obtained by this equation represents the eigenvector of the node.

In this study, the diffusion process on the network can be simulated in the following manner: given that some seed nodes are assumed as the starting nodes, the underlying network is sampled by the algorithm corresponding to the three different types of diffusion mentioned earlier, to get a subgraph.

Comin et al. measured the centrality of the nodes in the subgraph achieved after the sampling on the ER network and the scale-free network, and found that the degree of the nodes was almost unchanged after sampling because of local variables. Therefore, the deviation caused by sampling can be eliminated when the measured centrality value is divided by the degree of the node. The unbiased betweenness is defined as follows:

$$\hat{B}_i = \frac{B_i}{(k_i)^r} \tag{2.35}$$

where B_i is the biased betweeness, k_i is the degree, and an appropriate empirical value selected for r by experiment is $r = 0.85$. The result of measurement achieved using the improved method shows that the centrality of the source node is significantly higher than that of other nodes, and the source node can be well identified on the ER network and the scale-free network. In addition, Comin et al. experimented in three different modes of diffusion and found that the effect of this source location method is best when the diffusion mode approximates the Snowball.

Example 2.5 Example of centrality-based source location calculation

Calculate the relevant properties of node a in Figure 2.13.

Node a has a degree of 2. As this is a directed graph, both the in-degree and the out-degree are 2.

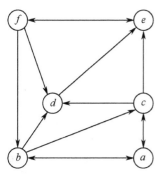

Figure 2.13: Example of centrality source location calculation

The shortest distances from node a to node b, node c, node d, node e, and node f are respectively 1, 1, 2, 2, and 3, so the average shortest distance to node a is $l = \frac{1+1+2+2+3}{5} = 1.8$.

The closeness of node a is $C = 1/1.8$.

The betweenness of node a is $B = \frac{1}{1} = 1$. because there is only one shortest path between node c and node b, and only the shortest path between node c and node b passes through node a.

2.7.3 Source location methods based on statistical reasoning framework

Nino et al. proposed a statistical reasoning framework based on maximum likelihood estimation, which is based on the observed diffusion process on any network.

In this study, the SIR model is used as the diffusion model. In the network G, the nodes have three states: susceptible (S), infected (I), and recovered (R). The diffusion process is simulated using discrete time steps. The probability that a susceptible node is converted to the infected state is p, and the probability that the infected node is converted to the recovery state is q. Let Θ be the original infection node, assuming that the time step experienced by the diffusion process is known and used as a parameter for estimating the source node by reasoning.

Based on the above assumptions, the source location problem is defined as follows:

The random vector $\vec{R} = (R(1), R(2), ..., R(N))$ represents the infection of the node before a certain time threshold T. The random variable $R(i)$ is a Bernoulli random variable, and if the node is infected before the time point T, the corresponding value is 1; otherwise, the value is 0.

Suppose we have observed the SIR model diffusion result of a known (p, q) and T, and the set of all nodes is $S = \{\theta_1, \theta_2, \cdots, \theta_N\}$, with a limited number of nodes. We get the following problem of maximum likelihood:

$$\hat{\Theta} = \arg \max{}_{\Theta \in S} P(\Theta | \vec{R} = \vec{r}) \qquad (2.36)$$

where $\Theta \in S$ is the all possible sources of diffusion. According to Bayes theorem, we can see that:

$$\hat{\Theta} = \arg \max{}_{\Theta \in S} P(\vec{R} = \vec{r} | \Theta) \qquad (2.37)$$

Algorithm 2.3 represents a process that uses a maximum likelihood estimation algorithm to perform calculations. The main idea of maximum likelihood estimation is, with the experimental result being already known, to find the experimental condition that is most favorable (i.e., of the largest likelihood) for getting the experimental result through the algorithm. The experimental result here means the observed diffusion result that is already known. At the same time, some conditions, including the parameters (p, q) and T of the SIR model, are also known. The unknown experimental condition is the source of diffusion.

Algorithm 2.3 Maximum Likelihood Based Source Node Estimation Algorithm: $(G, p, q, \overrightarrow{r_*}, T, S, n)$

Input: network structure G, SIR process parameter (p, q), possible source node set $S = \{\theta_1, \theta_2 \cdots, \theta_N\}$, observed dissemination result $\vec{r}$, cutoff time threshold T, number of simulations n

for each $\theta_j \in S$ (a prior set of possible source nodes) **do**

Likelihood estimation function calling $(G, p, q, \vec{r}_*, T, n)$

Save $\widehat{P}(\vec{R} = \vec{r}_* | \Theta = \theta_j)$

end for

Output 1: θ_k and maximum likelihood estimation $\widehat{P}(\vec{R} = \vec{r}_* | \Theta = \theta_k)$

Output 2: source nodes sorted based on likelihood $\widehat{P}(\vec{R} = \vec{r}_* | \Theta = \theta_k)$ in set $S = \{\theta_1, \theta_2, \cdots, \theta_N\}$

The n in the parameters is the number of simulations run for a set of source node candidates.

The similarity φ of two different diffusion results is judged in two ways (XNOR and Jaccard), which are denoted as $\overline{\mathrm{XNOR}}(\vec{r_1}, \vec{r_2})$ and Jaccard $(\vec{r_1}, \vec{r_2})$, respectively. Later, Nino et al. defined three different likelihood estimation functions: AUCDF, AvgTopK, and naive Bayesian. The first two uses the similarity calculation method mentioned earlier, and the naive Bayesian method uses its own similarity calculation method. Although the three algorithms are different, they share the same main idea; that is, to calculate the likelihood, i.e., the probability of achieving the experimental results under different experimental conditions. In the following part, we will intro-duce these three algorithms.

Algorithm 2.4 represents the algorithm for the AUCDF estimation function.

Algorithm 2.4 AUCDF Estimation Function $(G, p, q, \vec{r_*}, T, S, n)$

Input: network structure G, SIR process parameter (p, q), observed diffusion result $\vec{r_*}$, calculated source node θ, cutoff time threshold T, number of simulations n

for $i = 1$ to n (number of simulations) **do**

Run SIR simulation (p, q), wherein $\Theta = \theta$, get the propagation result $\overrightarrow{R_{\theta,j}}$, stop when the time threshold T is reached

Calculate and save $\varphi(\vec{r_*}, \overrightarrow{R_{\theta,J}})$

end for

Calculate the actual distribution function:

$$\hat{P}(\varphi(\vec{r_*}, \overrightarrow{R_{\theta,J}}) \le x) = \frac{\sum_{i=1}^{n} 1_{[0,x)}(\varphi(\vec{r_*}, \overrightarrow{R_{\theta,J}}))}{n}$$

Calculate the likelihood:

$$\mathrm{AUCDF}_\theta \int_0^1 \hat{P}(\varphi(\vec{r_*}, R_{\theta,J}) \le x)dx$$

Output: $\hat{P}(\vec{R} = \vec{r_*} | \Theta = \theta) = 1 - \mathrm{AUCDF}_\theta$

Algorithm 2.5 represents the algorithm for the AvgTopK likelihood estimation function

---

Algorithm 2.5 AvgTopK Likelihood Estimation Function $(G, p, q, \vec{r_*}, T, \theta, n)$

Input: network structure G, SIR process parameters (p, q), observed diffusion result $\vec{r_*}$, calculated source node θ, cutoff time threshold T, number of simulations n

for $i = 1$ to n (number of simulations) **do**

Run SIR simulation (p, q), wherein $\Theta = \theta$, get the propagation result $\overrightarrow{R_{\theta,j}}$, stop when the time threshold T is reached

Calculate and save $\varphi(\vec{r_*}, \overrightarrow{R_{\theta,J}})$

end for

Sort the ratings $\left\{ \varphi(\vec{r}_*, \overrightarrow{R_{\theta,J}}) \right\}$ in descending order;
Averaged of k maximum ratings:

$$\hat{P}(\vec{R} = \vec{r}_* | \Theta = \theta) = \frac{1}{k} \sum_{i=1}^{k} \left\{ \varphi(\vec{r}_*, \overrightarrow{R_{\theta,J}}) \right\} \text{sorted}$$

Output:
Likelihood $\vec{P}(\vec{R} = \vec{r}_* | \Theta = \theta)$

Algorithm 2.6 represents the algorithm for the Naive Bayesian likelihood estimation function.

Algorithm 2.6 Naive Bayesian Likelihood Estimation Function $(G, p, q, \vec{r}_*, T, \theta, n)$
   Input: network structure G, SIR process parameters (p, q), observed diffusion result
$\vec{r}_*$, calculated source node θ, cutoff time threshold T, number of simulations n
Where in $m_k = 0 : \forall k \in V$ *from* G;
   for $i = 1$ to n (number of simulations) **do**
   Run SIR simulation (p, q), where $\Theta = \theta$, get the propagation result $\overrightarrow{R_{\theta,J}}$, stop
when the time threshold T is reached
   Update $m_k = m_k + 1$ *for* k *being* $\inf ected\ in$ $\overrightarrow{R_{\theta,J}}$
   end for
   Calculate:

$$\hat{P}(\vec{r}_*(k) = 1 | \Theta = \theta) = \frac{m_k + \in}{n + \in}, \forall k \in G$$

Calculate log likelihood:

$$\log(\hat{P}(\vec{R} = \vec{r}_* | \Theta = \theta))$$
$$= \sum_{\{k : \vec{r}_*(k)=1\}} log(\hat{P}(\vec{r}_*(k) = 1 | \Theta = \theta))$$
$$+ \sum_{\{j : \vec{r}_*(j)=0\}} log(1 - \hat{P}(\vec{r}_*(j) | \Theta = \theta))$$

Output:
Likelihood $\log(\hat{P}(\vec{R} = \vec{r}_* | \Theta = \theta))$

Nino et al. tested the performance of the likelihood estimation algorithm on different network architectures. After the list of potential source nodes output by the algorithm in node set S is achieved, the ranking of the actual source node in this output list is checked. Experiments showed that this method performs well in various network environments.

2.7.4 Multiple information source location methods

Oftentimes, we can only observe some of the diffusion results. In a diffusion mode that fits the SIR model, part of the nodes will shift from the infected state to the recovery state, making it more difficult for information source location. In addition, the diffusion results derived from multiple-source diffusion make it harder for us to determine the true source of information. This section introduces a method of multi-point source location based on sparsely infected nodes, which solves the problem of incomplete observations and multiple-source diffusion. The method consists of the following three steps: first, detect the recovered nodes in the network using a reverse diffusion method. Second, partition all infected nodes using a partitioning algorithm, thus to turn the issue of multi-point source location into the issue of multiple independent single-point source location. Finally, determine the most likely source node in each partition.

1. Step 1: Reverse dissemination method
In real life, it is very difficult to locate the source of rumors only by observing several infected nodes. Considering the recovery of nodes from the infected state, to supplement such lost information and simplify the problem of source node location, we proposed a score-based reverse diffusion method to find the recovered nodes and infected node set. Algorithm 2.7 shows an algorithm for the scoring function based on the reverse diffusion method.

Algorithm 2.7 Scoring Function Based on The Reverse Diffusion Method
    Input: a social network G, node set V and connection set E contained in the network, and part of the observed infected node set $I \in V$; a constant basesore.
    Output: an extended infected node set $I^* \in V$, the infected node set which contains all the recovered nodes, the infected node set, both observed and unobserved, and the nodes that are associated with the infected nodes but are not infected. In addition $I \in I^* \in V$
    Initialize the nodes, assign the unique label C and the unique score S_c, $\forall n \in V$:

$$C_n, S_{cn} = \begin{cases} 1, & n \in I \\ 0, & \text{otherwise} \end{cases}$$

Initialize the node set $I' = I$
for iter 1 to N_{step} **do**
for $n \in I'$ **do**
for $i \in n_{neighbors}$ **do**
update $I' = I'U_i$, $C_i = 1$
update $S_{Ci} = S_{Ci} + S_{Cn}$, if $C_i = 0$
for $n \in V$ **do**

if $S_{Cn} >$ basescore, $I^* = I^* U_n$

Return extended infected node set $I *$

A new network is created for location analysis by implementing Algorithm 2.7, and is called the expanded infection network.

2. Step 2: Infected node partitioning

Use the "divide and rule" approach to change the multi-point source location into an issue of multiple independent single-point source location. In the following section, we will briefly introduce three methods of partitioning:

1) Method based on modularity

The result of a good partitioning method should exhibit relatively dense connections between nodes in the same partition, but relatively sparse connections between nodes in different partitions. This can be measured by the modularity function. Modularity refers to the difference between the proportion of the edges connecting the internal vertices of the community structure in a network and the expected value of the proportion of the edges connecting the internal vertices of the community structure in another random network.

The greater the value of this function, the better the effect of partition. This method can be rewritten in the form of a matrix, and the modularity is represented by the eigenvector of the matrix.

2) Method based on edge betweeness

Linton C Freeman first proposed to measure the centrality and influence of nodes in the network by using betweeness. Edge betweenness is defined as the number of the shortest paths passing an edge in the network. If an edge has high edge betweeness, it implies that it is the edge that bridges the two partitions of the network. The partitioning steps based on the edge betweeness method are as follows:

(1) Calculate the edge betweeness of all edges in the network;
(2) Remove the edge with the highest edge betweeness;
(3) Recalculate the edge betweeness of all edges;
(4) Repeat step (2) until all edges are gone.

3) MMSB (mixed membership stochastic model)

This method is based on the assumption that nodes infected by the same source node are more likely to have connections, and that nodes infected by different source nodes rarely generate connections. Given a graph $G = N$ (N, Y) which contains N nodes and the connection set $Y(Y(p, q) \in 0, 1)$. K is the number of potential partitions. The goal of MMSB is to obtain the parameters α and β by calculating the maximum likelihood of the edges.

$$P(Y|\vec{\alpha},\beta) =$$
$$\int \sum_{zs} (\Pi_{p,q} P(Y(p,q)|\vec{z}_{p\to q}, \vec{z}_{q\to p}, B) P(\vec{z}_{p\to q}|\vec{\pi}p) P(\vec{z}_{p\to q}|\vec{\pi}p) \Pi_p P(\pi_p|\vec{\alpha})) d\vec{\pi} \qquad (2.38)$$

$B\ (g,\ h)$ in $B_{K \times K}$ represents the probability that there is an edge between a node in partition g group and a node in partition h, and $\Pi = \pi_{N \times K}$ denotes the matrix formed by the probabilities of nodes in each partition.

3. Step 3: Node set source location
Through the above two steps, the multi-point source location issue is transformed into an issue of multiple independent single-point source location. Four measures related to centrality, i.e., degree, closeness, betweenness, and eignvector, are adopted for evaluation. Here, the method used by Comin et al. mentioned above in the single-point source location was adopted, which we will not describe here.

Experiment on three different types of artificial networks: random regular network, BA network, and ER network. All networks generate 5000 nodes through NetworkX. The probability of infection in the SIR model is 0.9 and the recovery probability is 0.2. Test the effect of different community detection algorithms on infected node partition. The experimental results show that the method based on the main features is superior to other community partitioning algorithms. Thus, the method based on the main feature is selected to evaluate the infected node in subsequent experiments.

Test the proposed multi-point source location solution on different networks. The three networks are: the random regular network with 5000 nodes, where the degree of each node is 3; ER network with 5000 nodes, where the probability of edge generation is 0.01; BA network with 5000 nodes, where each new node generates two edges to reach the existing nodes. The results of the experiment are shown in Figures 2.14 and 2.15. The solution achieved good results on the random regular network, which could effectively discover the source nodes.

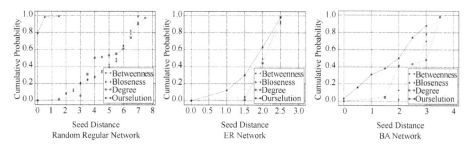

Figure 2.14: Cumulative probability distribution of the average distance between the real source node and the calculated source node, the number of source nodes $k=2$ [41]

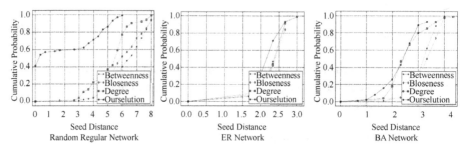

Figure 2.15: Cumulative probability distribution of the average distance between the real source node and the calculated source node, the number of source nodes k=3 [41]

2.8 Summary

The study of information diffusion in social networks has become one of the most challenging and promising fields of research. This chapter introduced a number of mainstream models of information diffusion in social networks and explored the methods for predicting the trend of information diffusion and tracing the source of information.

Despite numerous studies and certain achievements in the field of information diffusion in social networks, there are still many problems that require further exploration.

(1) Model validation and evaluation methods: the existing model validation methods are mainly based on random data for verification computer simulated data for analysis. However, for a more scientific approach, a unified standard test set should be established by screening the typical examples of diffusion to assess the advantages and disadvantages of different diffusion models, as well as to define the scope of applications of the algorithms.

(2) The intrinsic rule of multi-factor coupling: most reported studies discuss information diffusion from a single perspective, such as the topology of the network where the information is diffused and the rules of individual interactions. However, in reality, the diffusion of information is the typical evolution process of a complex system, which requires a comprehensive consideration of multiple factors including individual interaction, network structure, and information characteristics to describe information diffusion in online social networks in a more accurate manner.

(3) Dynamic changes in social networks: most existing methods of information diffusion analysis are based on the static network topology; however, in real social networks, the network of relationship between users changes over time. It is necessary to add dynamic change into the information diffusion model. In addition, the existing algorithms are mostly based on serial or time step models. Large-scale parallel distributed algorithms are needed to improve the efficiency of processing.

It is extremely important and challenging to study the mechanism of information diffusion in social networks and to understand the law of information diffusion. There are still a number of important issues that need solutions. We expect more exciting results in the future.

References

[1]   Mark S. Granovetter. The strength of weak ties. American Journal of Sociology, 1973:1360–1380.
[2]   Stratis Ioannidis, Augustin Chaintreau. On the strength of weak ties in mobile social networks. In Proceedings of the Second ACM EuroSys Workshop on Social Network Systems. ACM, 2009: 19–25.
[3]   Stephan Ten Kate, Sophie Haverkamp, Fariha Mahmood, Frans Feldberg. Social network influences on technology acceptance: A matter of tie strength, centrality and density. In BLED 2010 Proceedings, 2010, 40.
[4]   Paul S. Adler, Seok-Woo Kwon. Social capital: Prospects for a new concept. Academy of Management Review, 2002, 27(1):17–40.
[5]   Jichang Zhao, Junjie Wu, Xu Feng, Hui Xiong, Ke Xu. Information propagation in online social networks: A tie-strength perspective. Knowledge and Information Systems, 2012, 32(3):589–608.
[6]   Eytan Bakshy, Itamar Rosenn, Cameron Marlow, Lada Adamic. The role of social networks in information diffusion. In Proceedings of the 21st international conference on World Wide Web. ACM, 2012: 519–528.
[7]   John Scott. Social network analysis: Developments, advances, and prospects. Social Network Analysis and Mining, 2011, 1(1):21–26.
[8]   Mor Naaman, Jeffrey Boase, Chih-Hui Lai. Is it really about me?: Message content in social awareness streams. In Proceedings of the 2010 ACM conference on Computer supported cooperative work. ACM, 2010: 189–192.
[9]   Akshay Java, Xiaodan Song, Tim Finin, Belle Tseng. Why we twitter: Understanding microblogging usage and communities. Proceedings of the 9th WebKDD and 1st SNA-KDD 2007 workshop on Web mining and social network analysis. ACM, 2007: 56–65.
[10]   Mike Thelwall, Kevan Buckley, Georgios Paltoglou. Sentiment in Twitter events. Journal of the American Society for Information Science and Technology, 2011, 62(2):406–418.
[11]   Seth Myers, Jure Leskovec. Clash of the contagions: Cooperation and competition in information diffusion. ICDM. 2012, 12:539–548.
[12]   Mark Granovetter. Threshold models of collective behavior. American Journal of Sociology, 1978, 1420–1443.
[13]   Jacob Goldenberg, Barak Libai, Eitan Muller. Talk of the network: A complex systems look at the underlying process of word-of-mouth. Marketing Letters, 2001, 12(3):211–223.
[14]   Jacob Goldenberg, Barak Libai, Eitan Muller. Using complex systems analysis to advance marketing theory development: Modeling heterogeneity effects on new product growth through stochastic cellular automata. Academy of Marketing Science Review, 2001, 9(3):1–18.
[15]   Daniel Gruhl, Ramanathan Guha, David Liben-Nowell, Andrew Tomkins. Information diffusion through blogspace. In Proceedings of the 13th international conference on World Wide Web. ACM, 2004: 491–501.

[16] Xiaodan Song, Yun Chi, Koji Hino, Belle L. Tseng. Information flow modeling based on diffusion rate for prediction and ranking. In Proceedings of the 16th international conference on World Wide Web. ACM, 2007: 191–200.

[17] Kazumi Saito, Masahiro Kimura, Kouzou Ohara, Hiroshi Motoda. Behavioral analyses of information diffusion models by observed data of social network. Advances in Social Computing. Springer, 2010: 149–158.

[18] Kazumi Saito, Masahiro Kimura, Kouzou Ohara, Hiroshi Motoda. Selecting information diffusion models over social networks for behavioral analysis. Machine Learning and Knowledge Discovery in Databases. Springer, 2010: 180–195.

[19] Luke Dickens, Ian Molloy, Jorge Lobo, Paul-Chen Cheng, Alessandra Russo. Learning stochastic models of information flow. In Data Engineering (ICDE), 2012 IEEE 28th International Conference on. IEEE, 2012: 570–581.

[20] Wojciech Galuba, Karl Aberer, Dipanjan Chakraborty, Zoran Despotovic, Wolfgang Kellerer. Outtweeting the twitterers-predicting information cascades in microblogs. In Proceedings of the 3rd conference on online social networks. USENIX Association, 2010: 3.

[21] Adrien Guille, Hakim Hacid. A predictive model for the temporal dynamics of information diffusion in online social networks. In Proceedings of the 21st international conference companion on World Wide Web. ACM, 2012: 1145–1152.

[22] William O. Kermack, Anderson G. McKendrick, Contributions to the mathematical theory of epidemics, In Proceedings of the Royal Society of London, 1927, 115(772):700–721.

[23] Wiiliam O. Kermack, Anderson G. McKendrick. Contributions to the mathematical theory of epidemics. II. The problem of endemicity. Proceedings of the Royal society of London. Series A, 1932, 138(834): 55–83.

[24] Michelle Girvan, Mark Newman. Community structure in social and biological networks. Proceedings of the National Academy of Sciences, 2002, 99(12):7821–7826.

[25] Saeed Abdullah, Xindong Wu. An epidemic model for news spreading on twitter. In Tools with Artificial Intelligence (ICTAI), 2011 23rd IEEE International Conference on. IEEE, 2011: 163–169.

[26] Fei Xiong, Yun Liu, Zhen-jiang Zhang, Jiang Zhu, Ying Zhang. An information diffusion model based on retweeting mechanism for online social media. Physics Letters A 2012, 376(30):2103–2108.

[27] Dechun Liu, Xi Chen. Rumor Propagation in Online Social Networks Like Twitter-A Simulation Study. In Multimedia Information Networking and Security (MINES), 2011 Third International Conference on. IEEE, 2011: 278–282.

[28] Jaewon Yang, Jure Leskovec. Modeling information diffusion in implicit networks. In Data Mining (ICDM), 2010 IEEE 10th International Conference on. IEEE, 2010: 599–608.

[29] Thomas F. Coleman, Yuying Li. A reflective Newton method for minimizing a quadratic function subject to bounds on some of the variables. SIAM Journal on Optimization, 1996, 6(4):1040–1058.

[30] Seth Myers, Chenguang Zhu, Jure Leskovec. Information diffusion and external influence in networks. In Proceedings of the 18th ACM SIGKDD international conference on Knowledge discovery and data mining. ACM, 2012: 33–41.

[31] Alex Beutel, B. Aditya Prakash, Roni Rosenfeld, Christos Faloutsos. Interacting viruses in networks: can both survive? In Proceedings of the 18th ACM SIGKDD international conference on Knowledge discovery and data mining. ACM, 2012: 426–434.

[32] Gabor Szabo, Bernardo A. Huberman. Predicting the popularity of online content. Communications of the ACM, 2010, 53(8):80–88.

[33] Peng Bao, Hua-Wei Shen, Junming Huang, et al. Popularity prediction in microblogging network: a case study on Sina Weibo. In Proceedings of the 22nd international conference on

World Wide Web companion. International World Wide Web Conferences Steering Committee, 2013: 177–178.

[34] Kristina Lerman, Tad Hogg. Using a model of social dynamics to predict popularity of news. Proceedings of the 19th international conference on World Wide Web. ACM, 2010: 621–630.

[35] Changjun Hu, Ying Hu. Predicting the popularity of hot topics based on time series models. APWEB, 2014.

[36] Vincenzo Fioriti, Marta Chinnici. Predicting the sources of an outbreak with a spectral technique. arXiv preprint arXiv:1211.2333, 2012.

[37] Cesar Henrique Comin, Luciano Da Fontoura Costa. Identifying the starting point of a spreading process in complex networks. Physical Review E, 2011, 84(5):56105.

[38] Andrey Y. Lokhov, Marc M.E. Zard, Hiroki Ohta, et al. Inferring the origin of an epidemic with dynamic message-passing algorithm. arXiv preprint arXiv:1303.5315, 2013.

[39] Nino Antulov-Fantulin, AlenLancic, Hrvoje Stefancic, et al. Statistical inference framework for source detection of contagion processes on arbitrary network structures. arXiv preprint arXiv:1304.0018, 2013.

[40] Aditya Prakash, Jilles Vreeken, Christos Faloutsos. Spotting culprits in epidemics: How many and which ones? 2012. ICDM, 2012, 12: 11–20.

[41] Wenyu Zang, Peng Zhang, Chuan Zhou. Discovering multiple diffusion source nodes in social Networks. ICCS, 2014.

Xindong Wu

3 Topic discovery and evolution

3.1 Introduction

With the rapid development of information technologies and widespread information applications, online social networks are gradually replacing the traditional internet services and have become a more convenient and efficient channel for information dissemination and access. In social networks, news and events happening every second are reported timely in different regions and with diversified languages; moreover, they are spread in social networks across geographical boundaries. Social networks feature rich information and complex content, filled with topics that a large number of users may find interesting. How to extract and recommend topics of users' interest from the massive, dynamic, and multi-source social network data, track topic development, and dig into the development trend of events are very crucial for information decision in such a rapidly changing internet age.

In most research on topic discovery and evolution, a topic refers to an event or an activity that draws public attention and all related events and activities [1], where an event or an activity happens at a particular time and place[1].

In today's booming social networks, as a data-intensive application, topic discovery and evolution in social networks has the following data characteristics:

(1) The original location of topics in social networks is distributed. Users of social networks can launch topics at any time and place, and the corresponding locations are scattered. Basically, we cannot predict the exact time or place of the occurrence of a topic.

(2) Topics in social networks transmit rapidly with a large range. Through the globally-connected social networks, a topic can have a huge impact on the world within a few hours after its launch.

(3) Topics in social networks have a wide variety and almost cover and contain everything, which results in complex features of corresponding text requiring support from multi-domain feature knowledge. Therefore, traditional text analysis methods are not applicable to text analysis related to topics from social networks.

(4) The topic-related data from social networks are multi-source data. The initiator of a topic is usually not one person, which makes the structure of the topic complicated and results in contradictions and conflicts among opinions of the topic.

---

[1] Some research on topic discovery and evolution focuses on the discovery and evolution of a single event. However, from the point of algorithm there is no distinguished different from the most works on topics. Hence, in this book, we do not claim this difference particularly between event discovery and topic discovery.

https://doi.org/10.1515/9783110599435-003

(5) The topic-related data from social networks are massive and relatively concentrated. In large social networks, the data generated every day is massive. For example, Facebook usually handles about 2.5 billion messages on average every day. However, all these vast amounts of data are relatively concentrated in a few large social networks. With respect to Chinese networks, QQ, Sina Weibo, and WeChat include almost all topics of social network data.

(6) The topic-related data from social networks are dynamically and constantly updated. Because of the interaction of users in social networks, a user's attitude about a particular topic may change with that of the surrounding friends.

Based on the above features, the methods of topic discovery and evolution in social networks, unlike traditional media monitoring, should be able to automatically discover and track the evolution of the topic with no need for human intervention. In addition, because the topic data of social networks are multi-sources, dynamic, and massive, data discovering and tracking manually in social networks is almost impossible. Hence, it is necessary to propose algorithms for computer programs on topic discovery and evolution in social networks to ensure automatic topic detecting and tracking by computer programs.

As a relatively novel research subject, topic discovery and evolution in social networks, which is completely different from that of traditional media, has not been studied and explored in-depth before; thus, research on this issue still remains in a relatively preliminary stage.

This chapter is organized as follows: in section 3.2, as one of the theoretical base of topic-related research in social networks, the models and algorithms of topic discovery are introduced in detail, including topic model-based topic discovery, vector space model-based topic discovery, and term relationship graph-based topic discovery. In section 3.3, the models and algorithms of topic evolution, as another theoretical base of topic-related research in social networks, are introduced, including the simple topic evolution, topic model-based topic evaluation, and adjacent time slice relation-based topic evaluation. Section 3.4 is a brief summary of this chapter.

3.2 Models and algorithms of topic discovery

Traditional topic detection is generally based on news story or scientific corpus, such as the famous Topic Detection and Tracking (TDT) project [1], which regards discovering and tracking topics from news story as its goal. However, the difference between news corpus or scientific corpus and current social network corpus is huge, therefore, for social network data, direct application of traditional methods may not lead to good results. Therefore, we must propose new methods or improve the traditional methods to adapt to the characteristics of social network data.

As an emerging social media, Twitter, along with the development of internet, has attracted a large number of users. Meanwhile, the data published by Twitter users have also grown geometrically. We consider the following Tweets generated by Twitter as an example to analyze the data characteristics on the research of topic discovery in social networks.

(1) The scale of the data is large and the updating speed is fast; hence, for algorithm on Twitter data processing, the application efficiency under big data environ-ments should be considered and online dynamic requirements should be met.

(2) The data content is brief. A tweet is usually limited to 140 characters, hence, the messages on Twitter are relatively brief with some even only containing one or two words.

(3) The noise of data is too much. Tweets posted by Twitter users tend to be more casual whose main content usually consists of personal issues and personal viewpoints; owing to the length limit of the content, it is often mixed with mispronounced characters, new words, network slang, abbreviations, emoticons, special labels [such as Twitter in the # hashtag # (twitter tag)], etc. Of course, there are also stop words as in traditional text. These features are all noise information if they are handled with traditional methods. In short, Twitter data contains little text information, and usually of low quality [4]. Consequently, this presents a great challenge to text processing and topic discovery.

With regard to the features of Twitter data, we can propose targeted solutions to the problems of topic discovery. For example, regarding large-scale data, we can use a distributed algorithm; as for online demands, we can apply an online machine learning algorithm. With respect to data briefness, we can adopt aggregation strat-egy. Overall, we should pay special attention to the differences between data in social networks and traditional data on topic discovery, and only in this way can it guide us to propose reasonable and effective solutions to data in social networks.

3.2.1 Topic model-based topic discovery

Conceptually speaking, topic model refers to a statistical model applied to find abstract topic in a series of documents.

The topic model is derived from the latent semantic analysis (LSA) model [7], which was proposed by Scott Deerwester in 1990. LSA model mainly adopts singular value decomposition (SVD) method. Although probabilistic methods are not introduced in this model, it provides a foundation for the later development of the topic model. In brief, the probabilistic LSA is actually the probabilistic latent semantic analysis (PLSA) model [12], and afterwards, a more perfect latent Dirichlet allocation (LDA) model [5] is proposed with further probabilistic parameters, which forms a hierarchical Bayesian graph model. With the gradual research, the whole theory of the topic model tends to improve gradually, accordingly, the topic model has been widely applied in various fields. Topic model is now not only used in text processing but is also adopted in bioinformatics and image processing, achieving good results in all of these areas. Among all the topic models, LDA has been the most widely used because of its advantages such as a solid statistical base and flexibility to adapt to different task requirements.

1. LDA model introduction

Topic model is based on following assumption: it is based on the bag-of-words model, namely, in this model, words in the document feature interchangeability, i.e., each word is independent of others, and the exchanging order has no effect on the document. On this assumption, the true natural language has been simplified to facilitate computer processing.

After we have finished an article, there will be a term distribution[2], i.e., the proportion of each term in this document, here represented with $p(w|d)$ (because a topic model involves too many symbols, we listed all these symbols in Table 3.1). It is easy to calculate

Table 3.1: Involved symbols of a topic model

Symbols	Implication	Symbols	Implication
N	Document length (number of words)	M	Document number
D	Document	z	Topic
W	Terms	α	Dirichlet distribution parameter, determining the distribution of document topic
β	Dirichlet distribution parameter, determining the distribution of topic terms	E	Distribution parameter, determining the distribution of the document tags
K	Topic number	θ	Topic distribution in the document
ϕ	Topic term distribution	U	Users
θ^μ	Topic distribution of user μ	ϕ^z	Term distribution of topic z
ϕ^B	Term distribution of background B	Π	Binomial distribution, for select control

---

2 The difference between word and term: in a document represented by a term space, every term is a dimension, and the number of terms in a document refers to the number of different words. However, during the number counting for words, two same words can be counted repeatedly.

Table 3.1 (continued)

Symbols	Implication	Symbols	Implication
Λ	Topic distribution associated with tags	Z	Topic set
S	Term set associated with a topic	TF	Term frequency
DF	Document frequency	E	Edge formed by co-occurrence terms

the formula $p(w_i|d) = N_i/N$, where N_i represents the occurrence number of the word w_i in the document, and N represents the total number of words in the document.

Therefore, if $p(w|d)$ of a document is identified, we can quickly generate a document based on the probability distribution.

However, this process is not in line with our usual writing process. When we write an article, in general, we first select a topic, and then select a number of words related to this topic to enrich the article. In this manner, an article is generated. Therefore, according to this approach, the completion of an article is divided into two steps: first, selecting a topic of a document; and second, selecting words related to the selected topic, repeating this process in turn, and generating one word at a time until the number of words specified in the document is reached.

Topic model is a statistical modeling of the above-mentioned process where the differences remain in that there is more than one topic in the assumption document of a topic model. According to the generating process of a topic model document, a brief description is as follows:

Assume that we already know the topic distribution $p(z|d)$ of a document as well as the term distribution $p(w|z)$ of a topic.

When generating a word in a document, we first select a topic z according to the topic distribution and then select a term w according to the term distribution under the topic. Hence, the word generation in a document can be formulated from the probability perspective and simply interpreted as:

$$p(w|d) = \sum_z p(z)p(w|z)p(z|d) = p(d)\sum_z p(z|d)p(w|z) \tag{3.1}$$

Here, $p(w|d)$ is known and $p(w|z)$ and $p(z|d)$ is unknown; assuming that there are M documents, and the length of each document d is N, i.e., there are N words, and there are K optional topics, then $p(w|d)$ is a vector of $M \times N$, $p(z|d)$ is a vector of $M \times K$, and $p(w|z)$ is a matrix of $K \times N$.

From eq. (3.1), we can observe that this process inserts an intermediate layer more directly by the term distribution generated by words of the document – topic layer, which is invisible in an actual document. Therefore, in some studies, this layer is called the latent structures of a document, or by intuitive understanding this is what we want to express – topic.

A simple example is presented below (where although the data is artificially constructed, it is consistent with our understanding on real data).

Suppose that we have a document set D = {Document 1, Document 2, Document 3}, a term list V = {movie, music, tax, government, student, teacher, amount, art, principal}, and a topic set Z = {art, budget, education}, the optional words in each document are from V (actual term data is undoubtedly much larger than the set V here, and examples here are only for description convenience), and optional topics in each document are from the topic set Z. Here, we artificially construct the proportion of words of each document, however, in practice it can be obtained by taking the ratio of the frequency of a specific word and the total number of words.

In this example, the matrix $p(w|d)$ constructed by documents and terms is as below where the horizontal represents different documents, whereas the vertical represents different terms and the corresponding number is the probability of a term in a document.

	Movie	Music	Tax	Government	Student	Teacher	Money	Art	Principal
Document 1	0.27	0.19	0	0.027	0.06	0.083	0	0.36	0.01
Document 2	0.032	0.02	0.24	0.16	0.128	0.04	0.32	0.04	0.02
Document 3	0.06	0.12	0	0.006	0.48	0.174	0	0.08	0.08

The matrix $p(z|d)$ of documents and topics is as follows:

	Art	Budget	Education
Document 1	0.9	0	0.1
Document 2	0	0.8	0.2
Document 3	0.2	0	0.8

The matrix $p(w|z)$ of topics and terms is as follows:

	Movie	Music	Tax	Government	Student	Teacher	Money	Art	Principal
Art	0.3	0.2	0	0.03	0	0.07	0	0.4	0
Budget	0.04	0	0.3	0.2	0.01	0	0.4	0.05	0
Education	0	0.1	0	0	0.6	0.2	0	0	0.1

With eq. (3.1), the relationship of these matrixes can be expressed as:

$$p(w|d) = \sum_z p(z|d) \times p(w|z)$$

Back to the beginning, we assume that we already know the topic distribution of a document and the term distribution of a topic, then we can generate words in the document. However, it is just the opposite in reality: we can easily obtain the document set, i.e., the document has already been written. In addition, we have obtained the term distribution of the document, while the unknown part is the topic information of the document, namely, the latent structure of the document. Therefore, according to the document generation process, we know the results, and now we need to inversely infer the intermediate parameters based on the results, i.e., the topic distribution $p(z|d)$ of the document and the term distribution $p(w|z)$ of the topic. Before describing the calculation method about parameter estimation in detail, we will first introduce a formalized presentation and specific algorithm steps of LDA model.

2. Specific algorithm of latent dirichlet allocation model

LDA model is a hierarchical Bayesian model proposed by David Blair together with others in 2003. Here, we formalize the LDA model: we assume that the entire document set has T topics, each topic z is expressed as a polynomial distribution θ_z over a dictionary v, and each document d for the T topics has a specific polynomial distributed ϕ_d of a document.

In Figure 3.1, α and β are the parameters for Dirichlet distribution, which usually have fixed values and characterize a symmetric distribution. They usually can be represented by a scalar. θ indicates the topic probability distribution of a document; ϕ indicates the term probability distribution of a topic; and as parameters of a polynomial distribution, θ and ϕ are used for generating topics and words. z represents a topic, w represents a word, M indicates the document number, and N denotes the document length.

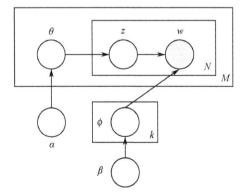

Figure 3.1: Graphical model representation of LDA

Algorithm 3.1: The generation process of LDA model into a document set
1: Extract the topic distribution over the term: $\phi \sim \text{Dir}(\beta)$
2: From $m = 1$ to M do
3:　　Extract N words: $N \sim \text{Poisson}(\phi)$
4:　　Extract the document distribution over the topic $\theta_m \sim \text{Dir}(\alpha)$
5:　　　For $n = 1$ to N do
6:　　　　Extract a topic $Z_{m,n} \sim \text{Multi}(\theta_m)$
7:　　　　Extract a word $w_{m,n} \sim \text{Multi}(\theta_{z_{m,n}})$
8:　　End for
9: End for

During the document generation process in LDA model, first the topic term distribution ϕ can be generated (Line 1 in Algorithm 3.1), where ϕ is a parameter in the document level, and it only needs to be sampled once, where the sampling conforms to the Dirichlet distribution with a priori parameter β. For each document, we first determine the document length on the basis of Poisson distribution (Line 3), namely the number of words N. Then, it comes to the step of generating every word in the document. More specifically, a topic can be generated by sampling according to the topic distribution of a document (Line 8), and then a word can be generated by sampling according to the topic term distribution obtained in the former step (Line 9). These steps are repeated until all words in the document set are generated.

In this process, in general, we use the collapsed Gibbs sampling method to get the values of the hidden variables (z values) and the probability distribution of the parameters in the model (the distribution of θ_m and ϕ). The collapsed Gibbs sampling process can generally be described as assigning every word in the document set to the corresponding topic. We will introduce Gibbs sampling process in detail below.

3. Gibbs sampling in latent dirichlet allocation model

The core procedure of LDA model is the relevant parameter estimation. As parameter estimation is a complex optimization problem, it is very difficult to propose approaches that can obtain precise solutions. Therefore, in general, we use approaches which lead to imprecise results, mainly including three ways: ① Gibbs sampling-based method; ② calculus of variations-based EM solver; ③ expectation advance-based approach. Because Gibbs sampling method is simple in reasoning with good results, in practice this algorithm is generally adopted to estimate parameters.

To obtain the probability distribution of the word, parameters ϕ and θ are not calculated first. Instead, the posterior probability $p(w|z)$ of the word for the topic is considered first and the value of ϕ and θ are obtained indirectly by using Gibbs sampling method. Markov Chain Monte Carlo (MCMC) is a set of approximate iterative methods to extract sample values from complex probability distributions. In this method, a component of the joint distribution is sampled each time, whereas the values of the other components remain unchanged. In case of joint distribution with higher dimensions, using Gibbs sampling can produce a relatively simple algorithm. As a form of simple implementation of MCMC, Gibbs sampling aims to construct the Markov chain that converges to a target probability distribution, and extracts samples considered to be close to the value of the probability distribution from the chain [27]. Regarding LDA model in this book, we need to calculate the word distribution over topic, i.e., sampling on variable z_i.

Gibbs sampling algorithm can be expatiated as follows [27]:

(1) As for each i from 1 to N, z_i is initialized to a random integer between 1 to K. This is the initial state of the Markov chain.

(2) As for each i from 1 to N, according to the posterior probability calculated by the following formula we assign words to the topic, and get the next state of Markov chain:

$$p(z_{i,j}|z_{-i},w_i) = \frac{\dfrac{n_{-i,j}^{(w_i)}+\beta}{n_{-i,j}^{(\cdot)}+w\beta} \cdot \dfrac{n_{-i,j}^{(d_i)}+\alpha}{n_{-i,\cdot}^{(d_i)}+K\alpha}}{\sum_{j=1}^{T} \dfrac{n_{-i,j}^{(w_i)}+\beta}{n_{-i,j}^{(\cdot)}+w\beta} \cdot \dfrac{n_{-i,j}^{(d_i)}+\alpha}{n_{-i,\cdot}^{(d_i)}+K\alpha}}$$

where β can be understood as the frequency of words obtained from topic sampling before seeing any word in the corpus. α can be understood as the frequency of topic sampling before seeing any word in the document. $z_{i,j}$ represents that term w_i is assigned to the topic j, and z_{-i} represents the distribution of all $z_k(k=i)$. $n_{-i,j}^{(w_i)}$ is the number of words assigned to topic j, which is the same as w_i; $n_{-i,j}^{(\bullet)}$ is the number of all words assigned to topic j; $n_{-i,j}^{(d_i)}$ is the number of words assigned to topic j in document d_i; and $n_{-i,\cdot}^{(d_i)}$ is the number of all words that are assigned with topics in d_i. All the numbers of words exclude the allocation of $z_{i,j}$ at this time.

(3) After a sufficient number of step (2) iterations, we can believe that Markov chain approaches the target distribution, and then takes the current value of z_i (i from 1 to N) as the sample recorded. To ensure the autocorrelation smaller, we need to record other samples after a certain times of iteration. Abandon word mark and set w represent words. For every single sample, estimate values of ϕ and θ according to the following formula:

$$\tilde{\phi}_w^{z=i} = \frac{n_j^{(w)}+\beta}{n_j^{(\cdot)}+w\beta}, \tilde{\theta}_{z=i}^{d} = \frac{n_j^{(d)}+\alpha}{n^{(d)}+K\alpha}$$

where $n_j^{(w)}$ represents the frequence of words w assigned to topic j; $n_j^{(\cdot)}$ represents the number of all words assigned to topic j; $n_j^{(d)}$ indicates the number of words assigned to topic j in document d; and $n_\bullet^{(d)}$ represents all the number of words which have been assigned with topics in document d.

Gibbs sampling algorithm starts from an initial value, and after being iterated enough times, it can be considered as the probability distribution of the sample close to that of the target.

Here, we use a simple example to illustrate the iterative process of Gibbs sampling. The selected five documents are from the Facebook about MH370 flight lost topic (for details, see Appendix), and their time is 20140309, 20140323, 20140325, 20140327, and 20140405. When the number of topics is set at 5, we get a series of Gibbs sampling results as follows:

	Iteration 1600 times	Iteration 1700 times	Iteration 1800 times	Iteration 1900 times	Iteration 2000 times
Topic 1	8.73	9.78	9.28	9.31	9.12
Topic 2	9.98	9.86	9.6	9.92	10.03
Topic 3	10.04	10.8	10.99	10.99	11.51
Topic 4	10.52	10.4	10.71	10.92	10.64
Topic 5	9.11	9.19	9.23	9.45	9.86

4. Application examples of latent dirichlet allocation model-based topic discovery

Although the theory of LDA model looks relatively complicated, it is mature and has been widely used. There are many LDA model implementation codes available for free downloading on the Web. In the application process of LDA, we can take full advantage of existing programs or tools concerning only with the results of the input and output without too much focus on the computational details. For example, in the application example of this section, the code of LDA model we used is Mallet Kit of UMass (MAchine Learning for LanguagE Toolkit)[3] using the default parameter settings.

In the examples in this section, using the five documents adopted in the above example of the Gibbs iterative process and implementing the algorithm, we get a series of results such as the relationship of topic and terms in a document, as follows:

Next we will take a document on Facebook from 20140323 as an example to illustrate the results obtained by LDA model. In this document, we use different underscores to represent the different topics (i.e., Topic1 Topic2 Topic3 Topic4 Topic5). After underlining the following documents, we can note which topic each word belongs to (words that are not underlined are prepositions or other words that cannot help in understanding the document, which should be ignored during processing).

---

3 http://mallet.cs.umass.edu/.

MH370: Indian aircrafts join search

KUALA LUMPUR: Two long range maritime reconnaissance aircrafts from India have departed the Subang Airport on Sunday to join in the search for the missing Malaysia Airlines (MAS) MH370 aircraft in the southern Indian Ocean.

This was despite reported bad weather caused by tropical cyclone Gilia which had forced a number of other aircrafts scheduled to go on the mission to be cancelled.

The High Commission of India to Malaysiaon Sunday said that both aircrafts were likely to encounter the cyclonic conditions enroute, but Captains of both aircrafts had instead "decided to skirt bad weather areas" to reach the search sectors.

The two aircrafts were the P8-I of the Indian Navy and the C-130J of the Indian Air Force. Both were expected to undertake a 10-hour mission in the area.

"Both aircrafts have long endurance capabilities coupled with state of the art electro optronic and infra red search and reconnaissance equipment on board," said the high commission in a statement here.

The P8-I aircraft has the added advantage of on-board radars and specially designedsearch and rescue kits.

Previously, the Prime Minister of India had committed to assisting Malaysia and "render all possible assistance to Malaysia in locating the missing Malaysian Airlines flight".

Both aircrafts arrived in Malaysia on March 21. After extensive briefings in Malaysia on Sunday, both Indian aircrafts took off to be part of the Australian-led search on Sunday morning.

India has been participating in the search and rescue operation beginning March 11 in the Andaman Sea and Bay of Bengal.

By the proportion of various underlined words in the document, we can see the distribution of various topics in this document, i.e., a large proportion of some underline words indicates that its corresponding topic takes a large proportion in the document.

Furthermore, we can obtain the following topic term distribution graph (as Mallet just gives the weight of each term, Figure 3.2 is not the real distribution graph but only depicts the renormalization results of each word corresponding to the weight in each topic, but it still indirectly reflects the distribution of the topic terms), where the horizontal axis represents each term (because there are a lot of terms, we have not marked them in the figure), and the vertical axis represents the weight of each term. From Figure 3.2 we can intuitively observe the difference between different topics, which is reflected by different term distributions.

The above examples with underlines provide an intuitive feel for topic distribution, and more specific values can be found in Figure 3.3, where it reflects the topic distribution of each document in the form of a line chart. Documents 1, 2, 3, 4, and 5 refer to the five aforementioned documents. As the five documents are in a chronological order, Figure 3.3 can simply be seen on the evolution situations of the topic of MH370 aircraft lost event (more specific analysis of topic evolution will be described in detail in Section 3.3).

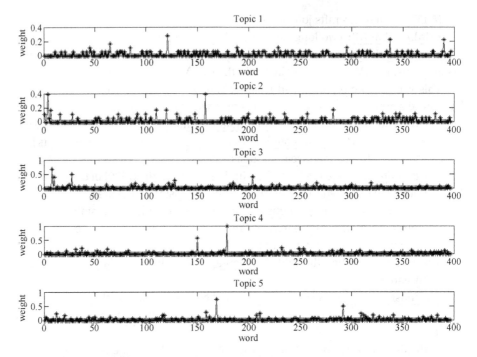

Figure 3.2: Topic term distribution graph

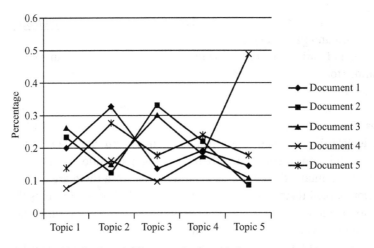

Figure 3.3: Distribution of different topics in each document

5. Research on topic model in topic discovery of social networks

Topic model is mainly used to discover the latent semantic structure in documents, i.e., the abstract topics in documents. Obviously, we will tend to apply the topic model to the topic discovery of contents in social networks. However, owing to certain features of social network data, relevant researches show that the direct application of the topic model to social networks (such as short text data) does not produce the expected results [17]. Therefore, we need to study how to use the topic model in the social networking environments.

Social network data includes the data from blog, microblog (e.g, Twitter, Weibo, etc.), instant message (IM, such as QQ, etc.), etc. Since Twitter was launched in 2006, it has covered more and more users, and thus, it has gradually become the most popular data source for social network researchers. With data from Twitter, researchers have done a lot of work. In particular, they try to use topic model on Tweets and try to find more valuable latent topic information.

Aiming at the problem that due to the content length limit of Tweets the direct application of traditional topic model is ineffective, some scholars study how to train the standard topic model in the short text environments. They combine Tweets with the authors' information, and present three topic modeling models [13].

(1) MSG Model: MSG refers to Messages Generated by the Same User.
  ① Train LDA model in training corpus;
  ② In the training corpus, the information generated by the same user is aggregated into a Training User Profile for the user;
  ③ In the testing corpus, the information generated by the same user is aggregated into a Testing User Profile for the user;
  ④ Take Training User Profile, Testing User Profile and testing corpus as "new documents", and use the training model to infer the distribution of their topics.

(2) USER Model:
  ① In the training corpus, the information generated by the same author is aggregated into the User Profiles, in which we train LDA model;
  ② In the testing corpus, the information generated by the same author is aggregated into the Testing User Profile for the user;
  ③ Take training corpus, Testing User Profile and testing corpus as "new documents,"and use the training topic model to infer the distribution of their respective topics.

Obviously, MSG model and USER model are not suitable for topic modeling of a single Tweet but can be applied to detect the topic distribution of Tweets posted by a specific author. Both models use the user-based aggregation policy, however, the order and the manner of training models are different.

(3) TERM Model: As the name itself suggests, it is the aggregation of all information that comprises a certain term.
  ① For each term in the training set, all information containing the term is aggregated into a Training Term Profile;
  ② Train LDA model on the Training Term Profile;

③ Establish User Profiles (namely aggregate the information issued by the same user) on the training set and testing set, respectively;

④ Take training corpus, Training User Profiles, Testing User Profiles and testing corpus as "new documents,"and use training models to infer the distribution of their respective topics.

The principle of TERM is based on the fact that Twitter users often use customized topic labels [the words surrounded with # called Tweets label (Hashtag)] which represents a specific topics or events. With the established Term Profiles, using TERM model can directly obtain topics related to these topic labels.

MSG model trains LDA model by a single Tweet. As the length of the content itself is limited, there is not enough information for the model to learn topic pattern. Specifically, compared with the long text, the words of short text have a lower distinction for text. The TERM mode and USER mode, however, use the aggregation strategy to train the model, and the results they obtained should be better.

For the difference between the content of Twitter and other traditional media, some scholars have proposed an improved LDA model – Twitter-LDA [32]. Clearly, because Tweets are brief, the standard LDA model does not work well on Twitter. To overcome this problem, the above-mentioned MSG, USER, and TERM modes use an aggregation strategy to merge the same user's Tweets to a longer article, which, by and large, is the application of the Author-Topic Model (ATM) [21]. However, this can only discover the same author's topic, which is useless for a single tweet. Hence, we need to improve the standard LDA model so that it can form a model which is useful for a single tweet.

In the Twitter-LDA model, we assume that a Tweet has K topics, and each topic can be represented by a distribution of terms. φ^t represents the term distribution of the topic t; φ^B represents the term distribution of background words; θ^u represents the topic distribution of the user u; and π represents a Bernoulli distribution (used to control the choice between background words and topic words). When writing a Tweet, a user first selects a topic based on its topic distribution, and then chooses a group of words according to the selected topic or background model. Twitter-LDA model is shown in Figure 3.4, with the generation process as follows:

(a) Sampling $\varphi^B \sim \mathrm{Dir}(\beta)$, $\pi \sim \mathrm{Dir}(\gamma)$

(b) For each topic t:

    a) Sampling $\varphi^t \sim \mathrm{Dir}(\beta)$

(c) For each user u:

    b) Sampling $\theta^u \sim \mathrm{Dir}(\alpha)$

    c) For each Tweet &

        i. Sampling $z_{u,\&} \sim \mathrm{Multi}(\theta^u)$

        ii. For each word n in &

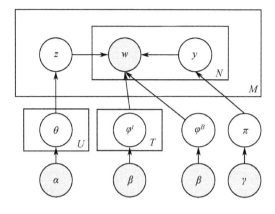

Figure 3.4: Twitter-LDA model

A. Sampling $y_{u,s,n}$~Multi(π)
B. If $y_{u,s,n} = 0$, sampling $w_{u,s,n}$~Multi$\left(\varphi^B\right)$
   If $y_{u,s,n} = 1$, sampling $w_{u,s,n}$~Multi$\left(z^{u,s}\right)$

Twitter-LDA is actually the extension of ATM, specifically, the background knowledge is introduced into the ATM model. Twitter-LDA models both users' background and the background of Tweets. Hence, to some extent, it overcomes the limitations of ATM which only models users' background.

Another variation of topic model used on Twitter is labeled LDA [20], which expands the LDA model and combines the supervision information. Labeled LDA assumes that there is a set of tags Λ, where each tag is represented by a polynomial distribution $\beta_k (k \in 1 \cdots |\Lambda|)$ of a term. Each document d only uses a subset of tags Λ, labeled as $\Lambda_d \subset \Lambda$, and document d represents a polynomial distribution of Λ_d. Labeled graph model is shown in Figure 3.5, with the generation process described as follows:

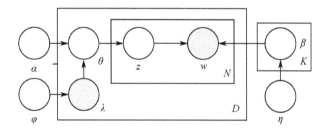

Figure 3.5: Graphical model as the representation of labeled LDA

(a) Sampling the topic distribution β_k~Dir(η)
(b) For each tweet d:
   a) Establish a label set Λ_d in describing the Tweet d from a hyper parameter ϕ
   b) Select a polynomial distribution θ_d from the label set Λ_d according to the symmetrical prior parameter α

    c)   For each lexeme i in tweet d

        i.   Sampling labels $z_{d,i} \sim \text{Dir}(\theta_d)$

        ii.   Sampling terms $w_{d,i} \sim \text{Dir}(\beta_z)$

To adopt labeled LDA to analyze the features of Twitter content [19], we can rely on the basis of the features of Twitter content and regard each hashtag as a label in Tweets, which to some degree uses the topic information that users tagged. However, a drawback of this approach is that the model cannot be directly applied to all Tweets without any hashtag.

In addition to the Twitter data, some scholars have studied the chat data from the Internet Relay Chat (IRC) [29]. Just like Twitter data, IRC data also includes misspellings, grammatical errors, abbreviations and other noise information. Along with such features as dynamic change, concise expression, intersected topic, etc., IRC data is not suitable for us to analyze with the existing text mining methods. To remedy these problems, researchers use the latent features of IRC data — social relationships among chatters, to filter out the irrelevant parts in discussion. This is similar to the use of PageRank algorithm that distinguishes highly interactive web pages from irrelevant web pages. However, it should be noticed that the score here is not for ranking but to improve the topic model via such correlation score. This method can be summarized as using some features of IRC data to construct user relationship graph, and then according to the features of the graph (such as indegree, outdegree, etc.) provide a score for the user, which is used to determine noise information and topic information. In addition, in accordance with relevant scores, noise information is decreased and useful information is enlarged so that the application effect of the topic model can be improved.

Topic model has receiveda significant amount of attention from scholars in various fields as it not only has a solid statistical theoretical foundation but also is simple to model and can be easily extended to accommodate different applications. Many scholars try to apply topic model on social networks. In addition to some of the models mentioned above, they also propose a variety of other topic models, which provides an effective means for us to analyze social network data.

3.2.2 Vector space model-based topic discovery

Vector Space Model (VSM) [23] was originally proposed by Gerard M. Salton et al. in the 1970s, and was successfully used in information retrieval. The basic idea of the VSM model is that the document or query is represented as the form of eigenvector, such that the processing of the text content can be transformed into vector operations in vector space, and the similarity of vectors reflects the similarity between documents. Specifically, first the features of these texts are usually represented as terms (the specific differences between term and word can be accessed in information retrieval section of this book). In addition, TFIDF value represents the weight of the feature. Finally, the similarity between vectors can be measured with a cosine function. This method is relatively simple and will not be introduced in detail here.

In the initial TDT project, the topic discovery was understood as the classification of a large number of different news stories; therefore, the methods focus on the VSM-based clustering method. Regarding different application scenarios, researchers have proposed different solutions. Regarding Retrospective Event Detection (RED), scholars have proposed a Group Average Clustering (GAC) algorithm. For online event detection, a Single Pass Incremental Clustering (SPIC) algorithm has been proposed. These methods well adapt to the needs of different scenarios and meet the task requirements.

The adoption of the vector space model for topic discovery is based on the assumption that the documents of similar topics have similar content. Thus, after transforming the document as eigenvector by VSM, the key step is to measure the similarity between features. However, the clustering algorithm used in traditional TDT mainly aims at the topic discovery in the data stream of news report, and migrating this method directly to the current social network environment has limitations. This is due to the fact that, in Twitter, Weibo, and other similar sites the data generated by users are relatively short with a frequent use of informal languages and there are specialized network terminologies, etc., which makes the VSM model that simply feature terms produce sparse data and other issues. Consequently, we need to improve VSM method to make it applicable to the data generated by social networks. When constructing eigenvector with the VSM model, it is necessary to pay much more attention to feature selection, the calculation of feature weight, and similarity measurement between features. In simple words, the chosen features and calculation of feature weight should be sufficient to represent the content of current text and reflect the difference between the texts. The similarity measurement should accurately reflect the difference between features.

Regarding the problems of feature selection and the weight calculation of text contents in social networks, researchers have done a lot of work. Here, we briefly introduce these efforts.

Paige H Adams and Craig H Martell compare the effect of several feature selection and weight calculation methods for the similarity measurement of Chat (i.e., instant messaging) data in the reference [1]. Authors analyze chat data and obtain the following characteristics:

(1) Topics tend to aggregate by time. New topics may come from the previous topics; before dying or being replaced by new topics, the current topic will remain for a while.

(2) Interleaving occurs between different topics. Messages containing different topics may be mixed together.

(3) The participants of a specific topic may change. But, generally speaking, the core participants of a topic dialogue tend to remain unchanged.

Based on the above data characteristics, the authors point out that it is necessary to improve the traditional weight calculation method of using TFIDF feature:

Regarding feature (1), during the similarity measurement, the time distance penalization coefficients are introduced to increase the similarity of data with similar time, as well as reduce the similarity of the data with larger time difference.

As for feature (2), with regard to term-featured aspect, the authors use Hypemym (i.e., topic words of conceptually broader denotations) to solve the problems that the different representations of the same topic result in high semantic similarity but low coincidence degree of terms.

Regarding feature (3), the author assigns each eigenvector with user's nickname information corresponding to the original document and gives the data published by the same user more weight, which implies that the information published by the same author has a higher probability under the same topic.

Hila Becker et al. analyzed rich context (i.e., background or contextual content) information in social networks in the reference [3], including text messages and nontext information, such as user labeled information (such as title, tags, etc.), automatically generated information (such as creation time of content, etc.) and so on. With the help of the above background information, the authors compared the various measurement techniques for the similarity of documents from social media. In this paper, the authors point out that the single feature of social media content remains with big noise and it cannot be used to effectively complete classification and clustering task, but the joint use of various features (including the document content and context of content, etc.) can provide us valuable information related to the topic or event.

In fact, although context features between different social medias are not the same, many social media still share some of the same features, such as author name (i.e., the user of document creation), title (i.e., the name of the document), description (i.e., a brief summary of the document content), label (i.e., a set of keywords describing the content of the document), date and time (i.e., the time of content published), and location information. These features can help measure the similarity between documents. For different features, researchers provide different approaches:

(1) For textual features, the eigenvector identifying with TFIDF as weights can be used to calculate the similarity by a cosine function.
(2) For date and time features, the similarity is calculated as $1 - \frac{|t_1 - t_2|}{y}$, where t_1 and t_2 respectively represent the time of publishing of document 1 and document 2, and y shows the number of minutes per year. In addition, if the time interval of two documents is more than a year, then the similarity of the two documents is regarded as zero.
(3) For geographical features, the similarity is calculated as $1-H(L1-L2)$, where L_1 and L_2, respectively, represent the latitude and longitude of document 1 and document 2, and $H(\cdot)$ function is to use a Haversine distance.

For topic discovery based on clustering algorithm, the key point is to determine appropriate similarity measurement approaches to reflect the similarity between documents. In regard to similarity measurement methods, Becker et al. proposed two ways in the reference [3], including the aggregation-based similarity measurement method and the classification-based similarity measurement method, of which the former adopts a variety of clustering methods, and the final result is determined by weighted voting based on different weights of clustering methods in the clusterers or weighted combination in the calculation of the similarity. The idea of classification-based similarity measurement takes similarity score as the classification feature for predicting whether two documents belong to the same topic or event.

After considering feature selection and similarity measurement, we also need to explore the selection of algorithms including clustering. Most data in social networks can be seen as a continuous incoming data stream, which can be categorized as large-scale and real-time. Hence, in the choice of clustering algorithms, we must choose a clustering algorithm which can be expanded and requires no prior knowledge of the number of clusters [4]. Thus, researchers have proposed an incremental clustering algorithm, which takes into account each piece of information in turn and decides the appropriate category based on the similarity between the information and current clusters.

Here, we briefly introduce a single-pass incremental clustering algorithm that only scans the data once and dynamically adjusts the parameters, perfect for online environment where there are continuous data and dynamic increase of the number of categories of clustering. The algorithm steps are as follows:

Algorithm 3.2 Single-pass Incremental clustering algorithm
1: Set two thresholds: clustering threshold t_c; creating a new type of threshold t_n
2: The input of a document x
3: For 1 to T do:
4:   Calculate the similarity $\text{sim}(x, t)$ between x and the current topic t
5:   If $\text{sim}(x, t) > t_c$ do:
6:     Refer x as the current topic t, and add into the document cluster of t
7:     Recalculate the center of the topic t (a document cluster), which represents topic t
8:   end cycle
9:   end If
10:   If $t_n < \text{sim}(x, t) \le t_c$ do:
11:   Without any treatment, continue to cycle
12:   end If
13: If $sim(x, t) \le t_n$ do:
14:     Create a new topic t', whose center point is represented by x, and add it into the topic set T
15:       end cycle
16:   end If
17: end For

Single-pass incremental clustering approach measures the similarity between each incoming data and each cluster (line 4). Specifically, if the incoming data is sufficiently similar to a cluster, it can be classified into this cluster (line 6); if it is not similar to any of the current clusters, we have to create a new category and put the incoming data into it (line 13). The center representing the cluster can be represented by a vector formed by the mean value of each dimension of the cluster.

In summary, the VSM-based topic discovery method is with the traditional clustering ideas, but for some of the new features in social networks, researchers have proposed improved scheme in feature selection, weight calculation and similarity measurement, and other aspects, which solves the encountered problems and improves the results of topic found to some extent.

3.2.3 Term relationship graph-based topic discovery

Term co-occurrence analysis is one of the successful applications of natural language processing techniques in information retrieval. It is established in the idea that the frequency of co-occurrence between terms, to some extent, reflects the semantic relation between terms. Scholars at the very beginning used term co-occurrence to calculate the similarity of the documents, and then applied this method to complete topic word extraction, topic sentence extraction, summary generation, among other tasks.

The method of term co-occurrence is mostly based on the following assumption: in corpus sets, if two terms frequently appear in the same document, the combination of these two terms is considered to be stable and semantically interlinked, where the frequency of co-occurrence reflects the closeness of semantics between terms. It can be further expected by such assumption that a topic or an event can be represented by a series of descriptive and parallel keywords, while according to intuitive idea, the same set of keywords tend to be used to describe the same topic or events among different documents, based on which the links between keywords will be closer, and the frequency of co-occurrence will be higher. In short, the closer the relationship between the term co-occurrence under the same topic is, the more the chance of co-occurrence is. In contrast, the weaker the co-occurrence relationship is between the terms under different topics, the less the chance of co-occurrence is. Thus, using the relationship of co-occurrence between terms in a document, we can reversely find out which words are related topics (used to describe the same topic) to achieve the purpose of topic detection.

Based on the above ideas, the term co-occurrence-based approach turned out to be useful on topic discovery. The term co-occurrence relationship can be shown in graphical form. The terms of close relationship can be intuitively found from the graph and futher forms a set of terms related to the topic, which has become a simple and effective method in topic discovery.

1. Basic idea
The basic idea of the term relationship graph-based topic discovery algorithm is to first construct a term co-occurrence graph based on the co-occurrence relationship between terms, then via the community detection algorithms commonly adopted in social network analysis to find the community formed by terms (i.e., a set of terms related to a certain topic), and finally to determine the topic of each document according to the similarity between the found term sets and the original document.

2. Method description
The term co-occurrence graph based topic discovery can be largely divided into the following three steps [25, 26]:
Step 1, construct a term co-occurrence graph according to the relationship of term co-occurrence;
Step 2, conduct a community detection algorithm in the term co-occurrence graph, which leads to a community (i.e., term set) with the description for a specific topic;
Step 3, specify a set of topic terms for each document in the original document set.

Next, we will conduct a detailed description for each of the above steps.

1) Step 1: Construct the term co-occurrence graph
In the term co-occurrence based topic discovery method, terms are generally taken as nodes in the graph. In the term co-occurrence based topic discovery method, terms are generally taken as nodes in the graph. However, because of the importance of different terms differs, it is unnecessary to construct a term co-occurrence graph with all words appearing in the document, instead, the keywords in the document should be regarded as the nodes, which is because the keywords of a document can better distinguish topics for a document. The keywords can simply be identified using document frequency (DF), and the words with the document frequency below a certain threshold node_min_df should be deleted [18, 25, 26].

After selecting terms as nodes, we start to construct edges between nodes and the edges in the term co-occurrence graph should reflect the co-occurrence relationship between terms, namely, if two terms co-occur at least in a document, then an edge between the two terms (nodes) can be established.

After constructing the term co-occurrence graph, we need to pre-process the generated graph to remove some edges to reduce the size of graph as well as remove noise information. Detailed process can refer to the following rules:

Now we need to calculate the total number of term co-occurrence (the number of documents with two term co-occurrence, here is equivalent to the document frequency of edges in the term co-occurrence graph), and referred as $DF_{e_{i,j}}$, representing the co-occurrence frequency of term w_i and w_j appeared jointly in the document set, and also representing the document frequency of edge $e_{i,j}$. We first remove edges whose co-occurrence frequency is below the threshold edge_min_df.

For edge screening, we can also calculate the conditional probability of the emergence between terms, and then remove the edge between corresponding nodes when the corresponding bidirectional conditional probability is below the threshold edge_min_prob. Conditional probability is calculated as follows:

$$p\left(w_i|w_j\right) = \frac{\mathrm{DF}_{i \cap j}}{\mathrm{DF}_j} = \frac{\mathrm{DF}_{e_{i,j}}}{\mathrm{DF}_j}$$

where DF_j represents the document frequency of term w_i; $p\left(w_i|w_j\right)$ represents the conditional probability that term w_i appears at the same time the term w_j appears; and $p\left(w_j|w_i\right)$ is defined similarly.

2) Step 2: Perform community discovery algorithm in the term co-occurrence graph

As mentioned earlier, we can make such an assumption that if there is topic relation with the same meaning between two words, the two words will appear together with a higher probability. Based on such an assumption, we construct the co-occurrence graph between terms and we also have formed a co-occurrence based term network from the previous step. In such a network, the terms used to describe the same topic connect closely, while the terms applied to describe different topics are the opposite. From this we can adopt the ideas of community discovery in social networks and divide the term co-occurrence network into "communities"—represents a set of terms corresponding to specific topics—to describe different topics.

Community discovery may draw support from betweenness centrality to discover the connected edges between two communities. This method is based on the intuitive understanding that when calculating the shortest path of nodes between two different communities, it is inevitable to pass through the edge connecting two communities, and then for this type of edge, its betweenness centrality value is relatively high. Therefore, by calculating betweenness centrality, the edges extending transversely across communities can be found. By removing the edge with higher betweenness centrality values, equivalent to cutting off the path between communities associated with the edge, the task of community discovery, i.e., the topic discovery, is achieved.

If the correlation between topics is weak, i.e., no basic connection between different topics, there is no edge connected between different topic term sets and then we can even use non-connectivity sub-graphs to discover topics directly.

Of course, there are other algorithms for topic cluster discovery, for example, for every term, it is first placed in a community; and for a neighboring node of the current community, if its connection with the current community exceeds a certain threshold, it can be added to the current cluster. Repeat the process until no additional nodes added to the current community, and then the community formed by the current terms is a term set describing a specific topic.

Definitely, the above topic clustering discovery algorithm is only an example for illustration. Because here the problem of topic discovery is converted to a community discovery task, theoretically the community discovery algorithm that can effectively detect a term set related to a topic can be applied to the topic discovery.

3) Step 3: Set topic marker to the original document set
After determining the topic cluster, we need to make a topic judgment about the original document sets, namely to determine the relationship between each document and the topic cluster. Intuitively, for each topic cluster, the more parts of the topic cluster appeared in a document, the more relevant the topic associated with the topic cluster in the document. In this step, we consider each term in the topic cluster as a feature of the topic, and then they can form an eigenvector of the topic. Our task is to calculate the similarity μ between the cluster and each document, and the similarity calculation can be simply represented by intersection with the calculation formula as follows:

$$\mu = \frac{\sum_{w \in d \cap s} f(w)}{\sum_{w \in S} f(w)}$$

Here, we define the topic cluster as S and the document as d, and $d \cap S$ represents the intersection of the document and terms in topic clusters. $f(w)$ can be a simple Boolean or other functions, and its value reflects the similarity between the topic cluster and the document.

Certainly, we can use a cosine function to measure the similarity between a topic and a document, hence, the probability distribution of each topic in document d can be calculated as:

$$p(z|d) = \frac{\cos(d, S_z)}{\sum_{z' \in Z} \cos(d, S_{z'})}$$

In general, the different features of the topic have different weights on this topic, so we can also on the basis of this feature improve the similarity measurement method for a topic and a document. For example, we can use TF*IDF value to evaluate the weight of different features (i.e., terms) under the current topic to obtain a more accurate topic distribution in the document.

Overall, the term co-occurrence graph-based topic discovery adopts a more matured term co-occurrence theory, which is intuitive and simple, providing new ideas and methods for topic discovery.

In summary, topic discovery technology originates from TDT project of DARPA [2], originally using VSM model-based clustering methods. Later, with the development of topic models, scholars gradually began to conduct text analysis with topic models. Meanwhile, other methods such as term co-occurrence analysis are also good. Definitely, not all topic discovery methods are mentioned in this chapter, for example, we can also use some of the new technologies from natural language processing. For instance, the recent deep learning method also provides a new technical means for topic discovery. In another example, focusing on extensive user participation and rich interactive features in Weibo social media, a group intelligence-based new topic/event detection method for Weibo streams is proposed in the reference [9]. The main idea of this approach is to first decompose the traditional single mode topic/event detection model according to Weibo participants, then create a language feature and sequential characteristic-based topic/event discriminant model for each participant, namely the Weibo user personal model, and finally determine the new topics/events by voting with group intelligence. As we have mentioned earlier, for various types of data, we cannot simply transplant these technologies and methods. Instead, we should analyze the features of these data and modify the traditional methods properly, only in this way can the effect of the adopted method and the accuracy of topic discovery be improved.

With the explosive growth of social networks, new social media represented by Weibo will surely get more widespread concern. Analyzing the content of social networks, better understanding their users' interests and providing valuable information for business decisions and public opinion monitoring can all find root in the topic discovery technologies in social networks. The rapid development of social networks provides plentiful research materials for topic discovery, which in turn requires topic discovery technologies advance with times, and adapt to the emerging new media and new data. In short, the prospect of technology application of topic discovery is bound to be more and more broad with the pace of the internet age.

3.3 Models and algorithms of topic evolution

Information in social networks is continuously updated due to the dynamic characteristics of data in social networks. In this case, how to track the development trend and future development of the topic interested to users becomes a key problem of user's concern and a key problem to be solved. With time, the content of a topic in social networks may change, and a topic strength may also undergo a change from a low tide to a high tide or backwards. Consequently, how to effectively keep detecting topics in social networks and obtain topic evolution in chronological order to help users of social network track topics has a very significant realistic demand and a practical value. Especially in public opinion monitoring in social networks, timely and effectively tracking the evolution situation of sensitive topics and making an appropriate forecast are core requirements for sensitive topic monitoring, which has broad applications.

In the early TDT research [2], the main consideration of topic tracking was the dynamics, development, and difference of a topic as time flies and the main technical approach is to use statistical knowledge to filter text information, followed by the adoption of classification strategy to track relevant topics. However, these earlier studies have not effectively considered time characteristics of terms and analyzed the distribution of topics across the timeline.

With the topic model proposed, how to effectively use the time characteristics of terms in the topic model and study the characteristics of topic evolution becomes a hot issue in study of social networking text. Unlike the earlier TDT study, each text in the topic model is a mixed distribution of topics and each topic is a mixed distribution of a set of terms. Because the topic model can capture the evolution of a topic and the introduction of topics may have a good effect on text prediction, the topic model has been widely used in the field of topic evolution.

This section focuses mainly on the most common and the most widely-used topic evolution methods in social networks. Firstly, we will introduce the most widely-used simple topic evolution method. Secondly, we will introduce the LDA model and other topic models with high precision which can meet various bonding time of a variety of application requirements. Finally, topic evaluation methods with better application effect in some special application environments will be introduced.

3.3.1 Simple topic evolution

In the study of the topic evolution in social networks, the most commonly-used method is the simple topic evolution method: using a topic discovery method in each time slice, and then analyzing and comparing the similarity of keywords obtained by the topic discovery algorithm of the adjacent time slices to analyze the situation of topic evolution [27].

A typical article [25] about topic evolution points out that, due to the fact that the social network continues to generate large amounts of data, it becomes impossible to perform topic discovery algorithm on the entire dataset after each generation of new data. Hence, they set a sliding time window with a fixed size in social networks, and use their proposed topic discovery algorithm to calculate the similarities and differences between the topic of this window and the topic of the previous window for analyzing the evolution of the topic.

There are many proposed topic evolution methods of the topic expression based on multiple words and supervised/semi-supervised algorithms which can solve the problems of topic evolution in traditional media. However, in topic evolution in social networks, these traditional methods have the following problems:

(1) There is more noise in social network text than that in traditional text, such as colloquial text, slang, advertising, etc.

(2) The text in social networks is shorter than that in traditional media, which make the accuracy of text mining algorithms greatly reduced.

(3) The topic in social networks is word of mouth, which makes the topic evolve very fast.

Taking into account the above-mentioned characteristics of the topic evolution in social networks, Tang et al. proposed a semantic graph model in reference [28] to study topic evolution. In this method, regarding the above-mentioned problems of semantic sparse, much noise, and short text, the authors introduced the existing knowledge base (such as Wikipedia) to solve these problems. Specifically, for any published blog, they take the name of the entity and concepts on Wikipedia as nodes, using the relationship between nodes and semantics measured by graph edit distance (GED) as the weight of the link to construct the semantic graph. Irrelevant concepts and noise will be filtered out by a graph clustering algorithm in the semantic graph. The model can be updated in line with the dynamic update of blogs to track the topic evolution. Moreover, this model also has the following characteristics:

(1) This semantic information-based model can solve the problem of synonymous. As traditional word classification methods cannot distinguish the semantic similarity of words, we cannot find synonyms that express the same topic. In contrast, in Wikipedia, synonyms are clustered together by links and all synonyms can be effectively mapped to the same concept.

(2) Graph clustering algorithm will effectively filter the noise and multi-topic texts. By analyzing the semantic distance between keywords, graph clustering algorithm will discover the main topic of a blog.

(3) There is no requirement for statistics on the training sets used in statistical methods because the graph edit distance is applied in this method.

(4) As this method uses the similarity between semantics, this method is particularly suitable for topic evolution.

The evolution analysis of public concerns is a variation of topic evolution analysis. In the case of Weibo, there is not only Weibo describing event information, but also Weibo reflecting public concerns. The event information in Weibo reflects the occurrence and development of events, while public concern in Weibo embodies the public's interest and expectations, opinions and attitudes, and emotions and tendencies for events. For example, in a commercial event, public concern reflects their demand for products and their evaluation for after-sale service and brand reputation. Therefore, understanding and analyzing the public concern become an important part on mastering Weibo events.

In the existing research on analyzing the public concerns in events, firstly we need to predict and specify the particular side of events required to observe, so this method is not suitable for unknown general event. Deng et al. take the long Weibo and the forward and comment Weibo as research object in the reference [10], and propose an unsupervised evolution analysis of public concern to reconstruct topic space with long Weibo, then map forward and comment Weibo to the space to perform correlation analysis with long Weibo and transform the evolution analysis of public concern into the position tracking of the forward and comment Weibo in the topic space. Therefore, under the situation without predicting public concerns in events, we can portray the evolution process of public concerns with the development of events. Interested readers can refer to the reference [10] for more details.

3.3.2 Topic model-based topic evolution

Topic model as the most popular and commonly-used approach in topic discovery also has very important applications in topic evolution in social networks.

1. LDA-based topic evolution

With respect to the topic research in online social networks, reference [7] proposes online LDA topic evolution with the basic idea as follows: firstly, a sliding window technique is adopted to divide the text stream of social networks into time slices; and then the LDA model is used to model the document within each time slice, where each document is represented as mixed topics with LDA and each topic is a polynomial distribution of pre-set words, which leads to the probability distribution of Topic – Word and Document – Topic. Moreover, the authors use the relationship between the posterior probability and the priori probability to maintain the continuousness between topics, namely, adding a weight W to the Topic – Word probability distribution of the previous time slice as the prior probability of the current time slice and establishing an online LDA calculation model. Under the guidance of KL similarity metric distance measurement, according to the changes of probability distribution of Topic – Word and Document – Topic over time, there are two fundamental topic evolution models: the topic evolution and the topic strength evolution.

Due to the fact that there is no requirement for data of the time slice when dealing with the current time slice, online LDA model thus saves the memory to handle large-scale corpus, which is suitable to online social network environments.

LDA model is also applied in another social networks, the topic evolution in research citation network. In research citation network, the reference naturally reflects the relationship between topics. Bolelli et al. [6] in 2009 first introduced the LDA in the research of research citation network, but they simply use references to identify and determine the weights of a few words that describe topics most properly. In reference [11], He et al. propose a systematic analysis approach for topic evolution in research citation network. First, the authors extended the LDA model, making it suitable for research citation network. For each time slice, they calculated the topic and then compared and analyzed it with the topic computed on the last time slice to get the evolution situation of the topic. In addition, each constraint in this simple algorithm was removed. For example, the topic not only relies on the document of the present time slice, but also relates to the information of previous time slice. Therefore, the authors propose a topic inheritance model where they clearly point out how to apply references to topic evolution. In this model, the reference is interpreted as the succession of the topic and the time properties of the document is carefully considered, even the time sequence of documents in a time slice is to be measured, ultimately reflected as a partial order of a reference graph.

In reference [30], the research topic evolution graph is proposed, which includes the following elements: topic milestone paper, topic time strength, and topic keyword.

(1) Topic milestone papers are the most representative of a topic in understanding a topic.

(2) The topic time strength indicates the number of relatively related topic citations at different times, which mainly reveals the changes between current citations and previous citations and the lifecycle of a topic.

(3) The topic keywords refer to the keywords that can accurately sum up the topic, which enables users to obtain a general understanding about the topic even before reading the relevant references and helps users to accurately locate papers they are most interested and are supposed to read the most in general references.

The biggest difference between this paper and previous research lies in that it not only considers the similarity between texts but also takes into account the dependencies between cited papers. The authors verify that there is topic similarity between the papers citing the same paper, which reflects the topic similarity between papers more accurately than that of the texts.

Another feature of this paper lies in regarding each paper as a set of references, which can be modeled with a topic generation model, with citations mainly represented by the latent topic variable. This is different from the traditional approaches using the probabilistic topic model to discovery topic in the document. The generated topic of this article is based on a polynomial distribution of research papers, while the topic generated in traditional methods is the polynomial distribution of words. Therefore, taking into account the time factors of papers and references, we can get the exact topic evolution graph.

2. Other topic-based topic evolution models

Although the LDA is the most commonly-applied topic model approach on the issue of topic evolution in social networks, some other type of topic models are proposed when taking into account the relevant background knowledge of topic research and the characteristics of data in social networks.

In the analysis of online social network community, an important task is to track the evolution situation of a topic in the community. However, the existing methods consider only the emergence of the topics or the evolution of network structures, ignoring the interaction between text topics and network structures. Therefore, Lin et al. puts forward a popular event tracking (PET) method in the reference [14]. This method takes into account the emergence of a user's new interest, information spread on the network structure, and the evolution situation of text topics. Gibbs random field is introduced to model the impact of historical status and dependency relationship on the graph, so that the topic model can be used to generate the corresponding keywords in the case of given interesting topics. As Gibbs random field and the topic model interact, topic evolution becomes an optimization problem of a joint probability distribution including historical factors, text factors, and structural factors. The authors also verify that the classic topic model is a special case of this model.

For the study of online social networks, especially the phenomenon of short text encountered during topic evolution in Twitter, the traditional text methods cannot solve this problem due to the requirement of short time, a large amount of data to be processed, and sparse data. Specifically, in the continuous generated data stream, we need to find Tweets related to a preset topic. In this context, the incoming data stream is huge, the specified data related topics are very limited and it is required to complete the topic evolution analysis with both time and space constraints. On account of the requirement of about only one millisecond to process a tweet in practice, Lin et al. use a simple language model in the reference [16], particularly, using the label appeared in parts of Tweets as an approximation to train the probability model, which can be applied to the continuous Tweets in online social networks, with even most of those unlabeled Tweets included. This paper adopts smoothing techniques to integrate timeliness and sparsity and also takes into account a variety of technologies for preserving historical information. Experiments validate that in this method the most appropriate smoothing technique is Stupid Backoff – the simplest smoothing technique. This paper shows that under the extreme circumstances of a large amount of data and the requirement of fast computing speed in online social networks and with consideration of equilibrium speed, availability, scalability and other demands for practical applications, the simplest way is the best way.

As for the cyclical phenomenon occurred in the topic evolution of social media (such as Flickr and Twitter), Yin et al. [31] in 2011 propose a latent periodic topic analysis (LPTA)-based probability model. This model mainly considers addressing the following several issues:

(1) The existing work on the periodicity is generally concentrated in the time series database, and it is not suitable for text processing required in topic evolution analysis.

(2) Periodic word analysis cannot satisfy the requirement of periodic topic analysis, because it is unlikely to see the same word again, but other words within the same topic.

(3) Due to the diversity of language, there are a lot of synonyms in text, which makes topic analysis a challengeable problem.

Therefore, the proposed LPTA method can be considered as a variant of latent topic model and the difference from traditional topic model lies in the time domain oriented period property. Specifically, it is to cluster the words of the same topic separated by about a time period. In other words, the problem is transformed into the estimation of the time period and the determination of the topic. Technically speaking, in this paper, the authors use the maximum likelihood probability approach to estimate the relevant parameters. The goal of LPTA is not only to identify latent topic space according to the data but also to discover whether there is a periodicity in topic evolution.

3.3.3 Adjacent time slice association-based topic evolution

In addition to the most simple and intuitive simple topic evolution model described in section 3.3.1 and the most commonly used topic model introduced in section 3.3.2, there are other types of models in the study of topic evolution, while the difference between these models and the aforementioned two models lies in that these models mainly focus on the link between history time slice and present time slice and relevant background of topics.

In the social media stream, users have the following natural requirements for the topic evolution:
(1) In social media, once there emerges a new topic, we need to detect it in time.
(2) The evolution of the interesting topics can be tracked in real time.
(3) The information provided should be ensured in a proper range to avoid information overload.

Saha et al. [22] point out that new information appears all the time in social media, leading to the fact that to send all topic information to users is impossible, which thus requires a model proposed to infer topics of users' interests according to the topic information of historical time slices. In this article, the authors propose a system based on the strict rigorous machine learning and optimization strategy for the online analysis of social media stream. Specifically, it applies the effective topic-related model and non-negative matrix factorization techniques. Different from the existing work, this article maintains the time continuity of topic evolution at the process of new topic discovery.

Unlike the above-mentioned papers on topic evolution, Lin et al. [15] also reveal the topic's latent diffusion paths in social networks except the simple analysis of topic evolution. After comprehensively considering the text document, social influence and topic evolution, they turn the problem into a joint inference problem. Specifically, the authors propose a hybrid model that on the one hand can generate topic related keywords based on topic evolution and diffusion, and on the other hand can adjust the diffusion process with Gaussian Markov random field using the social influence of users' personal layer. This paper believes that in social networks the information users acquire comes more from the social links rather than strangers. Hence, the researchers believe the topic is actually spreading in the social network structure. Based on the proposed topic diffusion and evolution model, for one thing the latent spread path graph can be determined for further determining the source of a topic; and for another, the properties of the time change of the topic can be inferred to track the new development of a topic and understand the regularity of its changes.

3.4 Summary

With the advancement of computing technologies and the popularization of internet, online social network has developed dramatically with an explosive growth of information. Therefore, traditional knowledge acquisition approaches have become obsolete to keep up with the pace of knowledge production in the era of big data, which demands intelligent processing of information in the network age and automatic discovery and acquisition of knowledge. Among these, social network contains a large amount of valuable information for its real reflection of people's life. Therefore, it is particularly important for text mining and analysis for social networks. Topic is the important information concerned by social network users. In addition, detecting accurately the topic and tracking the evolution of topic have a great reference value in monitoring and guiding public opinions, business decisions and other aspects. This chapter introduces the theories and technologies related to topic discovery and topic evolution with the hope that readers can have a general understanding of the relevant fields.

Topic discovery methods mainly include topic model, the traditional vector space model-based method, and the term co-occurrence graph-based method, where topic model is the current mainstream approach, whereas the above methods are all required to be suitably modified to suit the characteristics of text information in social networks to improve the analysis results. Research on topic evolution in social networks is relatively limited and the main method is still concentrated in the method of time slice segmentation, with the more complex considering the relationship between time slices, etc.

Overall, although the research on topic discovery and evolution has been carried out for many years, the initial research field is relatively narrow and the method used is not mature enough, which cannot simply be applied directly to the current online social network environments. In recent years, the research on topic discovery and evolution has made considerable progress and development, but we believe there are still many challenging issues to be solved:
(1) The formal definition and presentation of the topic. Although many researchers have made relatively complete definitions and presentations of the topic, the topic itself involves some subjective factors and researches have not established a more systematic concept to describe it, which leads to more or less differences

between researches of different fields of topic discovery and evolution and a barrier hindering more researchers from devoting to relevant studies.

(2) Online real-time processing of mass information. The world today is the era of information when timeliness of information has strategic significance. The requirements for timeliness of topic discovery and evolution in social networks has become higher and higher, so future research should focus much on topic discovery and evolution in massive online real-time information. Nowadays, Twitter, Weibo, and other applications generate thousands of data per second, therefore how to adapt to such a rapid information update speed has become a problem that we must consider first in constructing related applications. In addition, we should try to study new information compressing representations and online processing algorithms to better meet the requirements of online social networks.

(3) Aggregation of multiple source information. With the rapid development of Internet, various social applications have sprung up and users no longer focus on a single information source. Aggregation for the multiple sources information to construct multi-granularity and multi-level topic discovery and evolution application systems can better describe the topic and help users grasp the topic more intuitively and precisely.

References

[1] Paige H. Adams, Craig H. Martell. Topic detection and extraction in chat. 2008 IEEE International Conference on Semantic Computing, 2008.

[2] James Allan, Jaime Carbonell, George Doddington, Jonathan Yamron, Yiming Yang. Topic detection and tracking pilot study final report. In Proceedings of the DARPA Broadcast News Transcription and Understanding Workshop, 1998.

[3] Hila Becker, Mor Naaman, Luis Gravano. Learning similarity metrics for event identification in social media. In Proceedings of the third ACM international conference on Web search and data mining, 2010.

[4] Hila Becker, Mor Naaman, Luis Gravano. Beyond trending topics: Real-world event identification on Twitter. ICWSM 11, 2011: 438–441.

[5] David M. Blei, Andrew Y. Ng, Michael I. Jordan, John Lafferty. Latent Dirichlet allocation. Journal of Machine Learning Research 2003, 3:993–1022.

[6] Levent Bolelli, Seyda Ertekin, C. Lee Giles. Topic and trend detection in text collections using latent Dirichlet allocation. In ECIR'09, 2009.

[7] Kai Cui, Bin Zhou, Yan Jia, Zheng Liang. LDA-based model for online topic evolution mining. Computer Science, 2011, 37(11):156–159.

[8] Scott Deerwester, Susan T. Dumais, George W. Furnas, Thomas K. Landauer, Richard Harshman. Indexing by latent semantic analysis. JASIS, 1990, 41(6):391–407.

[9] Lei Deng, Zhaoyun Ding, Bingying Xu, Bin Zhou, Peng Zou. Using social intelligence for new event detection in microblog stream. 2012 Second International Conference on Cloud and Green Computing (CGC), 2012: 434–439.

[10] Lei Deng, Bingying Xu, Lumin Zhang, Yi Han, Bin Zhou, Peng . Tracking the evolution of public concerns in social media. In Proceedings of the Fifth International Conference on Internet Multimedia Computing and Service, 2013: 353–357.

[11] Qi He, Bi Chen, Jian Pei, Baojun Qiu, Prasenjit Mitra, C. Lee Giles. Detecting topic evolution in scientific literature: How can citations help?. CIKM'09, 2009.

[12] Thomas Hofmann. Probabilistic latent semantic indexing. In Proceedings of the 22nd annual international ACM SIGIR conference on Research and development in information retrieval, 1999.

[13] Liangjie Hong, Brian D. Davison. Empirical study of topic modeling in Twitter. In Proceedings of the First Workshop on Social Media Analytics, 2010: 80–88.

[14] Cindy Xide Lin, Bo Zhao, Qiaozhu Mei, Jiawei Han. PET: A statistical model for popular events tracking in social communities. KDD'10, 2010.

[15] Cindy Xide Lin, Qiaozhu Mei, Jiawei Han, Yunliang Jiang, Marina Danilevsky. The joint inference of topic diffusion and evolution in social communities. ICDM'11, 2011.

[16] Jimmy Lin, Rion Snow, William Morgan. Smoothing techniques for adaptive online language models: Topic tracking in Tweet streams. KDD'11, 2011.

[17] Yue Lu, Chengxiang Zhai. Opinion integration through semi-supervised topic modeling. In Proceedings of the 17th international conference on World Wide Web, 2008.

[18] Omid Madani, Jiye Yu. Discovery of numerous specific topics via term co-occurrence analysis. In Proceedings of the 19th ACM international conference on Information and knowledge management, 2010.

[19] Daniel Ramage, Susan Dumais, Dan Liebling. Characterizing microblogs with topic models. ICWSM, 2010.

[20] Daniel Ramage, David Hall, Ramesh Nallapati, Christopher D. Manning. Labeled LDA: A supervised topic model for credit attribution in multi-labeled corpora. In Proceedings of the 2009 Conference on Empirical Methods in Natural Language Processing, 2009.

[21] Michal Rosen-Zvi, Thomas Griffiths, Mark Steyvers, Padhraic Smyth. The author-topic model for authors and documents. In Proceedings of the 20th conference on Uncertainty in artificial intelligence, 2004.

[22] Ankan Saha, Vikas Sindhwani. Learning evolving and emerging topics in social media: a dynamic nmf approach with temporal regularization. In Proceedings of the fifth ACM international conference on Web search and data mining, 2012.

[23] Gerard M Salton, Andrew Wong, Chungshu Yang. A vector space model for automatic indexing. Communications of the ACM, 1975, 18(11): 613–620.

[24] Hassan Sayyadi, Matthew Hurst, Alexey Maykov. Event detection and tracking in social streams. ICWSM, 2009.

[25] Hassan Sayyadi, Matthew Hurst and Alexey Maykov. Event detection and tracking in aocial streams. ICWSM'09, 2009.

[26] Hassan Sayyadi, Louiqa Raschid. A graph analytical approach for topic Detection. ACM Transactions on Internet Technology (TOIT), 2013, 13(2): 4.

[27] Jing Shi, Meng Fan, Wanlong Li. Topic analysis based on LDA model. Acta Automatica Sinica, 2009, 35(12): 1586–1592.

[28] Jintao Tang, Ting Wang, Qin Lu, Ji Wang, Wenjie Li. A wikipedia based semantic graph model for topic tracking in blogosphere. In Proceedings of the Twenty-Second international joint conference on Artificial Intelligence, 2011.

[29] Ville H. Tuulos, Henry Tirri. Combining topic models and social networks for chat data mining. In Proceedings of the 2004 IEEE/WIC/ACM international Conference on Web intelligence, 2004.

[30] Xiaolong Wang, ChengxiangZhai and Dan Roth. Understanding evolution of research themes: A Probabilistic generative model for citations. KDD'13, 2013.

[31] Zhijun Yin, Liangliang Cao, Jiawei Han, Chengxiang Zhai, Thomas Huang. LPTA: A probabilistic model for latent periodic topic analysis. In 2011 IEEE 11th International Conference on Data Mining (ICDM), 2011.

[32] Wayne Zhao, J Jing Jiang, Jianshu Weng, Jing He, Ee-Peng Lim, Hongfei Yan, Xiaoming Li,. Comparing twitter and traditional media using topic models. In Proceedings of the 33rd European conference on Advances in information retrieval, 2011: 338–349.

Appendix

1 Document 20140309 in application examples

We are working with anti-terrorism units, says Hisham

SEPANG: Malaysia has informed counter-terrorism agencies of various countries in light of several imposters found to have boarded flight MH370 that went missing over the South China Sea early Saturday.

Defence Minister Datuk Seri Hishammuddin Hussein (pic) said Malaysia would be working with intelligence agencies, including the Federal Bureau of Investigation (FBI), on the matter.

"If it is an international network, the Malaysian immigration alone will not be sufficient."

"We have also informed the counter-terrorism units of all relevant countries."

"At this point, we have not established if there was a security risk involved (and) we do not want to jump the gun," Hishammuddin said when asked if there could be any hijack or terror elements in the disappearance of the MH370 flight.

On two impostors who boarded the flight using passports reported lost by an Italian and an Austrian, Hishammuddin said the authorities would screen the entire manifest of the flight.

2 Document 20140323 in application examples

MH370: Indian aircrafts join search

KUALA LUMPUR: Two long range maritime reconnaissance aircrafts from India have departed the Subang Airport on Sunday to join in the search for the missing Malaysia Airlines (MAS) MH370 aircraft in the southern Indian Ocean.

This was despite reported bad weather caused by tropical cyclone Gilia which had forced a number of other aircrafts scheduled to go on the mission to be cancelled.

The High Commission of India to Malaysiaon Sunday said that both aircrafts were likely to encounter the cyclonic conditions enroute, but Captains of both aircrafts had instead "decided to skirt bad weather areas" to reach the search sectors.

The two aircrafts were the P8-I of the Indian Navy and the C-130J of the Indian Air Force. Both were expected to undertake a 10-hour mission in the area.

"Both aircrafts have long endurance capabilities coupled with state of the art electro optronic and infrared search and reconnaissance equipment on board," said the high commission in a statement here.

The P8-I aircraft has the added advantage of on-board radars and specially designed search and rescue kits.

Previously, the Prime Minister of India had committed to assisting Malaysia and "render all possible assistance to Malaysia in locating the missing Malaysian Airlines flight".

Both aircrafts arrived in Malaysia on March 21. After extensive briefings in Malaysia on Sunday, both Indian aircrafts took off to be part of the Australian-led search on Sunday morning.

India has been participating in the search and rescue operation beginning March 11 in the Andaman Sea and Bay of Bengal.

3 Document 20140325 in application examples

New statement from Malaysia Airlines: Tan Sri MdNorMdYusof, Chairman of Malaysia Airlines:

The painful reality is that the aircraft is now lost and that none of the passengers or crew on board survived.

This is a sad and tragic day for all of us at Malaysia Airlines. While not entirely unexpected after an intensive multi-national search across a 2.24 million square mile area, this news is clearly devastating for the families of those on board. They have waited for over two weeks for even the smallest hope of positive news about their loved ones.

This has been an unprecedented event requiring an unprecedented response. The investigation still underway may yet prove to be even longer and more complex than it has been since March 8th. But we will continue to support the families—as we have done throughout. And to support the authorities as the search for definitive answers continues.

MAS Group CEO, Ahmad Jauhari Yahya, has said the comfort and support of families involved and support of the multi-national search effort continues to be the focus of the airline. In the last 72 hours, MAS has trained an additional 40 caregivers to ensure the families have access to round-the-clock support.

A short while ago Australian Defense Minister David Johnston said "to this point, no debris or anything recovered to identify the plane" He also said this is an extremely remote part of the world and "it's a massive logistical exercise." "We are not searching for a needle in a haystack. We are still trying to define where the haystack is," he said.

4 Document 20140327 in application examples

Chinese celebs lash out at M'sia over MH370

A number of big-name celebrities in China, including award-winning actress Zhang Ziyi, have hit out at Malaysia's handling of the search for Malaysia Airlines Flight MH370.

Several celebrities took to Weibo—a Shanghai-based Twitter-like microblogging service - to condemn Malaysia and urge a boycott of Malaysian products.

"The Malaysian government has offended the world! We are looking for the airplane but you are more concerned about timing."

"Malaysian government, today you have done wrong. You are wrong failing to take responsibility. You are wrong for prioritising political manoeuvres instead of respecting life."

"You are wrong for failing to respect the universal… quest for truth," wrote Zhang on March 25, 17 days MH370 went missing and a day after Prime Minister Najib Abdul Razak revealed that the plane went down in the Indian Ocean.

Among the 239 people on board MH370 were 152 Chinese nationals. One of them was Jo Kun, who was once Zhang's fight choreographer.

Chen Kun

Actor Chen Kun (right), another famous Chinese celebrity, accused the Malaysian government and MAS of "clownish prevarication and lies", also on March 25.

He added that he would boycott all Malaysian products and avoid coming to Malaysia indefinitely.

Posts by Zhang, Chen and other Chinese celebrities have been widely shared online by Chinese netizens.

Fish Leong

Some Chinese netizens have also urged a boycott of Malaysian artistes such as Fish Leong (right), Gary Chaw, Lee Sinje and Ah Niu, who are popular for their music and movies.

Bahau-born Leong, who is an expectant mother, drew scorn from Microblogging users after uploading a photograph of three candles as a mark of respect for MH370 victims.

Numerous Chinese netizens responded by cursing her and her unborn child. The photograph has since been removed.

In an apparent attempt to stem the anger and distrust in China, Malaysian officials have also met the Chinese ambassador to Malaysia Huang Huikang to ask for the Chinese government to engage and help clarify the situation to the bereaved relatives and the public.

"Malaysia is working hard to try and make the briefings to the Chinese relatives in Beijing more productive," read a statement sent out by the Transport Ministry today.

5 Document 20140405 in application examples

Chinese ship searching for missing Malaysia plane detects signal

BEIJING (Reuters) - A Chinese patrol ship searching for missing Malaysia Airlines flight MH370 detected a pulse signal with a frequency of 37.5 kHz per second in the south Indian Ocean on Saturday, state news agency Xinhua reported.

37.5 kHz per second is currently the international standard frequency for the underwater locator beacon on a plane's "black box".

A black box detector deployed by the vessel Haixun 01 picked up the signal at around 25 degrees south latitude and 101 degrees east longitude, Xinhua said. It has yet to be established whether it is related to the missing jet.

Xinhua also said a Chinese air force plane spotted a number of white floating objects in the search area.

(Reporting by Benjamin Kang Lim; editing by Andrew Roche)

Xiangke Liao

4 Algorithms of influence maximization

4.1 Introduction

Social network is playing a fundamental role in the spread and diffusion of information, viewpoints, and innovation. For discovering the most information-spread influential node set in social networks, the problem of influence maximization is one of the key issues being researched in the field of social network information spread. It is of high research and application value, with important applications including those in marketing, advertising publication, early warning of public sentiment, water quality monitoring, disease surveillance, and control. For instance, in the word-of-mouth marketing and advertisement publication, which are based on social networks, what kind of users will be used for promoting the product and advertising to maximize, through information and influence spread in the social network, the promotion profits of the brand and the spread scope of advertisement [1]. The solution of influence maximization directly affects the formulation and deployment of application strategies such as marketing, and has an important influence on the effectiveness and scalability of the system.

With the development of social network technology, the current social network is has become increasingly large, specifically reflected by numerous nodes and complex correlation between nodes; meanwhile, the network has become more dynamic, specifically reflected by the frequent variation in the number of nodes and the correlation between nodes, high randomness, and unpredictability. These characteristics of social network directly lead to a large amount of calculation and a long run time for seeking the most influential node in the network. As the requirement from practical applications for the execution time of algorithm is becoming increasingly strict, we urgently need to study the efficient processing technology of influence maximization in large-scale social networks.

This chapter is arranged as follows: in Section 4.2, influence spread models involved in the study of influence maximization is introduced and a formal definition of the problem of influence maximization is presented. In Section 4.3, three basic metric for measuring influence maximization algorithms are introduced, including the run time, algorithm precision, and scalability. In Section 4.4, algorithms of influence maximization are classified as Greedy Algorithms and Heuristic Algorithms. In Section 4.5, Greedy Algorithms of influence maximization, including BasicGreedy, CELF, and MixGreedy, as well as other Greedy Algorithms are introduced, and their advantages and disadvantages are discussed. In Section 4.6, several Heuristic Algorithms of influence maximization are introduced, and their advantages and disadvantages are discussed. In Section 4.7, related researches on the extension and deformation of influence maximization are elaborated.

https://doi.org/10.1515/9783110599435-004

4.2 Basic concepts and theory basis

The modeling basis of influence maximization is the topology of social networks and corresponding models of influence spread. Therefore, influence spread models involved in influence maximization research will be first introduced in this section, and the formal definition of influence maximization will also be presented.

Concept 1: Influence spread models
The influence spread models define the methods and mechanisms of influence spread in social networks, and is the basis for studying the influence maximization problem. Different from the afore-mentioned topology of social network, each node in the social network has two states, i.e., 0 and 1, where 0 represents an inactive state and 1 represents an active state. After a node v_i switches from an inactive state to an active state, it node v_i will try to influence other inactive neighboring nodes. If the activation succeeds, then its neighbors will switch from the inactive to the active state. As shown in Figure 4.1, the node a is in the active state at the beginning, and hence is capable of trying to influence other neighboring inactive nodes b, c, and e. There may be two situations at this moment: one situation is that, if the node a fails to activate the node c, then the node c will stay in the inactive state; the other situation is that, if the node a activates the node b successfully, then the node b switches from the inactive state into the active state and becomes capable of influencing other nodes; for instance, the node b may activate the node d. The process of influencing a node to switch from the inactive state into the active state is known as the spread of influence. It should be noted that the whole spread process is irreversible, namely, one node may be influenced to switch from the inactive state into the active state but not vice versa.

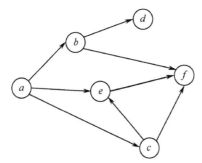

Figure 4.1: Diagram of influence spread

Detailed studies on the influence spread models have been made in the current academic community, where the independent cascade model [2] and the linear threshold model [3] are currently the two most widely researched influence maximization models.

The independent cascade model is based on the probabilities wherein each node, after switched into the active state itself, will try to activate its subsequent node at a certain probability, and the behaviors for multiple active nodes to try to activate the same neighboring node are independent from each other; hence, the model is named as the independent cascade model. The linear threshold model is based on thresholds; the behavior of multiple active nodes to try to activate the same subsequent node are dependent, and whether the influence is successful depends on whether the sum of the weights of the influences on the same subsequent node by all the active nodes surpasses the threshold of the subsequent node. The independent cascade model and the linear threshold model elaborate the process of influence spread based on probability and threshold, respectievely. Please refer to Chapter 10 for details, and pleonasm will be omitted here.

In addition to these models, there are also some other influence spread models in the research of influence maximization. A brief description is presented below.

(1) Triggering model [1]. The triggering model was proposed by Kempe et al. in 2003. In the triggering model, each node v is corresponding to a triggering node set T_v which defines the nodes capable of triggering the node v to switch from the inactive state to the active state; namely, at the time point of t, a nonactivated node v will be activated if and only if the precursor u of at least one node v is in the active state at the time point of $t-1$, and $u \in T_v$. Take Figure 4.1 as an example, suppose that $T_e = \{a, c\}$, $T_f = \{b, e\}$, and the node c is in the active state when $t = T_0$. Then, when $t = T_1$, c tries to influence nodes e and f. Since $c \in T_e$ but $c \notin T_f$, c can successfully activate the node e, while f is still in a nonactivated state. When $t = T_2$, the newly activated node e also tries to influence its neighboring node f. As $e \in T_f$ at this moment, the node e succeeds in activating the node f.

(2) Weighted cascade model [4] is a unique independent cascade model. The difference between the weighted cascade model and the independent cascade model lies in that, in the weighted cascade model, the probability for the node v to successfully activate the subsequent node w is the reciprocal of the in-degree of the node w, namely, $p(v, w) = 1/d_w$, where d_w is the in-degree of the node w. For instance, in Figure 4.1, the probability for the node e to successfully activate the node f is $p(e, f) = \frac{1}{3}$.

(3) Voter model [5] is a probability model which is widely applied to statistical physics and particle systems, and was first presented by Peter Clifford and Aidan Sudbury. In the voter model, each mode randomly selects one node from its precursor node set in each step, and takes the state of the selected node as its own state. Again take Figure 4.1 as an example, suppose that only the node c of all nodes is in the active state when $t = T_0$, while all the other nodes are inactive. Then, when $t = T_1$, the node e randomly selects one node from its precursor node set $\{a, c\}$; if the node a is selected, then the node e is still inactive at the time point of T_1; otherwise, if the node c is selected, then e will switch from the inactive state into the active state at the time point of T_1. It should be noted that, the states of nodes in the voter model can either switch from the inactive

state into the active state, or switch from the active state into the inactive state, so the voter model is more suitable for modeling those occasions allowing for the nodes to change their viewpoints, e.g., the public in democratic elections may change their votes due to the influence of the votees and other people.

Concept 2: Influence maximization

Based on the given influence spread model, the purpose of influence maximization is to find the K nodes having the largest ultimate influence spread in social networks so that the maximum nodes will be ultimately influenced through the influence spread in social networks with these K nodes as the initial active node set. For a formal description of influence maximization, when the symbol $\sigma(S)$ is used for representing the number of the nodes ultimately activated by the initial seed set S after the influence spread. Thus, a formal description of influence maximization is as follows:

Given: a social network $G = (V, E, W)$, a given influence spread model, and a positive integer K;

Goal: to select an initial active node set S from the network G so that $\sigma(S)$ is the largest;

Constraints: $S \subset V$ and $|S| = K$.

4.3 Metrics of influence maximization

Practical applications of influence maximization have lots of requirements for the solution of this problem, where run time, algorithm precision, and scalability are key factors that need to be considered in the current environment of large-scale social networks. Nodes of large-scale social networks are numerous, and the connections are tight and complicated; consequently, the run time is long and it is hard to deal with the problem. As the requirements for algorithm efficiency from modern applications are stricter, the run time becomes the primary standard for measuring influence maximization algorithms; moreover, in the problem of influence maximization, higher precision implies a larger ultimate influence range, so algorithm precision is also a key factor needs to be considered in the design of influence maximization algorithms. Meanwhile, the constantly increasing scale of social networks and mass data has brought serious challenges to the scalability of influence maximization algorithms. In a word, the run time, algorithm precision, and scalability are three essential standards for measuring the quality of influence maximization algorithms.

1. Run time

The computation time of influence maximization algorithm is important for policy formulation has important applications, hence, these applications are very sensitive to the computation time of algorithms, and have very high demands on algorithm efficiency. For example, in such application occasions as water quality monitoring as well as disease surveillance and control, delayed discoveries cause dangerous widespread pollution of water and massive disease outbreak. Therefore, the run time is one of the core optimal objects for designing influence maximization algorithms, and possibly the shortest run time can serve as the basic starting point for designing the solution scheme of influence maximization. However, traditional Greedy Algorithm of influence maximization calculates the influence range of a given node set through a large amount of repeated Monte-Carlo simulations, which causes a rather long run-time. In particular, in face of current large-scale social networks, existing algorithms cannot meet the requirements of applications for algorithm efficiency. Therefore, the run time of algorithm is one of the key metrics of influence maximization.

2. Algorithm precision
Regarding influence maximization, algorithm precision refers to the number of nodes ultimately influenced by the seed set selected by the influence maximization algorithm after the process of influence spread. In practical applications of influence maximization, many applications possibly require the largest ultimate influence range. Applications of this type are represented by marketing and advertisement publication or the like. In the above two applications, a larger ultimate influence maximization range indicates better promotion benefits of the product and more commercial profits. Therefore, exploring high-precision computation algorithm is also a key issue in the influence maximization researches. Influence maximization researches in recent years prove that it is a NP-Hard problem to find the most influential K nodes [1]. Traditional sorting algorithm, PageRank, among other methods pay no attention to the characteristics of influence spread, hence, the algorithm precision is too low to solve the influence maximization problem. As a result, high precision is also a goal sought by influence maximization algorithms.

3. Scalability
Scalability is an important metric for practical applications of influence maximization. Due to complicated algorithms and long run time, the current solution algorithm can be applied only to the social network of with less than a million nodes. Faced with large-scale social networks, influence maximization algorithms with fine scalability must be designed for handling the severe challenge due to the mass data of social network.

4.4 Classification of influence maximization algorithms

In recent years, influence maximization algorithms have resulted in extensive studies and attention from academic circles. As influence maximization has been proven to be a NP-Hard problem [1], its research can mainly be divided into two directions:

(1) Greedy Algorithm. Researches on Greedy Algorithm are basically based on the Hill-Climbing Greedy Algorithm [1], where one node capable of providing the maximum influence value is selected at each step, and a locally optimal solution is used for approximating the globally optimal solution. The advantage of Greedy Algorithm is its comparatively high precision, which can reach an approximate optimal of $1 - 1/e - \varepsilon$. However, Greedy Algorithm has a serious efficiency problem, namely, the high algorithm complexity and the long run time. As a result, it can hardly be applied to large-scale social networks. Numerous studies and related optimization have been made specific to the efficiency of Greedy Algorithm, and this problem is atill a hot topic in current research.

(2) Heuristic Algorithm. Different from Greedy Algorithm, Heuristic Algorithm selects the most influential node according to a designed heuristic strategy, and does not need to calculate the precise influence value of the node; hence, the run time of Heuristic Algorithm is short and the efficiency is high. However, its algorithm precision is too low to compare with Greedy Algorithm.

4.5 Greedy algorithm of influence maximization

To enable readers to better understand the Greedy Algorithm of influence maximization, first, the following two key concepts will be introduced in this section: marginal profit and submodular function; then, typical Greedy Algorithm of influence maximization such as BasicGreedy, CELF and MixGreedy will be introduced in detail, and advantages and disadvantages of Greedy Algorithm will be concluded.

4.5.1 Basic concepts of greedy algorithm

Concept 1: Marginal profit
For influence maximization, the marginal profit of the influence value function $\sigma(\cdot)$ refers to the growth of ultimate influence value that can be brought by addition of a node v_i as the initial active node on the basis of the current active node set S. That is

$$\sigma_{v_i}(S) = \sigma(S \cup \{v_i\}) - \sigma(S)$$

Concept 2: Submodular function
For an arbitrary function $f(\cdot)$ which maps the subset of a finite set U to be non-negative real numbers, if the function $f(\cdot)$ satisfies decreasing profits, then the function $f(\cdot)$ is a submodular function. Here, decreasing profits mean that the

marginal profit brought to the set S by the addition of any element v_i is not lower than the marginal profit brought to the superset $T \supseteq S$ of S by the addition of the element v_i, the formal description is as follows:

$$f_{v_i}(S) \geq f_{v_i}(T)$$

or

$$f(S \cup \{v_i\}) - f(S) \geq f(T \cup \{v_i\}) - f(T)$$

Basic theory 1:
If the function $f(\cdot)$ is a submodular function as well as a monotonic function ($f(S \cup \{v_i\}) \geq f(S)$ satisfies all sets S and all elements), when trying to locate the element set S with a size of K so that $f(S)$ is maximum, Hill-Climbing Greedy Algorithm can be used to obtain the approximate optimal solution of $1 - 1/e - \varepsilon$ [6, 7], where e is the base of a natural logarithm and ε can be any positive real number.

4.5.2 Basic greedy algorithm [1]

Pedro Domingos and Matt Richardson [8] studied influence maximum as an algorithm problem for the first time. The earliest method is to regard the market as a social network, model the individual purchasing behavior and the overall earning promotion after marketing as a model of Markov Random Field, and bring up Single Pass Algorithm and Greedy Search Algorithm so as to gain an approximate solution.

Therefore, Kempe et al. [1] first refined this problem to be a discrete optimization problem, that is to find K nodes capable of maximizing the ultimate influence range according to a given spread model. Kempe et al. proved that this optimization problem was a NP-Hard problem in both the independent cascade model and the linear threshold model. Later, the author proved that the influence value function $\sigma(\cdot)$ satisfied the submodular character and the monotonic character in both Influence Spread Models, and thus put forward a Greedy Hill-Climbing Approximate Algorithm BasicGreedy, which is capable of ensuring the approximate optimal of $1 - 1/e - \varepsilon$.

The Greedy Hill-Climbing Algorithm presented by Kempe et al. is shown as the Algorithm 4.1. The algorithm starts when S is a null set (Line 1), and later executes K rounds (Line 2), a node v capable of providing the maximum marginal profit will be selected in each round (Round 10), and then is added into the initial node set S (Line 11). To calculate the marginal profit s_v of each node in graph. G (Line 3), Kempe et al. designed to calculate, through R rounds of stimulation (Lines 5~7), the number of nodes which can be ultimately influenced with the set $S \cup \{v\}$ as the initial active node in each round, and finally seek the average value (Line 8) and select the node having the largest marginal profit to join the set S.

Algorithm 4.1 Greedy Hill-Climbing Approximation Algorithm Basic Greedy
Known: Social Network $G = (V, E, W)$, Parameter K
Seek: the most influential node set S with a size of K

1:   Initialize $S = \emptyset$;
2:   **for** $i = 1$ to K **do**
3:     **for** any node v in the set $V \backslash S$ **do**
4:      $s_v = 0$;
5:      **for** $i = 1$ to R **do**
6:       $s_v = s_v + |RanCas(S \cup \{v\})|$;
7:      **end for**
8:      $s_v = s_v / R$;
9:     **end for**
10:   $v = \operatorname{argmax}_{v \in (V \backslash S)} \{s_v\}$;
11:   $S = S \cup \{v\}$;
12:   **end for**

However, the complexity of BasicGreedy Algorithm is as high as $O(KnRm)$, where n and m are, respectively, the number of nodes and the number of edges in graph. G, R is the number of stimulation, which generally selects a value of 20000; therefore, BasicGreedy Algorithm has a rather long execution time and cannot be applied to large-scale social networks. There are two main reasons for it being time-consuming: ① The marginal profits of all nodes need to be calculated in each round of the algorithm; ② R stimulations are needed for calculating the marginal profit of each node. Therefore, although Greedy Hill-Climbing Approximation Algorithm ensures fine precision, its low calculation efficiency demands prompt solution. Basically, all subsequent Greedy Algorithm studies have tried to improve its efficiency.

4.5.3 CELF algorithm [9]

In 2007, Leskovec et al. [9] proposed CELF (Cost-Effective Lazy Forward), which is an optimization of BasicGreedy. As the influence value function $\sigma(\cdot)$ satisfies the submodular character, the influence value marginal profit brought by a random node v has to be smaller following the growth of the initial active set S. Hence, CELF Algorithm does not have to calculate in each round the influence value marginal profits of all nodes like the BasicGreedy Algorithm does. If the influence value marginal profit of the node u prior to this round is smaller than that of the node v in the current round, then the influence value marginal profit of the node u in the current round is bound to be smaller than that of the node v, therefore, it is impossible for the node u to be the node having the largest marginal profit in the current round, and there is no need to calculate its influence value marginal profit in the current round. Exactly, using the submodular character of the influence max-imization objective function, CELF Algorithm significantly reduces the number of calculations of the influence value marginal profits of nodes in each round, and narrows the selection range of nodes, thereby lowering the overall calculation complexity. Experiment results show that the precision of CELF Algorithm is basically the same as that of BasicGreedy Algorithm, whereas its calculation efficiency is far higher that that of the BasicGreedy Algorithm, and accelerates which is as high as 700 times. Even so, it still takes hours for CELF Algorithm to seek 50 most influential nodes in a data set having 37,000 nodes, and its efficiency can hardly satisfy the demand of short run time of current social networks.

4.5.4 Mix Greedy algorithm [4]

Chen et al. [4] presented the novel Greedy Optimization Algorithm, i.e., NewGreedy and MixGreedy. In the original BasicGreedy Algorithm, R simulations are needed for calculating influence value marginal profits of each node, so there are altogether nR simulations for all the n nodes in the network, which leads to a large amount of calculation. NewGreedy Algorithm makes improvement right on such a basis, and enhances the algorithm efficiency. The core thought of NewGreedy Algorithm lies in the calculation of the influence value marginal profits for all nodes in each stimulation, so NewGreedy Algorithm reduces the nR stimulations of BasicGreedy Algorithm to R. Specifically, in each stimulation, all the edges that fail to be influenced are removed from the original network, and a Network Spread Map will be obtained; then Breadth First Search (BFS) will be conduced for each node in the Network Spread Map and obtain the influence value for each node. As it is time-consuming to perform Breadth First Search for each node, a random algorithm, which was proposed by Cohen and et al., is adopted in the NewGreedy Algorithm for estimating the possible number of nodes in the Network Spread Map. Due to the Cohen Random Algorithm, on the one hand, the complexity of NewGreedy Algorithm is sharply reduced from $O(KnRm)$ for BasicGreedy to $O(KnTm)$, where T is the iteration times of Cohen Random Algorithm, and is far less than n; but, on the other hand, a method of estimation is used in Cohen Random Algorithm, so it is impossible to obtain the accurate influence value of nodes, which correspondingly lowers its precision. The design of NewGreedy Algorithm is shown in Algorithm 4.2.

MixGreedy Algorithm is a combination of NewGreedy Algorithm and CELF Algorithm. In the first round of CELF Algorithm, the influence value marginal profits of all nodes need to be calculated, so the amount of calculation is rather large; however, owing to its submodular character, it is not necessary to calculate the influence value marginal profits of a part of nodes after the first round, and the calculation amount is sharply reduced. For NewGreedy Algorithm, R simulations are needed in each round to calculate the influence value marginal profit for each node. The advantages of NewGreedy Algorithm and CELF Algorithm are orthogonal and are

Algorithm 4.2 NewGreedy Algorithm
Known: Social Network $G = (V, E, W)$, Parameter K
Seek: the most influential node set S with a size of K

1: Initialize the set to be a null set $S = \emptyset$;
2: **for** $i = 1$ to K **do**
3:      Provide the influence value sv of all nodes in Fig. G to be 0;
4:      **for** $j = 1$ to R **do**
5:          Remove the edges failed to be influenced in Fig. G according to IC Model so as to get the Fig. G';
6:          **for** any node v in Fig. G **do**
7:              Calculate the Influence Value marginal profit $MG(G', v)$ for node v;
8:              $s_v = s_v + MG(G', v)$;
9:          **end for**
10:     **end for**
11: $v_{max} = \text{argmax}_{v \in (V \setminus S)} s_v / R$;
12: $S = S \cup \{v_{max}\}$;
13: **end for**

not in conflict, so the MixGreedy Algorithm takes the advantages of these two algorithms, that is to use NewGreedy Algorithm in the first round and use CELF Algorithm in succeeding rounds so as to reduce the calculation amount, thereby further reducing the overall algorithm complexity. The experiment results show that the NewGreedy Algorithm and the MixGreedy Algorithm can significantly accelerate the discovery of most influential users in social networks, and ensure precision which is basically the same as that of BasicGreedy.

4.5.5 Other Greedy algorithms

In 2010, Wang et al. [10] proposed a solution algorithm, CGA, based on the concept of community. Social networks demonstrate good community characteristics, namely, the interaction between community members is close, so the probability of being influenced by each other is rather high; in contrast, connections between members of different communities is relatively few, so the probability of interaction is comparatively low. Exactly based on this community characteristic, Wang et al. presented the CGA Algorithm to approximate the most influential user in the global network using the most influential user inside of the community, thereby reducing the calculation complexity. The execution of CGA Algorithm is divided into two phases: in the first phase, specific to the problem that the information spread factor is not taken into consideration in the current community division algorithm, the author designs a new combination entropy division algorithm on the basis of influence spread; in the second phase, CGA Algorithm selects the most influential user from the divided community using the method of dynamic programming. Suppose that $k-1$ most influential nodes have been obtained in preceding $k-1$ rounds, each community will serve as the object of study in Round k, and MixGreedy Algorithm will be used in each community to select the most influential node, which will be selected as the globally most influential node in Round k. Through the experiments on mobile social network, the author proved that the operating speed of CGA Algorithm was significantly enhanced compared with MixGreedy Algorithm. However, the enhancement of speed is at the cost of precision because CGA Algorithm approximates the global influence of a node using its influence inside the community, which lowers the precision.

Goyal et al. [11] thoroughly analyzed CELF Algorithm, and presented the CELF++ Algorithm, which is an optimization method specific to CELF Algorithm. CELF++ Algorithm once again uses the submodular character of the influence value Function $\sigma(\cdot)$, and records in the current iteration for all nodes the most influential node ID: $prev_{best}$ after this node calculation. If the $prev_{best}$ node of the node v_i is selected as the most influential node in the current round after the iteration in current round, then the influence value of the node v_i does not need to be calculated in the iteration of the next round, thereby avoiding numerous recalculation of influence values existing in CELF Algorithm. The author proved by experiments that CELF++ Algorithm could reduce 35%~55% of the run time compared with CELF Algorithm.

On the basis of MixGreedy Alorithm, Liu et al. [12] analyzed the layer dependency and parallelizability of the nodes in the social network, designs, by the transformation of a directed acyclic graph and the bottom-up layer-by-layer scanning, an influence maximization algorithm BUTA having a high parallelizability to efficiently concurrently calculate the influence values of all nodes in the social networks. Later, a parallel computing system of CPU+GPU was taken as a representative of the existing heterogeneous-parallel computing frame, BUTA Algorithm was mapped onto the heterogeneous-parallel frame of CPU+GPU, and an IMGPU frame was proposed. In order to better make BUTA Algorithm adaptive to GPU hardware frame and programming models, the author provided the following three optimization methods: K-layer merging, data recombination and memory access merging to reduce the number of branches and memory access and to improve parallelism. Finally, a large amount of experiments were intensively performed in the real social networks, and the experiment results showed that the execution speed of BUTA Algorithm and IMGPU was notably improved relative to the aforementioned MixGreedy Algorithm.

4.5.6 Summary of Greedy algorithms

To summarize, Greedy Hill-Climbing Approximation Algorithm laid a foundation for the influence maximization approximation algorithm. Although Greedy Hill-Climbing Algorithm ensures a high solving precision, it has high complexity and requires large computation, resulting in a rather long run time. Numerous follow-up researches have been performed to optimize this efficiency problem, and have achieved notable effect of acceleration, but still fail to meet the demand of high algorithm efficiency. In particular, facing the current large-scale social networks, it is still the core object of current researches to design more efficient influence maximization algorithm.

4.6 Heuristic algorithms of influence maximization

Notable acceleration has been made for subsequently improving and optimizing Greedy Algorithms; however, due to the complexity of Greedy Algorithms, the run time after optimization still cannot meet the requirement of short run time of current large-scale social networks. Meanwhile, in the pursuit of higher algorithm efficiency, many excellent heuristic algorithms have been proposed for shortening the run time of influence maximization. Researches of existing heuristic algorithms will be introduced in this chapter.

4.6.1 Degree discount heuristic [4]

The most basic heuristic algorithms are Random, Degree, and Centrality Heuristics proposed by Kempe et al. [1]. Random Heuristic only randomly selects K nodes from all of the node sets V in the target social network G, and considers nothing about factors such as influence degree and influence spread. In comparison, Degree Heuristic and Centrality Heuristic are better, and both identify the most influential node in the network according to some network topological characteristics of the nodes. Degree Heuristic considers the concept of sociology, i.e., measuring the node influence spread according to its degree. So Degree Heuristic ranks all nodes in the network according to their degrees, and selects K nodes having the largest degree. Similar to Degree Heuristic, Centrality Heuristic believes that the node, the average distance between which and other nodes in the network is the smallest, has larger probability to influence other nodes, so it ranks the nodes according to the average distance between the node and other nodes in the network, and selects K nodes having the smallest average distance. Apparently, the design ideas of the above three basic heuristics are simple, so the execution time is as short as merely several seconds, or even several milliseconds. However, as they consider nothing about such factors as the actual influence value of nodes and influence spread, their algorithm precisions are pretty poor.

Based on the Degree Heuristic, Chen et al. [4] proposed DegreeDiscount in 2009, which is a heuristic algorithm specific to independent cascade model. The core idea of this heuristic is as follows: if a node u existing in the neighboring nodes of the node v is selected as an initial active node, the degree of the node v needs to be quantified and discounted due to the overlap existing between the two nodes. Details about the discounting method are shown in Algorithm 4.3. Experiment results show that the algorithm precision of DegreeDiscount Heuristic is much higher than that of Degree Heuristic, but still cannot be compared with the afore-mentioned Greedy Algorithms.

Algorithm 4.3 Degree Discount Algorithm
Known: Social Network $G = (V, E, W)$, Parameter K
Seek: The most influential node set S with a size of K
1:    Initialize the set to be a null set $S = \emptyset$;
2:    **for** any node v in Fig. G **do**
3:        $dd_v = d_v$;
4:        $t_v = 0$;
5:    **end for**
6:    **for** $i = 1$ to K **do**
7:        $u = \mathrm{argmax}_v\{dd_v | v \in V \backslash S\}$;
8:        $S = S \cup \{u\}$;
9:        **for** any neighbor $v \in V \backslash S$ of the node u **do**
10:        $t_v = t_v + 1$;
11:        $dd_v = d_v - 2t_v - (d_v - t_v) \cdot t_v \cdot p$;
12:        **end for**
13: **end for**

4.6.2 PMIA heuristic [13]

Specific to the independent cascade model, Chen et al. [13] proposed a new heuristic algorithm PMIA in 2010. First, the author proved that the calculation of the Influecen Value of the given initial active set in the independent cascade model was a #P-Hard problem, then the author provided a heuristic algorithm PMIA which is based on local influence. PMIA has high efficiency and good scalability as it approximates the global influence value of the node by using its influence value in its peripheral local area, constructs the maximum influence arborescence (MIA) model through the maximum influence path, and compromises between the algorithm execution efficiency and the algorithm precision through the regulation of the MIA size. The author proved that the influence function is still compliant with the submodular characteristics in MIA Model, so the Greedy Algorithms can reach an approximate optimal of $1 - 1/e - \varepsilon$. For higher execution efficiency, the author provided a heuristic PMIA, which is on the basis of MIA Model. PMIA merely needs to calculate the influence value of nodes in local area, and update the Influence Values of locally relevant nodes, so the calculation efficiency is higher. However, although PMIA heuristic improved the efficiency by local approximate optimal, but its precision is inevitably lost, which result in an over-low algorithm precision.

4.6.3 LDAG heuristic [14]

Also in 2010, Chen et al. presented for the first time the LDAG Heuristic specific to the linear threshold models. The author first proved that the calculation of the influence value of the given initial active set in the linear threshold models was a #P-Hard problem. The author discovered that the Influence Value of a node could be rapidly obtained in the directed acyclic graph (DAG), so the author provided the efficient LDAG Heuristic which is based on DAG. This Heuristic is based on the principle of locality, establishes a local DAG for each node in the social network by removing part of the sides having over-low weight, then calculates in the constructed DAG graph the influence value of each node, and selects the node with the maximum influence value as the algorithm result. The experiments prove that LDAG Heuristic can remarkably accelerate the resolving of the influence maximization problem in the linear threshold models. However, similar to PMIA Heuristic, the speed improvement of LDAG Heuristic is also at the cost of algorithm precision.

4.6.4 Other heuristics

In 2011, Goyal et al. [15] analyzed LDAG Heuristic, and noted the following disadvantages: ① Greedy strategy is used for constructing the directed acyclic graph, which reduces algorithm precision; ② LDAG Heuristic merely takes into consideration the influence spread within LDAG, while many other influence spread paths exist in reality, and the influence spread via these paths are neglected by LDAG; ③ All directed acyclic graphs need to be stored, so a large memory space is taken. With respect to these problems, the author designed the SIMPATH Heuristic, which can accurately estimate the influence value of the nodes by counting the number of paths starting from the seed node. Further, the author also provided the vertex cover optimization method and the Look Ahead Optimization method. The vertex cover optimization method is configured to reduce the time of influence value calculation in the first round of iteration to reduce the algorithm complexity and shorten the algorithm execution time of the first round. Later, the look ahead optimization method further reduces, via the parameter, the algorithm execution time in the process of influence value calculation in the follow-up rounds. Experiments on real datasets prove that SIMPATH Heuristic is better than LDAG and other heuristics in algorithm execution time, algorithm precision, and memory utilization, among other aspects.

Jung et al. [16] designed a new IRIE Heuristic in 2012 on the basis of independent cascade models. Traditional heuristics and PMIA Heuristic obtains the influence value of nodes through rounds of simulation or by means of local influence value calculation, and thereby selecting the node having the maximum influence value. However, for large-scale social networks, it is rather time-consuming to calculate the influence value of all nodes. Therefore, IRIE Algorithm is novel for that IRIE does not need to calculate the Influence Value for each node; instead, it is based on the method of belief propagation, ranks the influence values of the global node merely through rather few rounds of iteration, and then selects the top-ranked node as the most influential node. Moreover, IRIE is integrated with the method of influence estimation, estimates the influence of the most influential node on other nodes after each round of ranking, and then regulates the next round of influence ranking according to the results. IRIE combines the method of influence ranking and the method of influence estimation, and thus is on average two orders of magnitude faster than independent cascade model Heuristic PMIA, and is as precise as PMIA.

Furthermore, literature [17] has indicated that it is not necessary to precisely calculate the influence value of each node in social networks, and relative ranking according to node influence value will be enough. In addition, the distribution of social network nodes is subject to certain rules, so the nodes can be randomly sampled according to Monte Carlo Theory, and a distribution of overall sample can be approximated according to the distribution of the small sample, so as to approximate and estimate the node influence value, thereby decreasing the amount of calculation and improving algorithm execution efficiency. The author designed a supervised sampling method ESMCE based on power law index. Through deep analysis of node distribution features in social networks, ESMCE Algorithm determines the number of nodes in the initial sample according to power law index of the given social network; to minimize the number of the sample nodes and the number of sample rounds, ESMCE Algorithm proposed a method of forecasting the number of follow-up sample nodes based on a Grey Forecasting Model, which gradually refines the precision by iteration sampling till the error satisfies the predetermined requirement.

4.6.5 Summary of heuristic algorithms

The efficiency of influence maximization has been well improved through the aforementioned numerous researches on heuristic algorithms. These heuristic algorithms effectively shorten the algorithm execution time and also cause severe damage to the precision. The aforementioned heuristic algorithms select the most influential nodes by approximating or estimating the node influence value, or even without calculating the node influence value, so they have low complexity and short run time. However, their precision cannot be guaranteed, and cannot be compared to the aforementioned Greedy Algorithms.

4.7 Extension and deformation of influence maximization

As researches of influence maximization from academic circles go increasingly deeper, the influence maximization problem itself is continuously extended, deformed, and expanded, and is constantly used for solving more problems in social networks and other fields. Related researches about the extension and deformation of influence maximization will be elaborated in this section.

4.7.1 Extension of influence maximization

The subject of influence spread in basic influence maximization problem is a single subject, for instance, one certain kind of commodity is marketed in social network, and a certain piece of information is spread in network. However, in the real world, there are usually many kinds of subjects being spread at the same time in a single social network. In the process of spread, subjects of different kinds may not interacted, but it is more interesting that two or more kinds of subjects may compete with each other, or fight with each other for maximum spread range; or they may help each other and work together to fight for the maximum spread range. In the environment of competition, influence maximization problem has more applications, and thus attracts more attention from researches.

According to different problem targets, influence maximization problems in a competitive environment are basically divided into two kinds: one is to maximize the influence spread range of its own; the other is to minimize the influence spread range of competitors. These two targets seem to be consistent and complementary but are substantively different. When the target is to maximize the influence spread range of its own, it is not necessary to minimize the spread range of the competitors, or it may even have no effect on the spread range of competitors in extreme cases; conversely, when the target is to minimize the influence spread range of competitors, the influence spread range of its own may not be maximum. In a simple topological graph of social networks as shown in Figure 4.2, suppose that the spread probability of all edges is 1, two parties involved in the competitive spread are the Red party and the Black party, the Red party selects a node A as a seed node, and the Black party may select two of the remaining nodes as its seed nodes. If the target of the Black party is to maximize its own interests, the Black party will choose the nodes D and E as seed nodes, in this case, the Black party will be able to influence 12 nodes (the Black party realizes the maximum ultimate influence range); if the target of the Black party is to minimize the interests of the competitor, then the Black party will choose the nodes B and C, in this case, the Red party can influence only 6 nodes (the ultimate influence range of the Red party is minimal); if the Black party intends to win in the competition with the Red party, then the Black party will choose the nodes C and D, in this case, the Red party can influence 9 nodes while the Black party can influence 10 nodes, thereby realizing the Black party's target of winning the competition. Apparently, corresponding seed node selection strategies are needed for different targets of competitive spread.

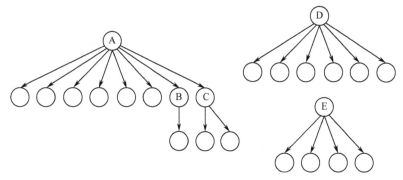

Figure 4.2: Schematic diagram of multi-target competitive spread

The earliest researches on influence maximization in competitive environment are from Carnes et al. [18] in Cornell University and Bharathi et al. [19] in the University of Southern California in 2007, and the studying targets of both are to maximize the influence of their own. Bharathi et al. expanded the independent cascade models to blend in competition factors, but the author merely provided an approximate algorithm FPTAS based on a special Bi-directed Tree Network Structure. Also in 2007, Carnes et al. presented two types of competitive spread models, i.e. the Distance Model and the Wave Model, and proved that the competitive influence maximization problems in both models were NP-Hard problems, and that an approximate optimal of $1 - 1/e - \varepsilon$ could be realized if the Greedy Hill-Climbing Algorithm can be used. Besides, Yang et al. [20] used the idea of swarm intelligence, and adopted Ant Colony Optimization Algorithm to solve the problem of competitive influence maximization. Nguyen et al. [21] had a different studying target. Their target was to identify a minimal number of initial active nodes to ultimately make, through diffusion and spread, the influence range of the competitor smaller than a given percentage. The author put forward the basic Hill-Climbing Greedy Algorithm at first, and proved that Greedy Algorithm could reach an approximate optimal result of $1 - 1/e - \varepsilon$. In addition, for the pursuit of higher resolving speed, this author proposed a heuristic strategy based on community, and testified the effectiveness of this method through experiments.

As for the minimization of the influence range of the opponent, Budak et al. [22] from University of California Santa Barbara initiated relevant researches in 2011. Based on the expanded independent cascade model, Budak et al. proved that the problem of competitive influence minimization is an NP-Hard problem, and compared the performances of Greedy Algorithm with three Heuristic Algorithms. Besides, He et al. [23] took into consideration multi-topic competitive factor in linear threshold model, and proved that the objective function in the problem of competitive influence minimization in linear threshold model conformed to the sub-modular character, as a result of which an approximate optimal of $1 - 1/e - \varepsilon$ can be realized when the Greedy Hill-Climbing Strategy is used; in order to enhance the calculation efficiency of Greedy Hill-climbing method, He et al. put forward an efficient heuristic algorithm CLDAG to make up the deficiency of long run time of Greedy Algorithms. In 2012, scholars including Tsai et al. [24] studied the problem of competitive influence minimization on the basis of Game Theory, and designed a heuristic mixed strategy for problem solution.

4.7.2 Deformation of influence maximization

Traditional problem of influence maximization tries to identify K initial active nodes so as to reach the maximum influence range; however, Goyal et al. studied how to choose minimum initial active nodes so as to ultimately influence a given number of nodes. Goyal et al. [25] proved that the objective function of this problem conformed to the sub-modular characteristics, as a result of which Greedy Hill-Climbing Algorithm can be used for approximating the solution. Moreover, Long et al. [26] proved that this problem was an NP-Hard problem. In addition, the author also considered the situation when the target node set is the overall network, and provided corresponding solving algorithm.

Furthermore, Goyal et al. [25] from the University of British Columbia also studied the minimization problem of Influence Spread time, namely, to ultimately influence a given number of nodes, how to identify k nodes so as to activate a given number of nodes in social networks in a shortest time. Similarly, the author provided basic Greedy Algorithms to solve this problem.

Besides, Lappas et al. [27] raised a new problem of K-Effector, namely, if a certain node set S in the network $G(V, E)$ is known, how to select an initial active node set with a size of K so that the ultimate active node set is most consistent with the set S after Influence Spread. The author proved that this problem is an NP-Hard problem in independent cascade models, and provided, based on a specific tree structure, a dynamic programming algorithm to solve the K-Effector problem.

Based on the problem of influence maximization, Lappas et al. [28] studied the problem of team formation, namely, if a task T (which needs to be finished by different skill sets), an alternative talent set X (each person has his own skill reserves), and a social network of talent set (the weight of edges between person and person represents the interaction price between them; the smaller the price, the more effectively they can cooperate) are given, how to organize teams in the set X and how to find the talent set X' to execute the task T so that the sum of interaction price in the set X' is the smallest. Based on the diagram diameter and the minimal spanning tree, the author defined two different methods of determining the interaction price, and proved that the problems of Team Formation in both methods were NP-Hard problems, and designed corresponding solving algorithms specific to these two methods.

4.8 Summary

For the past few years, with the rapid development of internet and Web 2.0 technology, and as a communication bridge in real human world, social network has become an important media and platform for inter-communication, knowledge sharing, and information spread. The problem of influence maximization aiming at discovering the most influential node set in social networks is a key problem in the field of social network analysis, and is widely applied to marketing, advertisement publication, early warning of public sentiment, and many other important occasions; hence, it is of high research and application values.

The problem of influence maximization in social networks and its main analysis methods are summarized in this chapter. With respect to algorithms, the current work focuses on the Greedy Algorithms and heuristic strategies. Existing researches have gained some research results in the efficient handling of influence maximization problem; however, because of the large scale of social networks, complex connection between nodes, and dynamic variation of the network structure, many new challenges have been resulted in efficient solutions of influence maximization. Therefore, there are many problems in this field that need further investigation.

(1) At present, there are numerous parallel computation frameworks which have already been widely applied to such field as massive scientific calculation and so on. MapReduce computation framework is good in programmability, has the advantages of automatic parallelization, load balancing or the like, and can be operated on large-scale clusters, so its computing power is very remarkable. Therefore, the parallel solving algorithm of influence maximization based on MapReduce framework is a feasible and meaningful solution. The key problem to be solved in this research direction is how to rationally assign the task of computing the influence value of each node in social networks to the computing

nodes in the computing cluster to ensure few interactive information between nodes and a short time of dependence and waiting.

(2) In the current independent cascade models or linear threshold models of influence maximization, the determination of influence probability or influence weight between nodes is on the basis of constant value assumptions, e.g., with an influence probability of 0.01 or an influence weight of 0.1. These assumptions facilitate the modeling and solving of influence maximization problem. However, these assumptions are unreasonable in reality. The determination of influence probability and influence weight between users are closely related to the relationship between users, as well as the communication content, users' interest, users' majors, and other contents. Therefore, it is an important research subject as for how to rationally provide the influence probability and the influence weight in the influence spread models. At present, in-depth research to this problem is lacking, and hence it may become the next research object.

References

[1] David Kempe, Jon Kleinberg, Eva Tardos. Maximizing the spread of influence through a social network. In Proceedings of the ninth ACM SIGKDD international conference on knowledge discovery and data mining, 2003: 137–146.

[2] Jacob Goldenberg, Barak Libai, Eitan Muller. Talk of the network: A complex systems look at the underlying process of word-of-mouth. Marketing Letters, 2001, 12(3):211–223.

[3] Mark Granovetter. Threshold models of collective behavior. American Journal of Sociology, 1978, 83(6):1420.

[4] Wei Chen, Yajun Wang, Siyu Yang. Efficient Influence Maximization in social networks. In Proceedings of the 15th ACM SIGKDD international conference on knowledge discovery and data mining, 2009: 199–208.

[5] Eyal Even-Dar, Asaf Shapira. A note on maximizing the spread of influence in social networks. Internet and Network Economics, 2007, 281–286.

[6] Gerard Cornuejols, Marshall L. Fisher, George L. Nemhauser. Exceptional paper—location of bank accounts to optimize float: An analytic study of exact and approximate algorithms. Management Science. 1977, 23 (8):789–810.

[7] George L. Nemhauser, Lawrence A Wolsey, Marshall L. Fisher. An analysis of approximations for maximizing submodular set functions—I. Mathematical Programming, 1978, 14 (1):265–294.

[8] Pedro Domingos, Matt Richardson. Mining the network value of customers. In Proceedings of the seventh ACM SIGKDD international conference on Knowledge discovery and data mining, 2001: 57–66.

[9] Jure Leskovec, Andreas Krause, Carlos Guestrin, Christos Faloutsos, Jeanne VanBriesen, Natalie Glance. Cost-effective outbreak detection in networks. In Proceedings of the 13th ACM SIGKDD international conference on Knowledge discovery and data mining, 2007: 420–429.

[10] Yu Wang, Gao Cong, Guojie Song, Kunqing Xie. Community-based Greedy Algorithm for mining top-k influential nodes in mobile social networks. In Proceedings of the 16th ACM SIGKDD international conference on knowledge discovery and data mining, 2010: 1039–1048.

[11] Amit Goyal, Wei Lu, Laks V.S. Lakshmanan. Celf++: optimizing the Greedy Algorithm for Influence Maximization in social networks. In Proceedings of the 20th international conference companion on World wide web, 2011: 47–48.

[12] Liu Xiaodong, Li Mo, Li Shanshan, Peng Shaoliang, Liao Xiangke, Lu Xiaopei. IMGPU: GPU accelerated influence maximization in large-scale social networks. IEEE Transactions on Parallel and Distributed Systems, 2014: 1.

[13] Wei Chen, Chi Wang, Yajun Wang. Scalable influence maximization for prevalent viral marketing in large-scale social networks. In Proceedings of the 16th ACM SIGKDD international conference on Knowledge discovery and data mining, 2010: 1029–1038.

[14] Wei Chen, Yifei Yuan, Li Zhang. Scalable influence maximization in social networks under the linear threshold model. In Proceedings of IEEE 10th International Conference on Data Mining, 2010: 88–97.

[15] Amit Goyal, Wei Lu, Laks V. S. Lakshmanan. Simpath: An efficient algorithm for influence maximization under the linear threshold model. In Proceedings of IEEE 11th International Conference on Data Mining, 2011: 211–220.

[16] Kyomin Jung, Wooram Heo, Wei Chen. IRIE: A scalable influence maximization algorithm for independent cascade model and its extensions. arXiv preprint arXiv:1111.4795, 2011.

[17] Liu Xiaodong, Li Shanshan, Liao Xiangke, Peng Shaoliang, Wang Lei, Kong Zhiyin. Know by a handful the whole sack: Efficient sampling for top-K influential user identification in large graphs, World Wide Web Journal.

[18] Tim Carnes, Chandrashekhar Nagarajan, Stefan M. Wild, Anke van Zuylen. Maximizing influence in a competitive social network: A follower's perspective. In Proceedings of the ninth international conference on Electronic commerce, 2007: 351–360.

[19] Shishir Bharathi, David Kempe, Mahyar Salek. Competitive influence maximization in social networks. Internet and Network Economics, 2007, 306–311.

[20] Wan-Shiou Yang, Shi-Xin Weng. Application of the ant colony optimization algorithm to competitive viral marketing. In Proceedings of the 7th Hellenic conference on Artificial Intelligence: theories and applications, 2012: 1–8.

[21] Nam P. Nguyen, Guanhua Yan, My T. Thai, Stephan Eidenbenz. Containment of misinformation spread in online social networks. Proceedings of the 4th ACM Web Science (WebSci'12), 2012.

[22] Ceren Budak, Divyakant Agrawal, Amr El Abbadi. Limiting the spread of misinformation in social networks. In Proceedings of the 20th international conference on World wide web, 2011: 665-674.

[23] Xinran He, Guojie Song, Wei Chen, Qingye Jiang. Influence blocking maximization in social networks under the competitive Linear Threshold Model technical report. arXiv preprint arXiv:1110.4723, 2011.

[24] Jason Tsai, Thanh H. Nguyen, Milind Tambe. Security games for controlling contagion. In Proceedings of the Twenty-Sixth National Conference in Artificial Intelligence, 2012.

[25] Amit Goyal, Francesco Bonchi, Laks V. S. Lakshmanan, Suresh Venkatasubramanian. On minimizing budget and time in influence propagation over social networks. Social Network Analysis and Mining, 2012: 1–14.

[26] Cheng Long, Raymond Chi-Wing Wong. Minimizing seed set for viral marketing. In Proceedings of the IEEE 11th International Conference on Data Mining, 2011: 427–436.

[27] Theodoros Lappas, Evimaria Terzi, Dimitrios Gunopulos, Heikki Mannila. Finding effectors in social networks. In Proceedings of the 16th ACM SIGKDD international conference on Knowledge discovery and data mining, 2010: 1059–1068.

[28] Theodoros Lappas, Kun Liu, Evimaria Terzi. Finding a team of experts in social networks. In Proceedings of the 15th ACM SIGKDD international conference on Knowledge discovery and data mining, 2009: 467–476.

Index